BICYCLE TOURING IN AUSTRALIA

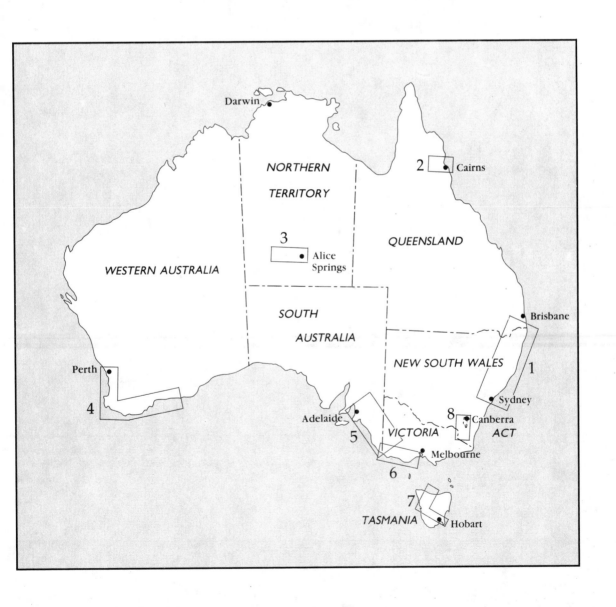

BICYCLE TOURING IN AUSTRALIA

Written and Photographed by Leigh Hemmings

The Mountaineers
Seattle

The Mountaineers: Organized 1906 '. . . to explore, study,
preserve and enjoy the natural beauty of the outdoors.'

Copyright © 1991 Leigh Hemmings

Published in the United States by
The Mountaineers
1011 SW Klickitat Way, Suite 107
Seattle WA 98134

First published in Australasia in 1991 by
Simon & Schuster Australia
20 Barcoo Street, East Roseville NSW 2069

Manufactured in Singapore.
Cover photos by Leigh Hemmings.
Designed by Kim Webber.
Cartography by Judy Trim.
Library of Congress Cataloging-in-Publication Data

Hemmings, Leigh.
    Bicycle touring in Australia/written and photographed by Leigh
  Hemmings.
        o.   cm.
    Includes bibliographical references (p.   ).
    ISBN 0 89886-302-3 (US)
    1. Bicycle touring—Australia—Guide-books. 2 Australia—
Description and travel—1981—Guide-books. I. Title.
GV1046.A8H46 1991   91-11093
786.6'4'0994—dc20   CIP

CONTENTS

HOW TO USE THIS BOOK

Each tour is described using a narrative day log, route slip, map, and height profile.

The narrative day log describes the route's significant features, attractions and possible detours. It also gives a daily account of my bike computer data (distance, time and average and maximum speeds).

The route slip and map follow a tour's progress, section by section. The route slips should be read from the bottom to the top, working upwards as you ride. The maps are all, as close as was practicable, north-oriented.

Each height profile shows altitude changes in the terrain ridden for each section, and are read from left to right. Note, road gradients are not as extreme as they appear on the profile; check the scale for each height profile — in most cases one grid square equals one kilometre (⅔ mile) on the horizontal axis, while vertically, one grid square equals 20 metres (65½ feet).

This book is designed for novices and experienced cycle tourers alike. If touring is new to you, match your daily destination to this day log. Generally, the log sets realistic goals. As your experience grows, adjust your touring goals to suit your cycling style. Potential body and bike troubles may be less likely if you follow the suggestions given in the chapters 'Organising Your Tour' and 'On the Road'. Remedies for typical breakdowns are set out in the chapter 'On the Road'.

Conversion Tables

For overseas readers, conversions for metric measurements mentioned in this text to imperial are as follows:

Length

1 centimetre (cm)	equals ⅓ inch
1 metre (m)	equals 1¹⁄₁₀ yards
1 kilometre (km)	equals ⅔ mile

Weight

1 gram (g)	equals ¹⁄₃₀ ounce
1 kilogram (kg)	equals 2⅕ pounds

Volume

1 litre (L)	equals 2⅛ pints
3.75 litres	equals 1 gallon

Area

1 hectare (ha)	equals 2½ acres

Keys to Maps and Height Profiles

- ● small town (basic shop/cafe, toilets, water, phone)
- ⬤ mid-size town (above, plus general store and accommodation)
- ○ major centre (above plus supermarket, medical, dental, post office, laundromat)
- △ youth hostel
- ■ bike shop
- ▲ information centre
- × railway station

——— ride
– – – train
·········· ferry

On ride line, each segment = 1 kilometre

INTRODUCTION

Bicycle touring is sensual travel, smoothly attuning mind and body to the surroundings. A bicycle tourer is an active traveller and yet one who is unobtrusive and sensitive to the environment. Sights, sounds and aromas bombard you in a sensory overload; sheaves of sunlight slipping through a tall canopy, the air pungent with eucalypt fragrance, your tyres crackling red-brown leaves on black tar, and sometimes, piercing rain stinging your skin. Dorothy Richardson described it in 1919 as '. . . On a bicycle you feel a different person, nothing can come near you, you forget who you are . . .', and today on a bicycle you still move to the sound of that different drum.

More correctly, though, you are pedalling, pushing, struggling, sweating, and persuading a bicycle into forward motion. Bicycle touring is, without doubt, an energetic endeavour, and I would not want to be accused of the same biased view of last century's hype writers who, according to Jerome J. Jerome (*Three Men on the Bummel*) tried to 'convince the hesitating neophyte that the sport of bicycling consists in sitting on a luxurious saddle, and being moved rapidly in the direction you wish to go by unseen heavenly powers . . . the sun is always shining, and the roads are always dry'. It is only like that some of the time.

There are tough hills, rainy days and hard bicycle seats, but the challenges are as much mental as physical. The key is to ease into the activity, taking advantage of bicycling's qualities as an excellent body-supported exercise. In Ivan Illich's words:

'the bicycle is the perfect transducer to match man's metabolic energy to the impedance of locomotion. Equipped with this tool, man outstrips the efficiency of not only all machines, but all other animals as well'.

Ivan Illich, *Energy and Equity*, 1979

Taken quietly, cycling is smooth and gentle on your body. You can begin touring whether aged nine or ninety. Leo Tolstoy learned to ride at the age of 67 and although his friends were offended by his riding, he said 'I feel that I am entitled to my share of natural lightheartedness, that the opinions of others have no importance, and that there is nothing wrong in enjoying oneself simply, like a boy'. It's this enjoyment that adds sparkle to life. Riders in the English Veterans Time Trial Association when tackling 40 kilometres (25 miles) against the clock, are allocated just 40 extra seconds for each year by which their age exceeds 70 years. Many can still post good times well into their 80s and often have the physical profile of someone 20 to 30 years younger.

Unlike bicycle racing, touring is concerned more with the enjoyment of travel, rather than hours, minutes and seconds. Whether pottering along or riding at athletic pace, staying in top hotels or camping out, your perceptions of time and distance undergo a radical transformation. A stretch of road which a motorist might absent-mindedly speed along in an hour in complete boredom, for a cycle tourer may provide a day of rewarding climbs, exhilarating descents and close encounters with wildlife and the elements.

'Such a day! Such a bicycle! Such sweet and merry air! . . . Before her there was a long slope down. To take it, brakeless, feet up on the rest, was like flying.'

Rose Macaulay, *Told By an Idiot*, 1928

Australia, which some people believe to be overwhelmingly vast, is in fact a superb country in which to go bicycle touring. There are plenty of quiet country roads, ever changing scenery and friendly, helpful people. You have a fantastic variety of terrain from which to choose, everything from sub-alpine peaks to ancient red ochre gorges. In a matter of half a day's riding you can travel from feeling giant rollers thunder into a wild, untrodden beach to being awestruck by the tallest hardwood trees in the world.

Designing, researching, riding, photographing and writing the eight tours detailed in this book has given me twelve months of inspiring discoveries, challenges and experiences. The tours cover all states, encompass great diversity in terrain and accommodation, from youth hostels, five-star hotels, motels and resorts to camping grounds. For me the tours are all favourites. I have presented them with Australia's seasons in mind so that, as far as possible, you will be touring in the peak time of year for that location. The order of tours was also established to minimise connecting distances between the end of one tour and the beginning of another. It is possible to start in Sydney during April and keep riding the whole eight tours, ending back in Sydney the following February.

The basic requirement for anyone contemplating riding these tours is to be able to handle a 10– to 21–speed bike and cope with derailleurs, brakes, descents and hills. When you are looking over the tours, please don't be alarmed at the height profiles. In order to fit each profile on the page, the relationship struck between height and distance greatly exaggerates the gradient. Something that looks impossibly steep may really be a long slow rise when you actually ride it — remember to look at the distance scale. The value of a height profile becomes apparent once you have covered some of the hills and can compare one to another. Each profile is immensely important in determining when and where you make rest breaks, or day's goals — 40 kilometres (25½ miles) of hard hills is not the same as 40 kilometres of billiard table riding.

The narrative of the tours follows my ride day-by-day, but naturally you can design overnight stops to suit your fitness and interests. The real value of the log is to give you a quick indication of what is usually a comfortable distance for which to aim. Keen readers will notice there is sometimes a discrepancy between distances shown on the height profile, route slip and distance log. This is the result of detours taken when I was riding the route and the difficulty in showing fractions of a kilometre on a small graph. Riding time is the actual pedalling time and the average speed also comes from my actual riding time. The computer was stopped when the bike was stationary; noting route slip information, morning teas, lunches, picture-taking, reviver breaks, etc.

Throughout the year this book has taken to come to fruition, with tours and training I have ridden more than 6000 kilometres (3850 miles). Fantastic, fun kilometres for the most part — two flat tyres and eight broken spokes aside. I've been snowed on in mid-summer and baked in the depths of winter, forced to push through desert sands and cracked the 80 kmph (50 mph) mark down smooth-as-silk roads. There have been sadistic headwinds and hedonistic tailwinds, agonising ascents and awesome downhills, sad and funny moments. The experiences have opened my eyes to a little of Australia's natural majesty, and reinforced my love of bicycle touring.

Pack your panniers and go. Australia awaits.

Leigh Hemmings
Sydney, 1991

THE HISTORY OF CYCLE TOURING

French, they say, is the language of cycling. The word bicycle itself comes from the French word, *bicercle*. It's a fitting origin, since it was in cultured streets of Paris that an unsteerable two-wheeled wooden horse made its appearance in 1790. Though it was more fun than functional — it had to be pushed — the glimmer of an idea had begun. Improvements to the design followed and by 1818 a French coach repairer was making steerable *velocipedes*. They still needed to be pushed, but in 1839 across the Channel in Scotland, a blacksmith improved the design by adding pedals and a brake. With this major improvement, new designs rapidly emerged including tricycles and even hand-cranked cycles. Sir Arthur Conan Doyle and his wife were keen tricyclists and Sir Arthur endowed his famous fictional character, Sherlock Holmes, with the ability to differentiate between 42 impressions left by bike tyres.

In Australia, the new fad of riding soon took hold and by 1867 it was reported that in Sydney there were races for 'bone shakers' as they were called. By 1869, *Scientific American* magazine confidently predicted, 'the art of walking is obsolete'.

No doubt a little money was placed on the outcome of races, hastening the desire for lightness and speed. This in turn encouraged a radical rethink. Nowadays we call it a 'Penny Farthing', but in the 1870s they called it the 'Ordinary'. Anything but ordinary, it had a front wheel 137 cm (54 in) high and a rear of 44 cm (17 in), both running on solid tyres. The large wheel enabled generation of greater speed from direct-drive crank pedals. Later developments replaced the solid radial spokes with wire spokes, and in 1876 Englishman James Starley developed the tangential spokes still used on modern touring bikes.

Despite being state-of-art for its time, the Ordinary was a tall and heavy machine. Just mounting the monster and propelling it safely was a balancing art. A writer in *English Mechanic* warned that 'unless anyone is possessed of legs of iron and thighs of brass, I would strongly recommend him to look before he leaps into the saddle of a bicycle'. Millions ignored this sage advice.

A Penny Farthing was, and still is, a difficult machine to ride. The transition from walking to cycling was neither a simple nor safe affair. Some people simply bought one and learnt to ride it by themselves, becoming intimately acquainted with the origin of the word 'header' (to tumble, head first, over the handlebars). Others took lessons and probably still found out what happend when the front wheel met any large obstruction. Catering for the rush for competency were the Royal Cycle Instructors who taught plain and fancy riding, as well as event riding including tent pegging, tilting the ring, polo and musical cycling. Despite even expert instruction, some people took an inordinately long time to get the hang of basic riding. H.G. Wells (a keen cyclist himself) described a learner:

> 'He did not ride fast, he did not ride straight . . . but he rode generously, opulently, using the whole road and even nibbling at the footpath . . .'
>
> H.G. Wells, *Wheels of Chance*, 1896

It seems that the bicycle and creative thinkers were made for each other. Henry James, Thomas Hardy and Leo Tolstoy all loved to cycle. For some it was a love–hate relationship. A bad fall caused Renoir to paint with his left, unbroken, hand and George Bernard Shaw seemed to have an annual accident. Though Shaw was an enthusiastic promoter of the joys of cycling, in the learning stages things were not so delightful. He confided in a letter dated 1895 to Janet Achurch:

> 'My God, the stiffness, the blisters, the bruises, the pains in every twisted muscle . . . that I have endured . . . But . . . I will not be beaten by that hellish machine'.
>
> George Bernard Shaw, *The Collected Letters of G.B. Shaw*, ed by Dan Lawrence, Reinhardt, 1965

The 'hellish' bicycle took hold in Australia. It was estimated that during the 1890s more than 200 000 of the demons were purchased by both men and women, despite the dire-warning editorials which decried the idea of women cycling. The activity was considered wild, unwomanly, indelicate and a wanton display of flesh — the ankles were shown when pedalling! Any woman rider was thought exposed to considerable peril, not the least from the bicycle seat rendering future miscarriages. Grudging acknowledgement was given that the act of bicycling was not in itself sinful, except for 'fallen' women. Women, upright and fallen, ignored this rubbish, became 'cyclistes' and revolutionised fashions by taking to Rational Dress — corsets were out, bloomers or knickerbockers in. The change was appreciated by both sexes, though there was considerable debate about which seat should be occupied by a lady on a tandem.

As thousands began to discover the joys of longer tours, they also found it was the simplest way to become lost. Sign posts in Australia were almost non-existent. Taking up the challenge, George Broadbent and Joseph Pearson began to research touring guides of Victoria and New South Wales respectively. On a typical expedition in the 1880s Pearson set off on a Sydney to Melbourne 900 km (576 mile) sojourn aboard a solid tyred 'Ordinary'. He took copious notes and utilised a measuring contrivance attached to the front wheel which tinkled a little bell at the completion of each mile. From these expeditions were born the first touring maps, hand books and road guides, published in 1896.

Some people weren't prepared to wait for guide books. In 1888, two adventurers, George Burston and H.J. Stokes, set out from Melbourne on the first leg of their round-the-world trip riding two 'Ordinaries'.

'. . . we rode in knee-breeches, Panama hats, and flannel shirts . . . In leather belts we had stuck our revolvers, ammunition, and nickel-plated wrenches. We are thus armed in case an emergency should arise in out-of-the-way districts.'

George Burston and H.J. Stokes, *Round about the World on Bicycles*, 1888

The quantum leap in bicycle technology came when a 'safety' cycle with a diamond frame and two equal-sized wheels, driven by a chain to the rear wheel, was first manufactured by Englishman John Kemp Starley (a cousin of James Starley who had invented the tangential spokes in 1876) in 1885. This, of course, had relied on two inventions, a ball-bearing race in 1877, which reduced the coefficient of friction by a factor of a thousand, and the bush roller chain in 1880. In New South Wales, Joseph Pearson imported a 'Safety' and took to it with gusto, eventually riding more than 257 500 km (160 000 miles), both in Australia and overseas.

Though the 'Safety' was a great improvement from the 'Ordinary', there were a few features to be invented before trouble-free cycle touring was unleashed. Pearson found that because solid tyres were attached to the rims with shellac, in hot Australian summers, the glue melted and the tyres frequently detached. 'Cushion' tyres (like a garden hose) followed but they proved exceptionally heavy. Then, a Scottish veterinary surgeon John Dunlop, reinvented a pneumatic tube in 1888. In *The Penguin Book of the Bicycle*, Watson and Grey credit the first patent being awarded to another Scot, Robert Thompson, in 1845 but he '. . . was too far ahead of his time'.

The Pneumatic Tyre Company swung into production but unfortunately, in Australian conditions excess heat on the early tyres would cause a blowout. Cycle tourers in the 1890s were frequently forced to look for streams in which to dunk their bicycle wheels. Blowouts were despisable as the outer tyre was laced on and repairs could take over an hour. Later developments made tyre changing far less odious and then blowouts became infrequent after the Dunlop Bushman Tyre, a Thorn Proof, was developed for Australian conditions.

In his excellent book, *The Bicycle and the Bush*, Jim Fitzpatrick credits Percy Armstrong and R. Craig with the first long distance cycle tour, or in his words 'overland ride' for their ride from Croydon in North Queensland, via Townsville, to Sydney. Armstrong continued to Melbourne on a bike with pneumatic tyres, but for their 3200 km (2000 mile) epic, they rode cushion-tyred safety cycles reportedly weighing 34 kg (74.8 pounds)! Many others followed: in 1897 William Virgin took 60 days to ride from Perth to Brisbane; Pat O'Dea averaged 169 km (105 miles) per day Perth to Adelaide; and Arthur Richardson rode a 243-day epic — the first person to ride around the country.

There is one bicycling overlander who stands out above all others — Francis Birtles. Birtles saw the bike as an ideal means for exploring Australia, making him famous and earning a living. His exploits were well recorded by pen, camera and a good imagination in many magazines such as *The Lone Hand*. In his book *Battle Fronts of Outback*, Birtles described an around-Australia trip in his typical over-the-top style — '... seething flies bespecked my swag, bike and body ... minute black ants had taken possession of my blankets ... the long cane grass ... was three times my own height ...'. Then later, 'In addition to the loneliness and the hazards of the desert, march flies came to plague me. They attacked my face so fiercely that I was rendered almost blind'. Despite such hardships and dangers, by 1912 Birtles had cycled across Australia seven times and twice around it — 115 500 km (71 800 miles) of overland cycling in six years, a great inspiration to anyone with a sense of adventure and a bicycle.

Thankfully, Australian bicycle touring clubs were founded in 1895, before they read Birtles' off-putting descriptions of overland cycling. England's The National Bicyclists' Touring Club (later CTC) was the first, established in 1878 to protect the rights of the cyclist. Like its earlier cousin, membership of a bicycle touring club in Australia had its privileges — route guides, guided tours and accommodation discounts were offered. *The Australian Cyclist — Tourist and Traveller* was a popular magazine of the late 1800s. Fitzpatrick outlines that in the NSW Cyclists' Touring Union guide they included such things as '... dangerous gradients; where pushing was required ... the specific soils ... where to cross rivers ... and facts important to particular areas ("look out for bullocks")'.

Not only were the hazards a little different than today, but cyclists in the early 1900s had a different relationship with motor vehicles. As Jim Dunning recounted in a touring newsletter '... we rode past the few cars we met on the road. The best they could do was fifteen miles an hour'.

Although safety cycles were less likely to decant you onto the roadway, most machines were originally of the fixed wheel variety — the pedals always turned. This was unsatisfactory in rough country where the pedals, in the lowest position, crashed into rocks and large tree stumps. The advent of the freewheel and back pedal brake was a vast improvement, but even then there was only one speed. Theoretically it was possible to carry different cogs to suit the terrain, but this was not really practical. In 1899 the French developed the forerunners of modern derailleurs and in 1902 the Sturmey–Archer three-speed-hub was patented.

The freewheel, back pedal safety cycle was a huge success in Australia. Unlike a horse, it was always saddled, didn't need to be fed, watered or hobbled at night and didn't die from eating poisonous plants. It was fast (160 km [100 miles] a day was a common distance), could be lifted over fences and carried across creeks when making short cuts and was capable of carrying a rider and 60–70 kg (132–154 pounds) of gear over the harshest terrain. And it was harsh, the so-called roads were atrocious: '... more like a plowed field than a road-way' was how one cyclist in 1897 described a road in Victoria.

Yet despite the obstacles, a multitude of riders chose that form of transportation for a variety of purposes. Rabbit fences were patrolled by bicycle, and kangaroo shooters on bicycles almost silently stalked their prey. Pastors with beautiful calf muscles administered their often far flung flocks by bicycle. Bicycle ambulances existed in the form of two bikes joined with a stretcher frame. Less altruistic motives were pursued by insurance salesmen and general hawkers who plied the outback by bicycle. The Coolgardie Cycle Express Co. was the predecessor of today's city couriers as its riders carried messages on Western Australia's goldfields. Even tricycles were discovered to be excellent strawberry planting platforms and they are still used on the Atherton Tablelands today (Tour 2 goes through this area). In her book *The Shearers*, Patsy Adam Smith describes shearer's rides of up to 4800 km (3000 miles) each season from shed to shed through sand or slush.

Even after the production of Thorn Proofs, the Australian bush was fierce on bicycle tyres, especially thorny plants such as three-corner Jack and bindi-eye which easily punctured tubes. Many a journey was completed on bare rims. On one trip, after bush fires had burnt his tyres, Birtles rattled into Gympie, Queensland on bare rims sounding like a travelling gypsy, much to the amusement of the locals. Tall tales were spun about various methods used to overcome tyre destruction. Ray Watley, a Tasmanian shearer claimed:

'Riding a bike from Bourke my tyre wore out so I killed a tiger snake and wrapped it round the rim, shoved its tail in its mouth and off I pedalled.'

Patsy Adam Smith, *The Shearers*, Nelson, 1982

In those early days of cycle touring, bikes were loaded down with canvas water bags, billies, bedroll, spares, rifle, flour, sugar and tea and forks, frame and handlebars were used as tie-on places. In the towns, some cyclists indulged in super energy drinks like raw egg in ginger beer and a commercial preparation 'Cykola', made from cola nuts, raisins and peppermint. If you rolled up to the Innamincka pub it might be a simple menu: goat or that ubiquitous bush bird, the galah. But that was probably better than the local wits' Barcoo Sandwich: a goanna between two slabs of bark. Birtles reckoned he did many gruelling miles dining on grilled 'gohanna' (goanna — a large lizard), boiled galah and solid damper (scone-like bread cooked in the coals of a campfire). More realistically it was probably 'underground mutton' (rabbit) which kept many a cycle tourer plugging onwards. Nights were spent under a strip of canvas slung like a lean-to. It was a case of dig a hipper in the sand, throw in a blanket then settle down for the night to yarn and watch the Southern Cross overhead. Some things never change.

ORGANISING YOUR TOUR

The Perfect Touring or Hybrid Bike

It weighs 250 g (8½ oz), has tyres that don't wear or puncture, unbreakable spokes and rims which never get out of true. Sitting astride the saddle is like being carried on a fluffy cloud. Gear changes are ESP activated and there's always a lower or higher gear. The chain never breaks or falls off and certainly never needs oiling. Steering is semi-automatic and senses changes in road conditions ahead. The rear vision mirror senses the size, speed and intentions of overtaking vehicles and shows it on a head up display. Within easy reach is a convertible lever marked Rough and Smooth. Coming down a big mountain with gay abandon? Set for Smooth and you are on board a sleek thin-tyred speed machine. Adventuring off road up a semi-vertical rock strewn track? Set for Rough and you are aboard an ultra-low geared all terrain bike. All camping equipment and clothes are slung in completely waterpoof, infinitely expandable, aerodynamic panniers which stay attached even when riding through foot deep corrugations. At night while it is cleaning and tuning itself, the bike maintains an unbreakable attachment to the nearest solid object. The brand of this touring bike? Why it's the Flight of Fantasy.

Okay, outside of my imagination the perfect touring or hybrid bike doesn't exist, yet. But if you were looking to buy a bike last century and accidentally slipped back to the future, what you would be offered today might seem very like the Fantasy. In the late 1800s between 10 and 15 pounds sterling (about four to five week's average wages, or today's equivalent of over $1400 Australian), could have purchased a steel-rimmed, one-speed bike with a back pedal brake. Today, for the equivalent money you get a very sophisticated piece of machinery. The power unit, however, remains the same.

Whilst it is possible to tour on an el-cheapo supermarket bike this is unlikely to be comfortable or trouble free. Two weeks fully-loaded cycle touring in the Australian countryside is probably

Touring or Hybrid Bike requirements checklist

Buy from specialist bike shop	Ensure bike greased when assembled
Frame size to suit your body	Anatomically correct saddle
Alloy 1¼ in rims and 1⅜ in (or 700 x 32 mm) tyres	Quick release hubs
	Alloy pedals and toe clips
Cotterless cranks	Indexed gears, bar-end shifters
Triple chainwheels	Double or triple butted frame
Cantilever brakes	
Sealed Bearings	40-spoke rear wheel

ESSENTIAL EXTRAS

Mudguards	Front (low rider) and rear pannier frames
Quality panniers	
Rear view mirror	Front and rear lights
2 Water bottles/plastic holders/carriers	Helmet

equivalent to two years unladen city riding and things have a habit of coming unstuck at the worst possible times. Brands aside, look for a double or triple butted frame — the strongest bicycle construction. Specialist bike shops, particularly those whose owner/salespeople do actually tour (ask them!), are more likely to set you up on a suitable machine. It may cost a little more, but there's less risk that the bike has not been carefully assembled and, given regular maintenance, chances are that it will last for many trouble-free years.

I have to own up here to a bias. I prefer classic style touring bikes to hybrid and all terrain bikes (ATBs). With the exception of the Red Centre Tour, I rode all tours in this book on a 21 speed Shogun touring bike. At times I have toured on and with ATBs, but to me on any surface other than 'terrible' they feel heavy, cumbersome, slow and ungraceful. I also have a problem with allowing ATBs onto national park walking tracks. The philosophy behind this book involves touring on quiet, well-made roads to scenically stunning places, then getting off the bike and walking.

Sizing

Like people, touring bicycles come in different sizes. Sometimes the two coincide, but usually, unless you have an open cheque book for a custom-made frame, you will have to compromise. The ready reckoner is to take your shoes off and see if you can comfortably straddle the bar leaving a 3–5 cm (1–2 in) gap between the bar and your pelvic bone when you stand with your feet flat. (I assume women will be buying a so called 'men's' bike since a 'ladies' pattern frame is weaker and less responsive.) Unfortunately top bar clearance is just a rough guide and doesn't guarantee the right fit. The length of your arms, trunk and legs all have a bearing. For short women, the top bar is usually too long. Your ability to reach the handlebars and brakes is crucial. One guide is to touch the seat front with your elbow and touch the handle bars (in centre near stem) with your fingers. There's no alternative to sitting astride a number of bikes with someone experienced in judging correct sizing. Expert fitting is generally available at a good bike shop.

Comfort

A touring or hybrid bike, with longer wheelbase and less upright frame angle, gives a more stable, comfortable ride. Body comfort is a vital factor in touring, but even on a correctly sized touring bike this is not assured. The palms of your hands contain many nerve endings which can be easily numbed, making well wrapped handle bars and padded cycling gloves essential. Though you will be continually asked how you can bear sitting on a bike seat for hours each day, your posterior will be fine if it is supported by an anatomically designed saddle. Men's seats are long and narrow, women's seats are shorter and wider. The seat should be adjusted so that it is perfectly level. Lycra cycling shorts with a chamois or synthetic crotch are also a major aid to comfort on long tours. I like the shorter triathalon style, and contrary to some writers, prefer to wear snug underwear while touring. In cold weather, support pantihose (which are thicker and tighter than regular pantihose) will help your legs stay warm and may also benefit your leg muscles. For long distance touring, feet need to be protected by strong soled shoes that can be walked in without crippling you. Cross training sneakers of medium to top quality are perfectly suitable.

Efficiency

A quality steel-framed touring bike absorbs about half a per cent of pedalling energy, the remainder goes into creating forward motion. Strong lightweight aluminium rims, quick release hubs (a rock-over lever loosens or tightens for fast wheel removal and replacement) and centre pull brakes all add to overall efficiency. Pedals should be of good quality with toe clips. Toe clips are essential touring aids since they position your feet correctly and enable you to partially lift the pedal with the top of your foot on the upstroke — a combined efficiency gain of about 15 per cent. At first, learning to ride with clips can be a bit tricky. Some people feel trapped and liable to fall over with the bike if they can't get their feet free. Start off with the straps of the pedal clips fairly loose, then tighten them as you become more proficient at getting your feet in and out on the move. In heavier traffic and on rough tracks keep the straps loose so you can whip your feet out for an emergency stop.

Gearing

In the days of one-speed bikes, gearing was no problem. Today the choices are a smorgasbord of confusion, compounded by the fact that the English use one way of defining gear sizes and the Americans use another. In simple terms; a small diameter gear driving a large gear equals power to get up hills, a large gear driving a small gear equals speed to fly along the road. When you push the pedal, your energy is transmitted from the outer edge of the chainwheel along the chain to the outer edge of the freewheel sprocket and then to the rear tyre. A roller bearing chain can achieve an efficiency of up to 98.5 per cent in energy transmission. How much power you want and how fast you wish to go will dictate the size gearing needed.

Chainwheels are flat metal circles or computer designed elipses with cut gear teeth on the outer edges which hook into the chain. Obviously, the greater the number of teeth, the larger the chainwheel, and vice versa. On my 27 in wheeled Shogun touring bike I have three front chainwheels with 24, 44 and 50 teeth. Attached to the rear wheel is a seven-speed freewheel with sprockets of 13, 15, 17, 20, 23, 26 and 30 teeth.

(Smaller diameter road wheels would give a lower overall gearing.) This gearing enables me to keep a reasonable pedal rotation rate (cadence) to travel up a steep hill at speeds as low as 5 kmph (3 mph) and to keep pedalling when travelling at speeds up to 60 kmph (37 mph). (See Riding Skills — Hills for the importance of this high speed.)

There is a tendency amongst people ignorant of the needs of long distance cycle tourers to set the gearing too high. They have not experienced the joy of pedalling a fully laden bicycle up a 30 km (18½ mile) hill. Of course, as you gain experience and become fitter, your need for super low gears reduces, but no matter how fit you are, I am sure that you will experience the sinking feeling on a big hill of going for a lower gear and finding there isn't one!

Getting Fit

Cycling is an aerobic exercise where you can burn in excess of 3000 kJ (715 calories) per hour. Yet some people have cycled around Australia by the simple expedient of riding a little further each day. That is probably the best way to prepare for a tour. Ideally, at least a month before your tour, commence regular training rides. Half an hour a day, three to four times a week of hills and level terrain is enough to build your cycling fitness. Be sure to stretch (See Touring section — Stretch) before climbing aboard the bike, take it easy for the first few minutes of cycling, then try to maintain 50–60 rpm, increasing to 80 + as your fitness improves. It's more fun if you can train with someone — my partner and I like to end our early morning ride with a race. On the first weekend following your training week, try to do a lightly loaded day tour of 30–50 km (18–30 miles). Increase this by 20 to 30 km (12–18 miles) each weekend before your long distance tour, but be sure to carry more in your panniers each time. Pre-tour training does lengthen the pain barriers, but the main ingredient to getting started in bicycle touring is enthusiasm — a desire to get out and have a go.

What to Take

While it is perfectly possible to tour carrying a toothbrush and a credit card, most of us prefer to take along a few garments and nicknacks — usually far too much. There are a few ways to deal with this, one is to lay out what you think is necessary then subtract a third of it, or take everything and use post offices to send back the stuff that proves to be unnecessary. To reduce your pile in the first place I have included my Luxury Camping Cycling Tour Checklist (over page) which was developed in the course of writing this book. Please feel free to photocopy it.

From this list there are a number of things which require elaboration.

When you are packing, equal the loads on each side of the bike, with an overall weight distribution of 40 to 60 per cent front to rear. Uneven front panniers will create interesting vibrations.

Luxury camping cycling tour checklist

Clothing and equipment worn

Cycling shorts
T-shirt
Bandana
Underwear
Sunglasses
Wool/cotton socks
Hard-soled sneakers
Fingerless gloves
Helmet
Watch (with alarm)

Attached to bike

Two 750 ml (1 pt 3 fl oz)
    water bottles
Hp pump
Rear and front light
Computer
Spare spokes taped to frame

Rear pannier (right-hand side)

Small rear pocket:

2 pr socks
2 bandanas
2 hankies
1 swimming costume
2 T-shirts
3 sets of underwear
(All in stuff sack)

(All in waterproof bag)

Large main pocket:

Lightweight towel
Woollen shirt
Thermal long johns
Walking shorts
Spare pr cycling shorts
Long-sleeved cotton shirt
Pr jeans and belt
Cotton T-shirt
Pr walk sneakers
Sun shade
Sleeping bag, preferably one
    that's compact, fully-zipped,
    hooded, filled with superdown
    and rated to − 5° Celcius
Silk inner sheet, youth hostel style
Woollen gloves

Rear pannier (left-hand side)

Small rear pocket:

1 Litre (2 pt) water bottle
Spare stuff sack
4-6 Litre (1 gal) water bag
    (empty)
Candle

Main pocket:

Accessible — Wet Weather
    Jacket
Toiletries and first aid kit
Cutting board and grater
Food cooler bag (for perishables)
Bowl and plate
One emergency dehydrated
    pre-packaged meal and
    aluminium foil
The day's food (bread, fruit etc)
Vitamin pills

Front pannier (left-hand side)

Small side pocket:

Washing up gear
500 ml (17½ fl oz) Methylated
    Spirits (fuel)

Large main pocket:

Stove (kettle, two pots, pot
    lifter, matches) fuelled by
    Methylated Spirits
Morning tea set (knife, spoon,
    fork, sharp knife, cup)
Coffee (or substitute — instant/
    ground with strainer), tea, hot
    chocolate, powdered milk
Muesli

Front pannier (right-hand side)

Small side pocket:

Bike lock and chain

Large main pocket:

Accessible — Wind Chill Jacket
(If solo: tent and pegs (no poles);
    if group: bivvy bag)
Tool kit in zipped bag:
Shifting spanner/crescent wrench
    (must fit freewheel tool)
Pliers
Side cutters
Cross and flat head screwdriver
Allen key tool
Crank remover suited to your
    bike
1 Set bottom-bracket, caged
    bearings
Freewheel remover to suit your
    bike
Tyre gauge
3 Electrical ties
Insulation tape
Puncture repair kit

Chain breaker
2 Tyre levers
Lithium grease
Chain lubricant
Spare tyre valve and cap
Spare brake and gear change
    inner cables
4 Spare bolts and washers
Spare pannier elastic straps
Toothbrush
Sponge
Spoke tightener
Clean rag
1 New tube
Cycle repair guide, cut-down to
    fit in your luggage

Handlebar bag

Front small pocket:

Lip cream
Sunscreen
Comb/brush
Insect repellent

Top (See-through section):

Day map/route slip/height profile

Main body pocket:

Photographic equipment
Notebook and pen
Photocopies of maps/route slip/
    height profile

Hand-held compass and whistle

Backpack   (On top of rear carrier — all of the following inside the backpack)

Tent poles
Insulated, high-density, closed cell, foam sleeping mat
Compact, self-inflating mattress
Backpack rain cover (optional)

Toilet trowel and toilet paper
Spare light cord
(If group, 3-person tent)
Camera tripod (optional)

Attached to Bike

Computer: To follow the route slip it is essential to have some means of measuring distance to a fraction of a kilometre.

Front and rear lights: I prefer bike lights which are removable. I rarely tour at night but very often use the torch capabilities around camp.

Rear Panniers

Water Bag: Empty, well-rinsed bladders from wine casks make good water carriers around camp (and on desert trips) but they need an extra outer cover to prevent leaks being created on rough roads.

Clothes: I use the rule of threes — wear one, carry a clean one and the third ready to be washed or in the process of drying out.

Bandanas: These have endless uses, for example as a cooling neck cloth when soaked in water, back of the neck sun protector, dust and fly inhibitor when worn in bushranger style; even as a sling for injured limbs.

Stove: I prefer a methylated spirits-powered stove of Swedish design which is simple, unpressurised, compact and lightweight, with great simmer controls and easily available fuel.

Backpack

Across the top of the rear carrier (lengthwise) I lash a frameless backpack. I secure it by wrapping its top strap around the seat stem and hang the pack's shoulder straps down the outside of the rear panniers, catching them underneath the pannier's top flap. An elastic strap holds the pack to the carrier at the rear. The backpack is large enough to fit sleeping bag and limited gear for a night or two camping out.

Spare Tyre

After a memorable tour in New Zealand where we destroyed four tyres in 500 km (310 miles) I always carry a spare tyre. It weighs very little and seems to have good karma to ward off tyre failures. It is hooked under one rear clip of a rear pannier, twisted in a figure eight and clipped down on the other side.

Camping

Though it carries a weight penalty, having the option of camping on a cycle tour gives you fantastic freedom and flexibility. It is also inexpensive accommodation. If solo touring, on dry nights I prefer to sleep under the stars using a light ripstop nylon groundsheet, a self-inflating mattress, superdown sleeping bag and a Gortex bivvy bag (a waterproof but air-permeable, outer sleeping-bag cover). In rain I use a tiny 1½ person tunnel tent and sling the nylon groundsheet as a fly over tent and bike, using the protected area as a dryish cooking space. When touring with my partner, we use a New Zealand designed three-hoop, double-skinned, tunnel snow tent which features vestibules at either end (one for the panniers and one in which to cook). In heavy rain you can take the inner section down and pack it away dry before pulling down the wet fly.

In keeping with cycling being an environmentally friendly means of travel, the bicycle tourer should also be a minimum impact camper. Many parks and reserves require the use of fuel stoves, but where fires are allowed, use the smallest amount of fallen timber for firewood and ensure that the fire is completely out before you leave. Please keep soaps, hair shampoos and bodily excreta far away from water courses. Many Australian streams still have pure, unpolluted water, but some are suspect. If you have any doubts, boil, purify or filter water before drinking (see Tour 8, page 154).

Helmet

It is now illegal to ride without a helmet in every state of Australia. But legal requirements aside, since brain matter has the consistency of barely set scrambled egg, it can be injured by the crushing effect of its own weight in severe jolts — like hitting the road. Studies have shown the first most common break was the collarbone, second was a skull fracture. Without a helmet, although you might survive a bad crash, parts of your brain may not, leaving you partially or totally paralysed. Buy and use the best helmet you can afford.

Whatever brand of helmet you use, it is essential that it has good ventilation and an adjustable visor. The latter is not only extra shade for your nose, but it seems to repel insects. The helmet is fitted correctly when it is comfortable but you can't whip it off by pulling it up from the rear.

Packing Panniers

On a full camping tour I use two UK-designed rear panniers (each 45 litres (11 gallons) in capacity), two 30-litre front panniers and another (with extra padding) as a handle-bar/camera bag (10 litres) — the luxury check list above defines where everything goes. It is vital when you pack that the leading edge of either rear pannier should not bulge. If it does, your heel will clip it on every pedal stroke.

Clothes: I pack, using the principle of layers of protection, in three sets of stuff sacks. Into the open clothes pannier I put a truly waterproof river bag (they are used by river rafters). Into this bag goes the down sleeping bag in a stuff sack — the Australian-designed sleeping bag I use is compact enough to fit lengthwise at the bottom of the pannier. On top of that go my 'better' clothes in one stuff sack and my warm clothes in another. I close the river bag and place spare shoes in a plastic shopping bag on top of that, then close down the pannier. Underwear, socks and the like go in a stuff sack inside the small rear-zipped compartment.

Food and utensils: A cutting board slides in on the flat side of the pannier, then in zipped nylon containers I pack food, plates and bowls. On top of that goes a soft-bodied, insulated bag — inside it are cheese, tomatoes, lettuce and margarine/butter. A loaf of bread and my wet weather jacket completes the load before the pannier is closed.

Front panniers: I try to pack them tall and thin, rather than squat. The broader they become, the more they tend to cause steering vibrations. I usually leave a space on the top of the left one to take my wind chill jacket — since it is taken on and off all day.

Handle-bar Bag: Extra padding on the sides and bottom helps to reduce vibration and protect its contents (in my case cameras) against knocks. Accessibility is the key to taking photographs on a bike so I pack the camera equipment with this in mind. At the bottom of the bag (in self-sealing plastic lunch bags) are 10 or 20 rolls of film — with the outer boxes removed. Then a spare camera body wrapped in a towelling sock. Beside it are two lenses in a soft, open-topped lens bag. In a flat-zipped purse I put reference material and maps to be used later. Placed in last is the camera mounted with a motor drive and lenses. Around the inner edges of the bag are the day's film, cleaning tissues, spare batteries, polarising and neutral density filters. In the front zipped compartment are nibbles, sun protection cream, insect repellant, and a camera puffer brush.

I place my day map in a clear map holder along with a photocopy of the height profile then slip that into the clear section on the top of the handle-bar bag. To research this book I also carried a small notebook and pen with which to note down the instructions for route slips. Under all that I slip my wallet. On days of heavy rain I place a clear plastic shopping bag over the whole handle-bar bag, threading the elastic, hold-down straps through the plastic bag's handles.

Information Sources

Please consult the Appendices for a list of valuable addresses, including bike shops, bicycle institutes and touring clubs. In most mid-sized towns, there is a local information centre. Call in and have a chat as you roll into town. Be sure to tell them you are cycle touring. This decreases the frequency of being told that a particular attraction is 'only 40 minutes away' — translated to bike language this can mean hours of riding.

ON THE ROAD

Your bicycle tour is about to commence, planning is done, packing completed, thighs and calves conditioned, the sun is shining and you have a heady exuberant feeling which manifests itself as an almost visible sign across your forehead which reads 'On Tour'. But, before you throw a leg over the saddle and ride off into the sunrise, let me hold you up for a couple of important minutes. Rather than have the day ruined by part of your bike coming adrift 10 km down the track, let's do a quick pre-ride check.

The Two-Minute Safety Check

After you have been touring for a while you may find that this check is better done at the *end* of each day. But if, like me, you always do it the last second before leaving, it's not the time to find that you broke a spoke yesterday. For repairs and replacements please see Running Repairs below.

Before starting, remove the panniers!

Bike Standing

Brakes: Standing beside the bike, pull firmly on one brake lever at a time. The pads must come to grip the edge of the rims, not clear air, and not on the tyre's edge. Adjust if necessary. While the brake is firmly on, rock the bike backward and forward and check that the brake arms don't flex too much. If they're loose, tighten them. Throw a leg over the top bar and pull hard on both levers. They should not come closer than 25 mm from the handlebars. Adjust by undoing the lock nut at end of the brake cable then, turning the knurled nut, retighten the locknut.

Headset: Still astride the bike with the brakes firmly on, rock the bike backwards and forwards. If there's a clicking sound, the headset bearings may be loose. Loosen the locknut, tighten the threaded top race until it is hand tight, then loosen it one quarter of a turn and tighten the locknut. Grip the front wheel between your knees and twist the handle bars from side to side. If loose, tighten the stem bolt.

Saddle: Look along the line of the top bar to check the saddle is not dipping at the front. Grip the saddle and try to twist it. If it's loose, tighten the bolts under the saddle.

Bike upside down

Wheels: Hold the frame down and wiggle the wheels from side to side. If it's loose, check that the wheel's quick release mechanism is tight. Older-style wheel bearings may need tightening — consult your manual.

Tyres: Spin each wheel very slowly, feeling the side walls with your fingers for any bumps and look at the tread for bumps or opening nicks and glass or burrs. Check for correct pressure in both tyres.

Rims: Rest a finger on the bike frame close to the edge of the wheel rim. Spin the rim and visually check for wabbles. Rest a finger close to the centre of the tread and check for hops. If either are excessive, try to discover why. Perhaps there is a buckle in the rim or maybe a spoke has broken — see below. Fix the problem if you can, or ride conservatively and check the wheel in to the next bike shop.

Spokes: To check for broken or loose spokes, feel them in pairs (on the same side) squeezing them together gently between your thumb and fingers. Adjust or replace — see Broken Spokes (page 26).

Chain: Inspect for dryness. As the chain dries, it will make more and more 'wash, wash' noises, particularly on steep hills. Lubricate it and wipe off excess.

Gear shifting: Turn crank with one hand and shift first the front then the rear derailleurs. Shifting to the smallest or largest chainrings and freewheel sprockets should not allow the chain to go past either and fall off. On freewheel sprockets, the changes should be without long hesitations. Consult the manual for your brand of derailleurs.

Bottom Bracket: Reach through the frame to grasp each crank (not the pedals). Push and pull enthusiastically from side to side. Any looseness indicates that the bearings may need tightening. When you are riding, particularly up steep hills, crunching, creaking or clicking noises will develop as the bottom bracket dries out, wears or loosens. This seems to occur more often after prolonged heavy rain. See Bottom Bracket (page 27).

Pedals: Grip and move each from side to side. There will be a slight sideplay but this should not make them feel sloppy. Undo the locknut, hand tighten the outer cone, back off one-quarter turn, then tighten the locknut.

Toe clips: Check for any looseness in the attaching nuts, and also check wearing of the straps.

Pannier frames: Hold the seat in one hand and grip the back of the rear pannier frame in the other. While looking at the top connecting bolts then the bottom bolts, briskly move the frame from side to side. Tighten if loose. Do the same for the front pannier frame, gripping the top bar and front of frame.

Panniers: Check for wear points. *Any* roughness is an early warning. Prevent holes forming by glueing (use contact adhesive) a pad over the wear point. If you have nothing else, use a tube patch, but don't leave yourself short of patches. Try to discover what the pannier is rubbing against. Check attaching straps for wear — carry spares.

Stretching

When your bike is ready to go, be sure to put your body in the same state with a few stretching exercises. (*NB.* For stretches 2–5, hold each steadily for a count of 15 and don't bounce.)

1. In a standing position with your arms beside body, breath in through the nose and raise your arms fully stretched over your head. Breath out through your mouth as your arms come down. Repeat twice.

2. Put the heel of one leg on the bike's top bar, gently reach with your opposite arm to touch the toe of your shoe, standing tall on the other leg. Feel the stretch at back of your knee. Repeat with your other leg and arm.

3. Lay your palms against a tree or wall, one leg straight out behind you and your foot flat on the ground and one leg bent and closer to the wall. Tighten your thigh muscles, feeling the stretch on your Achilles tendon. Reverse and repeat.

4. Standing side on to your bike, lift the foot of your outside leg up behind you and grasp it with your hand. Press your foot gently against your buttocks, balancing with your other hand on the saddle. Feel the stretch on the front of your bent leg, above your knee. Reverse and repeat.

5. Standing, feet together, turn your left foot 90 degrees out to the side and step out in that direction so your legs are now apart. Turn to face your left leg and gently lunge so most of your body weight is carried by your left leg. Feel the stretch in your inner thighs and crotch. Reverse and repeat.

6. Complete the exercises with five push ups, increasing these by one for each day of the tour.

You are now ready for a great day of touring.

Cycle Touring Riding Skills

Riding a bicycle is a deceptively skillful activity, particularly when the bike is fully laden with heavy panniers. The bike will feel very different to a pannier-free machine. Getting away from a standing start, use the gears and work up to each higher gear smoothly. There's an immediate awareness of heavier steering, headwinds have more force and sidewinds can nudge the bike with careless ease. Cornering a heavily-laden touring bike requires greater arcs and stopping takes much longer. Panniers add width as well as weight, so be sure to allow greater clearance when slipping past solid inanimate objects and slow moving pedestrians. Low-rider, front panniers also decrease ground clearance beside the front wheel — I managed an embarrassing side fall when a concrete flower pot 'grabbed' one of my front panniers. When stationary, be wary of the front wheel's tendency to turn by itself, and as the bike goes over, the chainring will gouge evenly spaced pieces out of your calf muscle. Standing a pannier carrying bike upright against a single post can be lots of fun, till you discover that it will stay put if you lean the front pannier and side of the handlebars against the post.

Setting Goals

The first day of touring you may tend to be keyed up, almost desperate to get down the road as fast as possible. Lots of people get cracking at sun up, then ride head down, bum up, eyes set on tunnel vision. Stops are brief, but anxious, and hills are an annoyance. A frayed wreck, they arrive at the day's destination by 11.30 a.m., wondering what they have just seen. Much better to relax, set a realistic distance to be travelled and take it easy. You have plenty of time — and you will get there.

Pace

Achieving your own pace is a matter of experience, but begin by finding out when you are at your best. I am a morning person. I like to be up with the sun, on the road and cruising by 8 a.m., and to be well beyond the half-way point before lunch. That way I can enjoy a relaxing lunch knowing that even though I'm less motivated in the afternoon, there isn't far to go. In summer, riding in the coolest part of the day is an advantage, but in winter it is sometimes better to wait until the sun has a little warmth, then use the middle of the day as the peak riding time.

While I believe it pointless to go fast just to clock up kilometres (downhills are a different story), it is wise not to dawdle. A body performs much better when it is used with vigour, the aim is to ride at a self-challenging pace. This is just under the point at which your heart rate soars and breathing becomes laboured. The optimum pace is a 'floater', decreasing as you climb hills, increasing as the tailwinds blow. Overall, however, it gradually increases as touring fitness increases (not the same thing as riding fitness on an unladen bike). While moderate exercise can be performed for a long time, strenuous exercise can be performed for only a short time, then you go into oxygen debt — repayed by quick, heavy breathing.

Cadence

Keeping just below serious oxygen debt is the way to enjoy cycle touring, and cadence is the key factor in both not becoming exhausted and yet developing touring fitness. In essence, cadence is how many times you spin the cranks each minute, and virtually everyone starts touring at a cadence which is too slow. Put too much effort into each pedal stroke and you are working too hard; exhaustion and sore muscles are the result. The whole point of having 18 or 21 speeds on a touring bike is to enable you to maintain a constantly high cadence, i.e. more than 80 rpm, no matter what the ground speed. To establish what 80 + rpm feels like, use a cycling computer with this function, ride beside someone who has a computer while in the same gear as that person, or count while touring yourself. To achieve a cadence of more than 80 rpm does, at first, feel unnaturally quck, but it won't tire you nearly as fast as slow pedal thrusts in too high a gear.

21

Rhythm

The keys to establishing and maintaining a good pace are rhythm and smoothness. Cycling is a naturally smooth activity, but it can become a syncopated jumble if you are forever charging and dying. Instead of becoming a thrashing machine for 200 m (210 yd), then a steam engine for the next 50, establish as high a cadence as is comfortable and maintain it as the terrain changes. At the mere hint of an incline you smoothly slip the gear to the next larger freewheel sprocket, so although, your ground speed slows, cadence has been maintained.

Gear Changing

Sound, or lack of it, is an indicator of good gear changes. Even in this wonderful age of indexed gears it is possible to make a noisy hash of it. Riding an unladen bike, there's no drama if you miss a gear change — going two clicks will let you catch up, but when touring this is a sure way to quadruple the effort required to ascend hills. Choosing the correct moment to change gears only comes with experience. Essentially, on rises, you feel the bike is just about to lose momentum, which would result in pedal speed dropping. Before that happens, click to the next largest freewheel sprocket.

Now just to complicate life, if it is already on the largest sprocket, you have to go to the next smallest chainring. This is no problem when changing from the largest to the middle chainring. But, when on the start of a serious hill, going from the middle chainring to the smallest is often too big a step — cadence spins off into infinity. That's when you need to juggle two things in very quick order. At the same time as you move the chainring to the granny gear, drop down a couple of freewheel sprockets. This means the overall gearing changes slightly and you can maintain the same cadence to keep momentum.

Momentum is vital when 'charging'. Some hills are small enough to be charged, or follow good downhills. That's when you are on the largest chainring and small freewheel sprocket and it's the

reason that touring bikes need high gears. By maintaining a fast cadence just before starting the rise, as gravity starts to bite, quickly and smoothly stepping down through the gears, you can make the bike almost fly over the next hill.

Hills

Some hills, though, fight back. Such hills need to be negotiated rather than attacked. Try not to consume a large meal just before a substantial ascent, use the height profiles to plan your day. Assuming your bike has sufficiently low gears, climbing really large hills is a process of patience and persistence. Sit as upright as possible to allow maximum intake of oxygen, find a speed that doesn't stress your legs too much and cruise a little in those tiny dips one often discovers on big hills. And use your arms to pull on the handlebar tops — not in a upwards motion but parallel to the level of the road. On extremely steep climbs, where possible, stay well away from the inside edge of any curve, always prefer an outside, less extreme gradient.

Over time — maybe ten minutes, maybe an hour (depending on touring fitness) — your legs may begin to 'scream'. No one else will hear, but you will. That's the time for a little 'honking', or, put more delicately, riding 'en danseuse', out of the saddle. Honking on a fully laden touring bike needs good balance and an unhassled approach. Treat it as if you are now gently walking up a set of tall stairs. As you rise off the seat, change the freewheel sprocket to one smaller. This slows the cadence and makes honking easier. Racers throw their bikes from side to side in a wonderful display, but try that with full panniers and the bike will bite, dumping you on the deck. Tour mode honking must be done slowly and gently, with a minimum of side to side movement. When going back to seated pedalling, put in a couple of faster strokes, then ease pressure and change to the next largest freewheel sprocket.

To walk or not to walk?

Believe it or not, on a steep slope it is metabolically about one-third more efficient to keep riding than it is to get off and push. If a loose bit of gravel or an errant vehicle forces you to get off and walk, it is easier to proceed by gripping the handle bars with your left hand and grabbing behind the seat with your right hand. Extend your right arm straight and use it to pull the bike along.

Flying Descents

Whether you ride or walk, in the end there's little to surpass the sense of relief at feeling the hill's resistance melt at the apex of a long hard climb. This is perhaps heightened by the anticipation of an exhilarating, long, tarred road descent. Okay, I acknowledge that fast, freewheeling descents can be dangerous, but why do we climb hills if not to admire the views then blast down the other sides?

Before you enter terminal velocity it is comforting to remember the morning's pre-ride check showed that all was perfect with your bike. A dab on the brakes will confirm they are still working, then you are away. Road speed increases as quickly as you can click through the gears into the largest chainring and smallest freewheel sprocket. Once above 20 kmph your body position has a dramatic wind resistance effect. On the flat at 32 kmph nearly 80 per cent of rider's power is used to overcome wind resistance and by 64 kmph this has risen to 93 per cent.

One unbreakable rule about fast descents is *don't brake in the corners!* In the straight sections, even short ones, by sitting up straight in the saddle your body acts as a wind brake. This, assisted by a firm, simultaneous squeeze of both front and rear brakes, will wash off enough speed to set you up for a smooth handling of the next corner. As you approach the corner, ensure that the inside pedal, i.e. left for left corners, is at the 12 o'clock position and coast. On corners that decrease in radius, force yourself to look to the inside of the curve (turn head firmly) — looking outwards will take you there.

On corners through which you can see clearly (and only when you are sure there are no cars nipping at your heel), keep on your half of the road but take the racing 'line', i.e. on a left-hand bend you start the corner beside the centre line, at the half-way point you are on the far left-hand edge of the road (beware of rough or loose patches) and by the end of the corner you are back near the centre line again. This, in effect, 'straightens' the corner. At high speed you need to be reading the road a good distance in front. Even if you see some danger ahead, you must try to avoid it in smooth, minimal movements only. Any harsh steering changes can produce spectacularly painful results.

Falls

Though it can easily reach speeds in excess of 80 kmph, a touring bike has a minute footprint on the bitumen and even tinier strips of brake rubber. Add into the equation a wet road and a speeding cyclist is skating on the very thinnest veneer of ice. Speeding in some circumstances could be exceeding 15 kmph! Given those factors it is more than likely, sometime, somewhere, you will have a fall. None are pleasant, and there is very little I can offer as advice in coping with them, other than two maxims:

1. If you are going to hit something try to pick the softest inanimate object; and

2. If you are heading for a hard inanimate object, lay the bike down and put it between you and that object.

Surviving Traffic

'I went ahead gallantly, and hit the horse fair and square on the breastbone with my front tyre . . . I hit the dust . . . and though I managed to roll over and spring upright . . . just clear of the wheels, my bike came out a mangled, shrieking corpse . . .'

This was G.B. Shaw to R. Golding Bright on 22 September 1896, describing his confrontation with a baker's van, and amply demonstrates that traffic hazards are not new.

For the great bulk of kilometres in these eight tours you will be away from heavily trafficked highways, but unavoidably you will still be sharing the roads with other users. With this in mind, when shopping for cycling clothes, a wind chill jacket and wet weather gear choose dazzlingly, gaudily bright designs — colours that you might otherwise not want to be seen dead in, which is the point. To high-speed vehicle drivers, a bicycle simply doesn't register on the consciousness unless it is obvious — and that's in overhead sunlight. Change the conditions to heavy rain or sun-in-their-eyes and if dressed in muted earthy colours you have really ceased to exist.

Assuming now that you are emitting a rainbow-like luminosity, the best defence in traffic is to start acting paranoid. In traffic if you believe every other road user is able to kill you, then you are perfectly right. Every parked car contains a driver who just bent down to pick up a dropped set of car keys. They find the keys and innocently open the car door just as you pass by the rear bumper. When a vehicle overtakes a bike, the bike ceases to exist, that's why the driver pauses up ahead then turns hard left, right in your path. If an over-taking vehicle finds that there's an oncoming vehicle, you are the softest thing to hit. Get out of the way, pronto. On a narrow road every vehicle behind you is being driven by a very important person, who is late for a very impor-tant meeting. Pedestrians believe touring cyclists are able to stop in a space the length of a dollar coin's diameter. Surviving traffic is more likely if, no matter what the circumstances, you remain alert, take care and always have an escape route.

Wind

'The wind too has its destination, but in the opposite direction', wrote Wendell Berry in *Harper's Bazaar* magazine, September 1977, a case of heads you lose, tails you win. Not many tourers like headwinds, particularly solo travellers. In designing the eight tours in this book I have tried to select the best travelling direction with prevailing winds in mind. If, when you ride them, the breeze has only Wendell's direction, I offer my condolences and claim the fickle finger of fate. Sometimes the only escape for solo riders is to

adopt the strategy of riding in the evening if the winds have died down.

If you are touring with a friend or a group and encounter headwinds, learn to 'draft' off each other. This entails riding *en echelon*, closely in the lee or sheltered quarter, of the rider in front — sometimes only 15 to 30 cm (6 to 12 in) off their real wheel. It requires a modicum of skill not to come too close and get a wheel overlap, and a degree of confidence in the rider in front. Lead riders must be smooth and constant and not prone to sudden photo stops, or radical last-minute swerves to avoid huge pot holes. When you are drafting, try to soft pedal (ease pressure) rather than touching the brakes — the latter can cause a chain reaction of problems.

Road Surfaces

Although the days of following a camel train to get a smooth, padded riding surface are long gone, for most of the tours in this book, road surfaces are conducive to pleasant riding. Unavoidably there are some tough sections. The second day of Tour 8 lives strongly in my memory. Rocks and potholes not only drain your energy when con-centrating on finding the best path, but they increase the tyres' rolling resistance. Heavy rains can create brake-jamming quagmires, though they can also make sandy sections much firmer. The condition of dirt roads often depends on recent weather and when they were last graded. When I rode the tours there weren't too many corruga-tions big enough to shake your eyeballs out, nor did I have the experience of the Reverend Sussex who, in 1902, after riding 402 km in three days on Western Australian roads wrote:

'Could not write yesterday. My hand was quite numbed with the vibration of the bike through travelling over rough roads. Took me all my time to hold the knife and fork at meals.'

Animals

An anonymous cyclist from the past is quoted as saying 'To run over a dog — not too large — is the ambition of every cyclist possessed of any self

respect.' After being chased and bitten on some memorable occasions I can appreciate how one could come to this conclusion. For dealing with dogs it's a good plan to try all five of these recommended methods of defraying a dog attack:
1. Command it to stop.
2. Spray it with your water bottle.
3. Wield the pump.
4. Sprint.
5. Stop the bike (keeping it between you and the dog).

Though you may be regaled with stories of savage koalas and sabre-toothed possums (both fanciful), there is also one hard-to-believe account of a cyclist being chased by a pack of dingoes. There are frequent, credible accounts of panniers being raided at night (it happened to me whilst riding Tour 1), so it is wise not to leave food accessible in unattended panniers overnight.

Getting Lost

Given the detailed route slips and maps contained within this book I sincerely trust you will not become lost on any of the tours. Detours of course can be a little confusing, leading you to become geographically embarrassed. Those of us who have experienced this sensation will identify with the words of Jerome Murif who was the first person to pedal across Central Australia. In 1897 he wrote:

> 'The cyclist who is sure of his road can never imagine the weakening effect which uncertainties on that most vital point can produce. Such doubts involve sickening, depressing, unhappy sensations which make themselves felt more acutely than do the mere bodily disablements associated with hunger and thirst.'

Dehydration

Murif may have rated getting lost of greater hardship than thirst, but dehydration is a major problem for bicycle tourers. Hill climbing is the obvious time sweat is flowing, but on a hot day you don't appreciate how much sweat is being generated because it is being rapidly evaporated by a constant breeze. Headache, muscle tiredness then cramps, faintness and dizziness may be the first signs, not thirst. It is essential to drink before you get on the bike, then keep drinking pure fresh water all day. In extreme conditions your body needs as much as 500 ml (17½ fl oz) fluid per hour! Avoid sugar drinks or too much coffee and tea — alcohol when riding is a no no. When overstressed I use a fizzy vitamin drink for a much needed boost.

Running Repairs

These are purely by-the-roadside repairs and maintenance designed to get you to the next town. The segment is not intended as a workshop manual. Buy and carry a good general maintenance book, e.g. *Richards Bicycle Book* by R. Ballantine or *Bicycle Maintenance Manual* by Eugene A. Sloane and use it to do a complete service (or pay for one to be done) before the tour. The service should include removing, lubricating and reassembling the freewheel.

Flats — the five-minute tyre change.
Symptoms: Painfully obvious.
Needed: Two tyre levers, good tube, pump.

1. First, remove the water bottles and have a calming drink of water. Then get out the tool kit, lay a ground sheet down in the shade, invert the bicycle, release the quick-release mechanism on the hub. Undo the quick release mechanism on the brake (a knurled end on brake cable at brake end). If a rear tyre, shift the gear to the smallest sprocket, hook the chain up on a little frame peg (if the bike has one), tilt the body of the derailleur to the rear. Slide the wheel out. Retire to the ground sheet and shade.

2. Undo the valve cap. Opposite the valve, using two tyre levers, insert one between the rim and tyre and lever the tyre over the edge of rim. Hook the tyre lever on a spoke using the lever's cut-out section. Do the same with the second tyre lever on the same side, but a few spoke widths away. Remove the first lever and continue to gently prise the tyre off the rim for a full circle on one side.

3. At the valve, gently remove the valve from the hub and pull out all of the tube. Fold and set aside. Hold the rim, grip the freed edge of tyre and pull it off the rim. Check the tyre and rim for sharp, protruding objects.

4. Get out a new or previously repaired tube. A puncture can be repaired later at lunch or dinner or before breakfast. Put a few pumps of air into the new tube to give it shape. Put tyre levers in the tool kit and forget they exist.

5. Slip one bead of the tyre on the rim. Find the valve hole, *gently* grip the thin rubber strip around the rim and hold away from the rim. Slip the tube valve through this hole, then insert it between the tyre and rim, then through the hole in the rim.

6. *Begin near valve* to reseat the tube into the rim. Take care not to twist the tube or to leave creases.

7. *Using only thumbs*, begin at the valve to roll the tyre bead over the rim. Take care not to pinch the tube. As the tyre bead goes over, push down on the tread to seat the bead in the bottom of the rim. On either side of the valve, work for a few spokes clockwise, then a few spokes anticlockwise.

8. The crux: The last 10 cm is a no-go? *Go back to the valve and push down on the tread getting the bead to seat. Work the tyre down all the way around heading back to the hard bit.** It should be easier. Still no-go? Relax, have another drink of water. Do * to ** again. Trust me, it will go.

9. Slide the wheel back on the bike. If a rear wheel, pull the derailleur towards the rear first.

10. Refit the brake quick-release mechanism. Pull tightly on the brake, tighten the quick-release hub mechanism. Spin to ensure there's no rubbing. Pump up the tyre.

Broken Spoke

Symptoms: A 'crack' as it brakes, or a 'tinkle' after the event.
Needed: Two tyre levers, spare spoke, flat head screwdriver, spoke key, freewheel remover, adjustable spanner.

Complete steps **1–3** for flats, above.

4. Unless you are truly blessed, the broken spoke will be on the rear wheel, close to the freewheel cluster. This means removing the freewheel before you can replace the spoke.

(a) For a cassette cluster, lay the bike on the left-hand side. Wrap the chain around the largest chainring, and ask an assistant to hold it (wrap the chain in cloth first). Fit the freewheel remover, adjust the spanner to fit the remover, and turn the spanner firmly in direction of the arrow as shown on outer edge of cluster. Ignore the creaking — it is just the ribbed underside of the locknut. Once it is off, the whole cluster comes off in one unit.

(b) For an older-style freewheel, have a calming drink and then offer a small sacrifice to the gods of cycle tourers. Choose members of your cycling party whose knuckles drag on the ground, and ask one to hold the rim, adjust the spanner to tightly fit the freewheel remover, turn it against the direction of resistance with as much force as you and the gorilla can manage. No go? Flag down a motorist and beg a large spanner and length of pipe. Apply considerable force to the freewheel removing tool. Success? Go to step 5. Still no go? Bad kharma, utter expletives. Do Flats steps 5–9, above. Lighten the load on the wheel with the broken spoke by sharing it out to all members of the party. Ride to the nearest bike shop and get it fixed there.

5. Using near spokes as a guide, insert the threaded end of new spoke in from the hub and thread it through the companion spokes. This is tricky but persistence will be rewarded. Insert the threaded end through the hole in rim. Wind on the spoke nut. With the screwdriver, tighten until the new spoke is close to the tension of others. Lay the rim flat, push down on the outer edges at the 3 and 9 o'clock points, then 12 and 6. Don't worry if it creaks.

6. Do Flats, steps 5–9, above.

7. At the next bike shop get the wheel tuned.

Bottom Bracket Bearing Replacement: cotterless cranks
Symptoms: Crunching grinding feel when pedalling
Needed: Crank removal tool, shifting spanner, flat head screwdriver, spare caged bearing set, grease, clean rag.

1. In the shade, invert the bicycle over a ground sheet. *At the bearing end of the right-hand crank (chainring side), remove the cover plastic with a screwdriver. Fit the socket end of the crank-removing tool (CRT), hold the crank in one hand, turn the locknut *anti*-clockwise with a shifting spanner. Reverse the CRT, back off the puller shaft (inner plunger), screw the CRT into the crank at least four or five complete turns. Hold the crank, turn the puller shaft clockwise with the shifting spanner. The crank should slide off the bottom bracket axle.**

2. For left-hand side crank, repeat * to **.

3. If you are not carrying a bottom bracket spanner set (costly and heavy), the inelegant solution is to use a flat end screwdriver and pounding implement (rock, crank end, flat side of shifting spanner). The lockring has square serrations, place the end of screwdriver in the bottom of a serration and tap firmly to move the lock ring in an *anti*clockwise direction. You may need to do this on a number of serrations.

4. Undo the outer cup by inserting the point of a screwdriver in the indentation and turning *anti*clockwise. Remove the cup, caged bearings (note which way it goes — flanged edge of cage towards axle bearing surface), axle, plastic dirt protector and other side caged bearings.

5. Clean the inside housing and inner face of cup, then grease them, grease the spare set of caged bearings and refit, hand tightening the outer cup, then back one quarter of a turn. Hold in this spot and tighten the lockring.

6. Reassemble the cranks by sliding them on the axle and tightening the locknuts.

Catastrophes!

My only suggestion is to be innovative. In the past, broken frames have been held together by fencing wire, a saw, strong pair of pincers and a piece of hardwood batten. Broken forks have been repaired by inserting a stick in the tube or putting a splint on it.

Food

The most important factor is to eat when your body tells you, rather than trying to impose your wishes on it. Beware of becoming so tired that you don't feel like eating. Naturally, what you eat is a very individual thing but here are two menus, both presume you are in contact with shops at least every second day.

1. Meat Eater (male, never gains weight):
Breakfast: Natural muesli, chopped banana, low-fat fruit yoghurt, hot water. Wholemeal toast, margarine/butter, peanut butter, honey. Coffee with powdered low fat milk. Note: Local bread in small Australian towns is often a disappointment, unless you are into white cardboard.
Lunch: Wholemeal bread, margarine/butter, tomato, cheese, lettuce (ham sometimes). Slice of fruit cake, coffee with powdered low-fat milk.
Dinner: Meat or fish, stir-fried mushrooms, carrots, potato, beans.
Dessert — chopped banana, kiwi fruit, low-fat fruit yoghurt, milo with powdered low-fat milk.
Nibbles: Chocolate-coated peanuts, dried fruits, nuts.

2. Vegetarian
Breakfast: Two pieces wholemeal toast, peanut butter, water or juice.
Lunch: Carbonated sweet drink, peanut-butter sandwich.

Dinner: Rice or pasta with lentils, chilli pasta, vegetables and fruit cut up into it, yoghurt or cream or milk mixed into it. Tea and juice or milk.

Nibbles: Apple and malted barley sugar for bottom of hills and chocolate for the tops.

Body Pain

I presume you religiously stretch before and after each segment of riding (i.e. breakfast to lunch and lunch to dinner), and that you are riding a bike which is vaguely close to the correct size and sitting on an anatomically correct seat. If so and the pain persists then the following may help.

Knees: Until you are warmed up, spin the pedals easily as if there was a fresh egg between the sole of your foot and the pedal. Find the most comfortable riding position on the bike. Check that your shoes really do fit. Micro adjust the seat — 2 mm max, up or down, forward or back.

Back and/or Neck: You need variety — change your seating position often. Learn to ride on the finger tips for a few hundred metres sitting as upright as possible. Long periods of tuck riding can antagonise your neck. Check that your saddle is dead level. Ride with your arms slightly bent, not dead straight. If all this fails, micro adjust your head set height — 1 mm max at a time.

Hands, Wrists and Arms: Same as above, plus ensure many changes of hand grip. Better gloves may help.

Bum: Check the seat angle. To give yourself a break, on gentle downhills and tailwind flat sections, extend one leg straight, slide forward till your backside is off the seat and lean the inside of your thigh against the top bar. *Note* — this position is not recommended unless you are a confident and very competent rider.

Personal Details

If your pubic bone area becomes painful try a little talcum powder each morning and rub a small amount of face cream into the chamois crotch of your cycling shorts. On long tours, some women may initially stop menstruating, then become more regular than before the tour began. Men can sometimes lose sense of feeling in genitals — relax, it is only temporary.

Okay you brave souls who have read everything to this point, eight of the loveliest tours in Australia await you.

TOUR 1
SYDNEY TO THE GOLD COAST

1 SYDNEY TO THE GOLD COAST

This is a 900 km camping and accommodation tour which could be ridden at any time of year (though it can be very wet and very hot during January and February). The route will take you through some of the most beautiful national parks on the east coast of Australia, and probably provide many opportunities to see the local wildlife. For most of the time, the route keeps you away from the overly busy Highway One by utilising ferries and a train. I rode it solo during May taking a total of 15 days (including two rest days), averaging 71 km per day. The tour could be ridden in reverse, though you would miss out on a beautiful first day descent.

Sydney

Sydney (pop^n 3.6 million) is Australia's largest city. As you would expect, there is a multitude of accommodation to choose from — youth hostels, serviced apartments, budget to expensive hotels. Check the yellow pages or the free 'What's On' (in Sydney) magazine available from most hotels and travel agents.

Transport and Tours

Getting from the airports (international and domestic) **to Central Station** (train): Riding all the way to Central Station is not recommended as you will be fighting Sydney traffic, literally. An airport bus (bright yellow) runs every 20 minutes but will take a bike only if it is boxed. Sedan taxis will transport one bike (remove front wheel) and there are a small number of station-wagon taxis that can take two bikes.

An **alternative** is to ride (10-15 mins) to Arncliffe station, then catch the train to Central (preferably not during the morning peak hours 7-9 a.m.). You will need to buy a bike ticket, put the bike in the companion way, then hold onto it. **Route** for this is:

From *Domestic terminal*, towards city along Keith Smith Ave/Shiers Ave, L-Ninth St, S-Qantas Dr. to *International terminal*, Centre Rd, L-Cooks River Ave, L-Marsh St, L (lights) West Botany Rd, R-(lights) Wickham St, cross railway, R-Firth St, Arncliffe station on R.

For **train, bus and ferry information** call Metro Trips (955 4422 — at time of writing), or check the front of the white pages phone book.

For **general touring information**, visit the Bicycle Institute of New South Wales (BINSW), 802 George Street, Sydney (near Central Station). They have an excellent escorted day-tour program usually on weekends and public holidays. For 22 self-guided short tours around Sydney, I recommend *Sydney Bicycle Rides* published by BINSW. **Commercial bike tours** are run in the Blue Mountains by Out and About Bush Ventures.

Other Contacts: NSW Information Centre, Castlereagh St, Sydney.

Youth Hostel Association, 176 Day St, Sydney.

NRMA, 151 Clarence St, Sydney — District maps are excellent. Reciprocal arrangements with members of interstate and overseas motoring organisations (bring your card).

National Parks and Wildlife Service Office, Cadman's Cottage, The Rocks.

DAY 1: Sydney to Newcastle

Distance ridden: 35.4 km;   Riding time: 2 hrs 12 mins;   Average speed: 16.0 kmph;   Maximum speed: 51 kmph

You begin the tour by catching the Newcastle train from Sydney's Central Station to Cowan. As the train eases out of Central Station you can look at the lines of congested traffic and be thankful for this effortless method of escape from Australia's largest city. Within about 40 minutes, licks of orange sandstone can be seen amid green-treed hills, along with enticing glimpses of secluded bays. You are now passing through Ku-ring-gai Chase National Park. The 150 000 hectares of sandstone plateau is one of Sydney's gems, and day rides through it are both challenging and immensely rewarding. Thanks to the foresight of local conservationists, this national park was established in 1894. For many thousands of years before that, it had been home to the local Daruk and Eora tribes of Aborigines. Now the only remaining visible legacy from their culture is a rich

ROUTE SLIP

Directions	R/S km	Ride for	Destination	Cum route km
END OF SECTION 1			**TOTAL FOR ROUTE**	**84.7**
Soldiers Point	84.7			84.7
L	78.7	6	Salamander Bay	78.7
L-Port Stephen Dr	74	4.7	Soldiers Pt	74
L-rejoin (122)	69.1	4.9	Nelson Bay	69.1
L-Marsh Rd	60.9	8.3		60.9
S-roundabout	58.4	2.5		58.4
BR	51.4	7	Williamtown Air Base	51.4
R-main road	40.8	10.6	Nelson Bay	40.8
R-Fullerton St	38	2.8		38
L-Caragan St	36.8	1.2		36.8
S-Mitchell St	35.8	1		35.8
ferry to Stockton				
R-Ncl Ferry Terminal	35.8		Stockton	35.8
L-Wharf St	35.6	0.2		35.6
L-from station	35.4	0.2		
train to **Newcastle**			Newcastle	
L-**Gosford** Station	35.4			
L-traffic lights	33.4	2	over train lines	33.4
R-traffic lights	32.5	0.9	Gosford	32.5
R	24.7	7.8		24.7
S-roundabout	24.2	0.5	West Gosford/Woy Woy	24.2
S-rejoin road	19	5.2		19
L-at T-intersection	17.9	1.1	No Through Rd	17.9
R-at T-intersection	17.7	.2		17.7
S-Diamond Rd	17	.7		17
L-Crystal Ave	16.5	0.5		16.5
R-service trail end	16.4	0.1		16.4
R-walking track	14.6	1.8	Warrah Lookout	14.6
S-track on L	14.2	.4	Warrah Trig	14.2
R-service trail	13.1	1.1	Pearl Beach	13.1
R-end of wharf	11.4	1.7		11.4
board ferry to Patonga			Patonga	
L-Dangar St	11.2	0.2	Ferry	11.2
R-Brooklyn t'off	7.9	3.3	Brooklyn	7.9
R-Cowan Stn	0.0	7.9		0.0
Central Stn, **Sydney**	0.0	0.0	Cowan	Train
(Country Trains Platforms)				
BEGIN SECTION 1				

KEY

L = left   **R** = right   **S** = straight

BL = bear left   **BR** = bear right

X = cross   * = detour directions

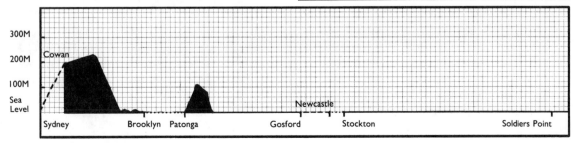

On ride line, each segment = 1 kilometre

assortment of cave paintings and rock engravings.

Alight at Cowan and after a few minutes of stretching exercises you can begin cycling on a beautifully constructed highway, and luckily a road that most motorists reject. Your morning will begin by carving high speed turns on a predominantly downhill glide and far below, you can see the Hawkesbury River. It's an immense waterway - more than 480 km long - which begins life as a bundle of swift, fresh streams in the Blue Mountains, then grows into long river reaches before finally broadening out into mangrove fringed bays and fjord-like inlets.

Turning off the old highway there are a couple of little rises on the outskirts of a sleepy hollow called Brooklyn. Being a boating/fishing village and located on one of the largest waterways in New South Wales, there are always the freshest of fish and oysters to be purchased at excellent prices from the local co-op. However, if the river is in flood, it is wise to check whether the oysters have been affected.

Head towards the river and catch the ferry to Patonga. As you skirt Juno Hill, take a look out to sea. From here Lion Island, which usually resembles a big crouching cat, actually looks more like a scaled-down version of the giant Central Australian monolith — Ayers Rock.

Barely off the ferry, a quick climb becomes a steep ascent and you'll need to get off the seat and pump up the hill. The fire trail is to your right and looks like a rough little bush track but, unlike the main road which goes straight up the hill, the track follows a contour and, in doing so, meanders through a section of Brisbane Waters National Park (12 000 hectares), a place where cars are banned.

With only the jingle-jangle of panniers to disturb the quiet, you can ease yourself into the bush. Walking sometimes, cruising at others, your attention will probably alternate between choosing a boulder-free route and admiring the bird calls and flowering banksias. While small bush birds are hard to spot, banksia cones, like giant orange bottlebrushes, seem to leap out of subtle grey-green bush like hazard lights. Take the short detour to Warra Lookout. From here the view is a panoramic vista of waterway and forested headlands — it's hard to believe this alluring, wild place

is on Sydney's doorstep.

After a skittery descent along what at times becomes a charming leaf-strewn path, the route passes an immense cave right beside the track before rediscovering suburbia at Pearl Beach. Instead of climbing Mt Ettalong, skirt around its seaward side on a little walking track which, during rough seas, would be easily within salt-spray distance of the ocean. Back on a tar surface again near Woy Woy, you'll unfortunately have to share the road with more and more cars through to Gosford. Leave them behind by boarding the next train to Newcastle.

Newcastle

Newcastle (pop $259\,000$) is NSW's second largest city. Predominately an industrial centre, it fronts some of the best surfing beaches on the east coast and has produced world-class surfers. To ride and surf the **beach circuit**, turn right at Wharf Rd (see Section 1 Route Slip) and ride to Nobby's Beach. Then, by keeping the ocean on your left, you can experience a line of stunning beaches and some good hill climbing. Many of the beaches are patrolled by lifesavers and if you are body surfing, swim between the boundaries set by the flags onshore. There is a range of accommodation available.

Information Centre: Queens Wharf, Wharf Rd. No change given from machines for Newcastle Ferry to Stockton.

Hunter Valley Detour

The Hunter Valley is an unusual combination of coalfields, agriculture and wineries. Take the train up to Maitland, then ride to Cessnock via Rutherford and Sawyers Gulley. Cessnock (pop $17\,000$) — camping areas, hotels and a bike shop — is a perfect base for **winery touring**. A circuit of about 30 km — Cessnock, Pokolbin, Nulkaba, Cessnock — would take in roughly 15 wineries, if your taste buds can hack the pace. Check at the **tourist information centres** in both Sydney and Newcastle for a map of the area and addresses.

TOUR 1: Secluded
bliss in Smoky Cape
bush camping area,
New South Wales

DAY 2: Newcastle to Port Stephens

Distance ridden: 50.1 km;   Riding time: 2 hrs 23 mins;   Average speed: 20.9 kmph;   Maximum speed: 41 kmph

The ferry across the Hunter River to Stockton (it leaves from Queen's Wharf) is very civilised — it actually has a bike rack on board! From Stockton, there is often a gentle south-westerly breeze that provides a tailwind and would normally be good news, but for the first few kilometres the wind will be coming straight off the BHP works which can leave an acid-like gritty taste in your mouth. If you rejoin the main road to Nelson Bay at mid-morning, the traffic is usually light. Early morning and late afternoon this road is tight with commuters.

As you are cruising along this dead flat road, don't think you are hallucinating if you come across a landscape of grass-chewing cows with a backdrop that looks like a giant snowfield shimmering in the bright sunlight. On closer inspection the 'snowfield' yellows a little and is transformed into a series of immense sand dunes being driven inland from the sea.

Your attention may also be diverted by a less than subtle shaking of the earth, accompanied by a deafening roar. The road is running parallel to the Williamtown air base and when the Royal Australian Air Force jets take off in pairs, it seems that the sky has been ignited.

Marsh Road is a shorter, less-used detour which barely manages to keep above the high-tide wash. You cycle beneath the calming shade of a natural grey-green arch formed on the left by a lush mangrove forest and on the right by the soft-fingered branches of casuarina groves. It's not a road where you can relax, however. Countless patching attempts have produced an incredible mosaic of tar dollops, interspersed with newly formed potholes. This, combined with mottled shade from the overhanging trees, gives an exacting 10 km.

If you arrive at Port Stephens mid-week, the little section of beach just short of Soldiers Point will be virtually deserted, except perhaps for a patrolling pelican. You can coax one of these large birds into coming close to you by tossing a few handfuls of sand in the air. Then you can inspect its enormous bill, yellow-ringed eyes and pouch, and it can weigh up the chances of a free feed.

Port Stephens

Port Stephens is a large waterway and very popular tourist area, so camping, unit, motel and hotel **accommodation** is extensive. Cycle east to Shoal Bay and south to Fingal Bay. Zenith is one of the prettiest beaches and from the top of nearby Tomaree Head is one of the best views. **Sail and powerboat cruises** can take you to attractions like Moffat Oyster Barn and remote quiet reaches like Fame Cove. **Day boats** travel to Tea Gardens and Myall Lakes ($15 for you and bike to Tea Gardens).

Information Centre: Victoria Pde, Nelson Bay.

DAY 3: Soldiers Point to Myall Lakes National Park

Distance ridden: 34.3 km;   Riding time: 2 hrs 4 mins;   Average speed: 16.6 kmph;   Maximum speed: 43 kmph

An early morning ride along the foreshores of Port Stephens gives you time to stock up on supplies prior to joining a day boat on its journey across to Tea Gardens.

When the wind blows from a particular direction, the high-arching concrete and steel bridge which joins Tea Gardens and Hawks Nest becomes a giant windchime, and you may hear this uncanny sound as you ride across it. The bitumen surface peters out on entering Myall Lakes National Park. On a mountain bike this would be pure fun, but on my thin-tyred touring bike I clicked to a lower gear and began to concentrate on finding the smoothest passage along a pebbly sand track.

It is usually the shiniest patch, but getting from one patch to another and keeping upright is a challenge needing firm hands on the bars and vigilance in not making any sharp turns.

It is slow going, but with plenty of the day left and a blue sky above, there's no hurry. Big dunes rise up close to the track and it's a good opportunity to wander amid a desert of sand. Back on the road a negative aspect is introduced by occasional thoughtless drivers who don't consider slowing down when passing you. If unlucky, you can be showered with small stones and dust.

You will probably share lunch with a gaggle of pied currawongs at Mungo Brush, the main National Parks camping area. They get their name from one of their calls, which does sound like 'curra-wong', though their other calls are sweeter and more melodious. They are aggressive birds with atrocious table manners. When I left the table for a moment to fill up my water containers, all hell broke loose over the ownership of a loaf of bread. Mungo Brush is pleasant enough, but I prefer one of the tiny bush camp sites on the northern shores of The Broadwater.

Myall Lakes

Myall Lakes National Park (31 000 hectares) contains the largest fresh-brackish water system on the NSW coast, as well as long expanses of beach, rolling sand dunes and extensive forests. It is a great place to get off the bike for a while and enjoy using other muscles: **On foot** — the Mungo Track (21 km) begins just past the park entrance, 5 km north of Hawks Nest. On the track,

Brambles Green (see Section 2 Route Slip) is particularly beautiful. Using the Old Gibber Track (see Section 2 Route Slip for track head), a memorable multi-day walk can be organised stopping at the bush camping sites at Johnson's Beach, Tickerabit, Shelley Beach and Kataway Bay. After heavy rain, tracks can be more water than land, but drinking water should always be carried.

Canoeing — Canoes can be hired from Bombah Point to reach the same locations as on foot, but with additional delights of Boolambaytye Creek and Violet Hill. From Bulahdelah you can hire yachts and houseboats for luxury exploring of the lakes system, or join a two- to five-day canoe tour.

This is one of the most beautiful campsites on this tour. At sunset on a still evening, the water becomes a reflective silver and the trees turn gold. The camp I chose was only a few metres from the water's edge due to previous heavy rain in the upper catchment, causing the Myall Lakes network to break its banks and lap at the feet of fringing melaleucas. *Melaleuca* means black and white and refers to the usually singed appearance of the tree's bark. The bark actually resembles ancient parchment and its multi-layered wrapping effect protects the tree from fires, as well as giving it the commonname of 'paperbark'.

Don't be too distraught if your peaceful breakfast in the wilderness is shattered by a noisy bunch of interlopers — choughs. They will simply march through camp en masse, chattering incessantly, tearing at the undergrowth and rooting around in the leaf litter beside your feet. White-winged choughs are gregarious birds resembling crows, but with red eyes, rather than white.

DAY 4: Myall Lakes National Park to Forster

Distance ridden: 85.1 km; Riding time: 4 hrs 25 mins; Average speed: 19.0 kmph; Maximum speed: 64 kmph

At one time in NSW, cable ferries were prolific, but now there are only a few left. The little wooden-planked craft at Bombah Point is one of the last.

Bombah Point Ferry, 8 a.m. — 6 p.m.

Just short of Bulahdelah, the road surface changes colour and most touring bike riders will enjoy being back on the bitumen. Just as my wheels started to glide on the tar again, a posse of parrots — probably rainbow lorikeets — screamed past in noisy pleasure sharing my enjoyment.

ROUTE SLIP

Directions	R/S km	Ride for	Destination	Cum route km
END OF SECTION 2			**TOTAL FOR ROUTE**	**180.1**
Pacific Palms	95.4			180.1
R*-Smith Lake t'off	90.4	5		175.1
L*-Wallangat t'off	85	5.4	*camping area	169.7
R*-Seal rocks t'off	84.5	0.5		169.2
L*-Grandis t'off	66.3	18.2	*tall tree	151.0
R*-Violet Hills t'off	65.5	0.8	*camping area	150.2
R-Lakes Way	58.4	7.1	Forster/Tuncurry	143.1
R-Pacific Hwy	54.2	4.2		138.9
S-restart bitumen	50.5	3.7		135.2
S-leave NP	43.3	7.2		128
BL	43	0.3		127.7
Ferry	38.5	4.5		123.2
BL	38.1	0.4	Bulahdelah	122.8
R*-track head	36.9	1.2	*walking track	121.6
BL-old road closed	36.2	0.7		120.9
L*-North Shore	34.3	1.9	*bush camping sites	119
L*-Mungo Brush	31.5	2.8	*camping area	116.2
L*-Brambles Green	26.9	4.6	*walk in	111.6
S-end of bitumen	16.4	10.5		101.1
L-T-intersection	12	4.4	Myall Lakes NP	96.7
L-at wharf	10.3	1.7	over bridge	95
day boat			Tea Gardens	
L-Nelson Bay	10.3		Information Centre	
L-Sandy Pt Rd	5.9	4.4		90.6
L-Foreshore Dr	3.2	2.7		87.9
leave **Soldiers Point**	0.0	3.2	Nelson Bay	84.7
BEGIN SECTION 2				

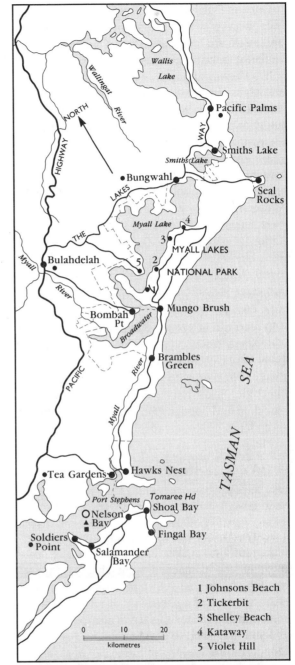

1 Johnsons Beach
2 Tickerbit
3 Shelley Beach
4 Kataway
5 Violet Hill

0   10   20
kilometres

On ride line, each segment = 1 kilometre

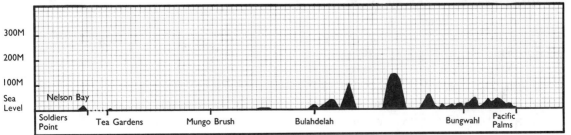

Once in Bulahdelah, be sure to detour to the local bakery where the loganberry, peach and apple pies are legendary. One of them is enough to fuel you through a cluster of densely-wooded hills — beautiful stands of regrown blackbutts — and across open valleys all along the Lakes Way to Pacific Palms. After a morning of climbs, once beside Wallis Lake the road has nary a rise, though if you have the same deliciously warm conditions that I experienced, then a nor'east breeze might buffet your bike all the way to Forster. Luxury for me was a hot shower and warm bed at the Belavilla Motor Inn.

The Lakes Way and Forster

Off to the left of the Lakes Way between Bulahdelah and Bungwahl (see Section 2 Route Slip for turnoff) is **The Grandis**, 76 m high and more than 400 years old, it's reputed to be the tallest tree in New South Wales. Nineteen km further along the Lakes Way is **Wallingat Forest Drive**. Although this is a dirt road with some occasional steep pinches, the 24 km circuit takes in lofty stands of blackbutt and flooded gum trees. Highlight of the meander is an hour's stroll amid the exuberant Cabbage Tree Palms of Sugar Creek Flora Reserve. There is a **bush camping area** at Wallingat River (9 km off the Lakes Way). **Other interesting detours** off the Lakes Way (see Section 2 Route Slip) are to the little coastal village of Seal Rocks (11 km, with 6 km dirt) where Australian sea lions can still be seen occasionally, and Smiths Lake to the Frothy Coffee Cafe (3 km).

The twin towns of **Forster—Tuncurry** (popn 15 500) are at the mouth of Wallis Lake. Extensive camping, motel, hotel and unit **accommodation** is available and the area has some great **scuba diving**. Beginning at North Street take the **Bicentennial walk** along the coast via Pebbly Beach and The Tanks Rockpool (a saltwater waterfall at high tide) to Bennetts Head. Stretching south from here is One Mile Beach where, believe it or not, dolphins can be seen surfing (see the photograph in the information centre). **Tour boats** give an introduction to Wallis Lake, but for an overnight adventure hire an inexpensive little power boat at Forster and navigate across the water to the only **camping area** on the shores of Wallingat River.

Information Centre: Little Street, Forster.

DAY 5: Forster to Crowdy Bay National Park

Distance ridden: 83 km; Riding time: 4 hrs 35 mins; Average speed: 17.6 kmph; Maximum speed: 57 kmph

Twenty-one km on an infrequently-used road makes for a great start to a day's riding. Unfortunately, it's dampened somewhat when you rejoin Highway One, which sometimes adopts the characteristics of a speedway. It's wise to wear something bright for this leg of the journey, but you still may need to revive your nerves with a cappuccino in Taree.

Gratefully part company with the highway at Moorland, and the bitumen a kilometre later. In this region there is a strange anomaly, older road maps are more likely to be accurate. Bitumen roads are proving too expensive to maintain so they are being turned back into dirt roads.

The track aims for Diamond Head, a prominent bump on a fairly flat landscape. On entering Crowdy Bay National Park, the track is a delight; smooth clay meandering timelessly through an angophora forest. But the track soon turns into soft sand. I was mesmerised by the pulse of shadows and light as I glided along, when suddenly an outstretched shadow paced along with me. I glanced up to look straight into the eyes of Australia's second largest bird of prey. This magnificent white-breasted sea eagle was using its immense wings to lazily beat the air. Dangling from its talons was a freshly-killed rabbit.

My euphoria at such an experience was swamped by the reality of encountering soft sand. Fat-tyred, all-terrain bikes will revel here, but a thin-tyred, heavily-laden touring bike takes an instant dislike to corrugated sand. If you are on

ROUTE SLIP

Directions	R/S km	Ride for	Destination	Cum route km
END OF SECTION 3			**TOTAL FOR ROUTE**	**285.6**
R-**Diamond Beach**	105.5			285.6
R*-rest area	102.7	2.8	Indian Head	282.8
R*-to beach	100.2	2.5	via camping area	280.3
L	98.7	1.5	Laurieton	278.8
BR	91.8	6.9		271.9
S-enter NP	89.4	2.4		269.5
S-end of tar	83.9	5.5		264
R-at corner store	82.6	1.3	Moorland/Crowdy Bay	262.7
BR-roundabout	60.9	21.7		241
Taree				
R-end of bridge	59.6	1.3		239.7
R-Highway One	43.1	16.5		223.2
R-Diamond Bch t'off	35.8	7.3		215.9
S-Failford t'off	34.9	0.9		215
BR-end of bridge	23.2	11.7	Taree	203.3
Forster	21.9	1.3	Taree	202
L*-picnic area	2.1	19.8		182.2
Pacific Palms	0.0	2.1		180.1
BEGIN SECTION 3				

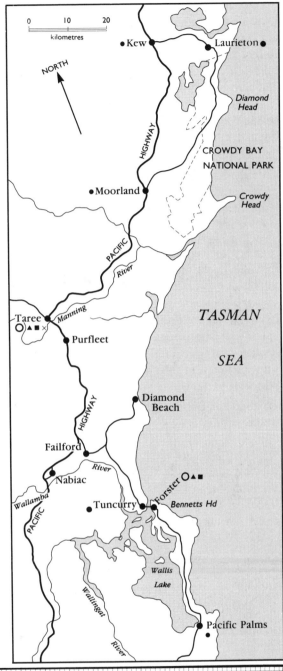

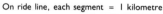
On ride line, each segment = 1 kilometre

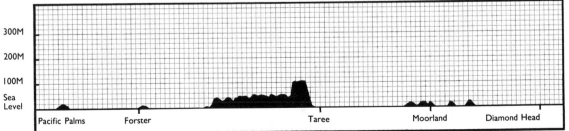

a touring bike, like me, you may be forced to walk a little on this section.

At the Diamond Head National Park Service camping area there's a resident family of eastern grey kangaroos. The campsite is within a grove of ancient melaleucas and the nights are soothed by sounds of the nearby surf washing the beach.

Crowdy Bay National Park

Crowdy Bay National Park (7412 hectares) is dominated by a craggy 113 m headland, Diamond Head, named after the quartz crystals found there.

The park has a wild landscape of rocky foreshore, beach, coastal heaths, littoral rainforest and wetlands. Outside of school holidays, kangaroos can outnumber the campers. At low tide try the **Cliff Base walk**, beginning at a stunning, eroded rock formation just near the Diamond Head rest area. When you are walking close to the water's edge be wary of a bunch of rough, tough looking dollops strongly attached to the rocks — *cunjevoi*, an Aboriginal word for sea-squirt.

Information Centre: Pacific Highway, Taree.

DAY 6: Crowdy Bay National Park to Port Macquarie

Distance ridden: 42.5 km;   Riding time: 2 hrs 20 mins;   Average speed: 18.1 kmph;   Maximum speed: 51 kmph

Diamond Head to Port Macquarie is an easy morning ride on a quiet road which meanders through small coastal communities and retirement havens. Larger and uglier developments only emerge at Port Macquarie, where your fitness will be tested by some Everest-like rises.

Port Macquarie

Port Macquarie (pop^n 27 000) is one of the larger north-coast resort towns. What makes it different are koalas and Kooloonbung. The koala is a marsupial, not a bear — but it's a marsupial in trouble. In the 1900s millions of koalas were shot and skinned, and their fur exported. This barbarism ceased by the mid 1920s, but their habitat areas have continued to be cleared. This, plus other factors such as cars, wild dogs, fires, pesticides and stress-induced disease, has caused an alarming drop in numbers. The **Koala Hospital and Study Centre** (off Lord St) grew out of local concern. Staffed by dedicated, knowledgeable volunteers and run on a shoe-string budget, the centre does caring work of inestimable value. Visit the centre, see koalas close up and please make a donation.

The ability of local people to restore the ecosystem rather than destroy it is evident in the remarkable rebirth of **Kooloonbung Creek Nature Park**. Today you can enjoy the tranquillity of eucalypts and casuarinas, and tread the boardwalks through mangrove and melaleuca wetlands — and it starts just off the southern end of Port Macquarie's main street.

Port Macquarie has a variety of accommodation available — I stayed at the Youth Hostel.

Information Centre: Horton St, Port Macquarie.

DAY 7: Port Macquarie to Hat Head National Park

Distance ridden: 86.6 km;   Riding time: 4 hrs 19 mins;   Average speed: 19.9 kmph;   Maximum speed: 47 kmph

Pedalling towards Kempsey beside a roadside forest in the early morning means the road is streaked with flickering shadows. Fifteen km out from Port Macquarie is Cairncross Forest picnic area, an ideal place to refuel with water and nibbles, and admire a few remnant tall trees close up — a token reminder of thoughtless destruction. Out of the forests, the land looks abused and tired.

ROUTE SLIP

Directions	R/S km	Ride for	Destination	Cum route km
END OF SECTION 4			**TOTAL FOR ROUTE**	**377.4**
South Kempsey	91.8			377.4
R*-beside road	84.5	7.3	Maria Picnic Area	370.1
L*-beside road	58.3	26.2	Carncross Picnic Area	343.9
R-rejoin Hwy	52.1	6.2		337.7
R-roundabout	44.1	8.1	Kempsey	329.6
Port Macqaurie	42.5	1.5		328.1
L-roundabout	42	0.5		327.6
R*-Pacific Dr	38.5	3.5	Beaches Route	324.1
S-info sign	34.7	3.8		320.3
BL	25.5	9.2		311.1
R*-side road	17.1	8.4	Grants Head	302.7
L-Ocean Dr	12.7	4.4		298.3
R-T-intersection	10.1	2.6	Port Macquarie	295.7
S-Lauriton	9	1.1		294.6
S-rejoin tar	6.3	2.7		291.9
S-leave NP	5.7	0.6		291.3
R*-side track	5	0.7	Blackbutt Picnic Area	290.6
R*-side track	2.9	2.1	Cheese Tree Picnic Area	288.5
R*-side track	1.6	1.3	Geebung Picnic Area	287.2
R-rejoin main track	0.3	1.3		285.9
Diamond Beach	0.0	0.3		285.6
BEGIN SECTION 4				

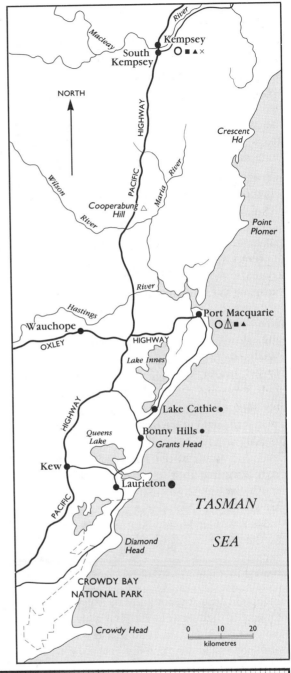

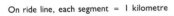

On ride line, each segment = 1 kilometre

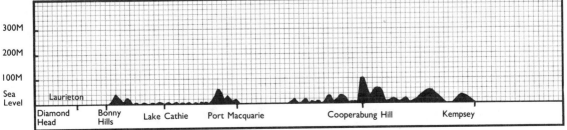

Stock up with supplies in Kempsey before the route becomes a quiet secondary road. A 400 m granite outcrop called Big Smoky beckons, but the road follows the Macleay River. Beside the road is a depressing grassed wasteland. It should be regarded as a national disgrace to allow mazes of paddocks with not a native tree in sight. It struck me as strange how people can manage to raise crops and cattle, yet tree cultivation seems unimportant to them.

Hat Head National Park, Arakoon & South West Rocks

Hat Head National Park is a 3990 hectare ribbon of preserved coastline, butting on to Arakoon State Recreation Area. The **Smoky Cape bush camping area** in the north of Hat Head National Park provides a rough camp, wilderness experience — no showers, no water, pit toilets — but, bonuses include a great chance to interact with a wide range of Australian native fauna, including falcons, hawks, sea eagles, black swans, egrets, herons, spoonbills, redneck and swamp wallabies, grey kangaroos, possums and goannas. After rain a waterfall forms at the back of the beach near the camping area. A 15 km beach runs south to Hat Head. Just south of Hat Head is **Hungry Head bush camping area** (reached via the Hat Head

turnoff) and nearby are an outstanding set of sand dunes.

Arakoon State Recreation Area (465 hectares) has two **camping areas** complete with all facilities including barbecue and picnic areas. Within Arakoon are the historic ruins of Trial Bay Gaol (1886) and it is possible to walk from the gaol through to Smoky Cape Lighthouse. The nearby township of **South West Rocks** has a full range of **accommodation** and **supplies**.

Entering Hat Head National Park is like gaining admittance to a priceless treed fortress. In afternoon light the stand of white-barked scribbly gums just near the park entrance positively glow. In Smoky Cape bush camping area you can pitch your tent amid a stand of angophoras and lean the bike gently against an ancient tree. Sometimes called crab apple trees, they are regarded as commercially useless — thankfully — but have red-barked limbs which writhe into the most voluptuous shapes.

The beach is but a few minutes stroll from your campsite. North of a posted sign is a restful haven from trail bikes and four-wheel drive vehicles. Their tracks have not yet ground into the beach's delicate natural sculptures: a sensuous curve of a tannin-stained creek snaking across the beach, and curious fan-like shapes painstakingly constructed with tiny balls of sand by burrowing ghost crabs.

DAY 8: Hat Head National Park to Nambucca Heads

Distance ridden: 89.3 km;   Riding time: 4 hrs 10 mins;   Average speed: 19.6 kmph;   Maximum speed: 66 kmph

You might hear a cacophony of noisy friarbirds living up to their name. A long bill with an upright knob on it, bald black head and red eyes don't combine to make for a conventionally pretty bird, but these honeyeaters certainly seem to enjoy life.

Take a detour towards Smoky Cape lighthouse (open Tuesday and Thursday). Naturally enough, it is built on the highest, furthest seaward position possible, and reaching this heady plateau is a lung-taxing fitness test. Once my head cleared, I could appreciate infinite rollers cruising into a seemingly endless beach stretching southward, and admire

Dorrigo Detour

At Raleigh (23 km north of Nambucca Heads) take the road to Bellingen and then to Dorrigo (84 km return). Getting up to the Dorrigo Plateau is a tough climb, but the Dorrigo National Park contains some of the most spectacular rainforest on the north coast.

the landlocked secluded patches of northern sand just waiting for a keen walker to explore. The views are almost as exhilarating as the free-wheeling descent.

ROUTE SLIP

Directions	R/S km	Ride for	Destination	Cum route km
END OF SECTION 5	*(This is roughly the half-way point)*			
			TOTAL FOR ROUTE	**483.1**
Macksville	105.7			483.1
L-T-intersection	101.7	4	rejoin Pacific Hwy	479.1
	(Note: road passes **under** highway before rejoining it)			
R*-Scotts Head Rd				
L-T-intersection	94.7	7	Pacific Hwy	472.1
R*-side road	87.7	7	Grassy Head	465.1
L	83.3	4.4	Grassy Head	460.7
R	81	2.3	Stuarts Pt	458.4
R-side road	73.8	7.2	Stuarts Point	451.2
R-T-intersection	60.7	13.1	rejoin hwy	438.1
BR-near pine trees	56.6	4.1		434
R-over bridge	50.3	6.3	Pacific Highway	427.7
L-T-intersection	46.2	4.1		423.6
S	45.7	0.5	Kempsey	423.1
South West Rocks	45.7			423.1
BR	45	0.7		422.4
L-T-intersection	42.6	2.4	South West Rocks	420
R*-Trial Bay Gaol				
S-rejoin tar	42.1	0.5		419.5
S-dirt road	40.7	1.4		418.1
R-T-intersection	40.6	0.1	Arakoon	418
L-from camping area	37.3	3.3		414.7
Smoky Cape				
R-side road	37.3		camping area	
S-enter NP	34.2	3.1	Hat Head	411.6
R	34.1	0.1	lighthouse	411.5
R	32.5	1.6	Arakoon	409.9
S	31.2	1.3	South West Rocks	408.6
BR-after bridge	30.6	0.6		408
R*-side road	20	10.6	Hat Head Rd	397.4
S	14.9	5.1		392.3
R-before bridge	0.0	14.9	South West Rocks	377.4
South Kempsey				
BEGIN SECTION 5				

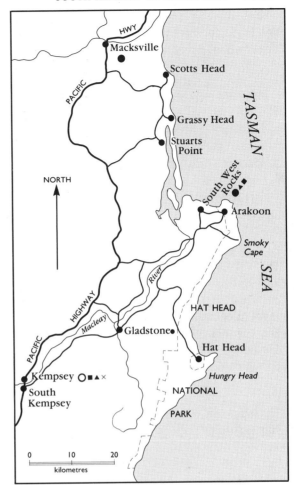

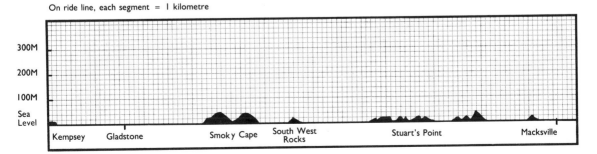

On ride line, each segment = 1 kilometre

300M
200M
100M
Sea Level

Kempsey   Gladstone   Smoky Cape   South West Rocks   Stuart's Point   Macksville

After taking in the old gaol at Trial Bay, South West Rocks and a detour around Scotts Head, quiet back roads give way to an unavoidable section of dreaded Highway One through to Nambucca Heads.

DAY 9: Nambucca Heads to Coffs Harbour

Distance ridden: 47.2 km;   Riding time: 2 hrs 19 mins;   Average speed: 20.3 kmph;   Maximum speed: 53 kmph

Nambucca Heads to Coffs Harbour is all on Highway One — and just bearable.

Coffs Harbour for me was a 2-day luxury rest stop — at Aanuka, a resort just north of town.

Coffs Harbour

Coffs Harbour (pop^n 44 300) is a major regional centre and tourist destination. Reflecting this is the range of **accommodation** — six major resorts, 23 caravan parks, 31 motels, 45 holiday apartments, nine hotels, and two hostels. There are also 55 restaurants and 60 fast food outlets. Passive **tourist attractions** include sunsoaking on the beaches — the winter average is 18°C (68°F) (the nudist beach is at the northern end of Diggers Beach), the Big Banana, Agradome and botanical gardens. For a more energetic break, you could try **white-water rafting** on the Nymboida River, go **canoeing** or **rainforest trekking, hot-air ballooning, horse-trail riding, four-wheel drive safari-ing** or tramp out to **Mutton Bird Island**.

Information Centre: Centre City Mall, Coffs Harbour.

DAY 11: Coffs Harbour to Grafton

Distance ridden: 83.4 km;   Riding time: 4 hrs 15 mins;   Average speed: 19.5 kmph;   Maximum speed: 54 kmph

Red Hill 'gets all the triathletes' I'm reliably informed just prior to heading off toward Grafton on a quiet backroad. Halfway up you will appreciate why. The crest comes, eventually, but instead of a mind-blowing descent it is a sort of half-hearted affair as if the terrain doesn't want to yield up any given altitude. The road progresses through rolling tree-clad hills, but between Glenreagh and the Orara River (a nice lunch stop) it seems to climb the same altitude countless times; falling into little gulleys, crossing numerous creeks and then jumping up pinchy ascents to regain the lost height.

A dry road, speckled sunlight and warm air is always encouraging, but when I rode this section just as the forest closed in and the road began a longer than normal curve downhill, everything became very cold and very dark. Rounding the next corner I was confronted by a white cloud of torrential rain. By the time I had grabbed my wet weather jacket, the world seemed to be underwater. Visibility was reduced to 20 m. The appalling conditions encouraged me to discover a room in the Royal Hotel at Grafton, overlooking the Clarence River — a room with a giant bath where a tired bicycle tourer can soak into oblivion.

Grafton

Grafton (pop^n 17 000) is a major regional centre on the Clarence River with banks dominated by sugar cane fields. There is an **arts festival** in May/June and a **Jacaranda Festival** in October/November.

Information Centre: 49 Victoria St, Grafton.

ROUTE SLIP

Directions	R/S km	Ride for	Destination	Cum route km
END OF SECTION 6			**TOTAL FOR ROUTE**	**593.1**
Orara River	110			593.1
L-traffic lights	56.6	53.4	Grafton	539.7
Coffs Harbour	56.6			
S	8.6	48	Coffs Harbour	491.7
Nambucca Heads t'off				
S	0.0	8.6	Nambucca Heads	483.1
Macksville				
BEGIN SECTION 6				

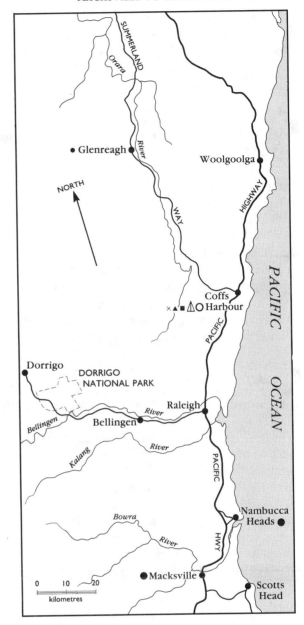

PACIFIC OCEAN

Glenreagh

Woolgoolga

Coffs Harbour

Dorrigo

DORRIGO NATIONAL PARK

Raleigh

Bellingen

Nambucca Heads

Macksville

Scotts Head

NORTH

0 10 20
kilometres

On ride line, each segment = I kilometre

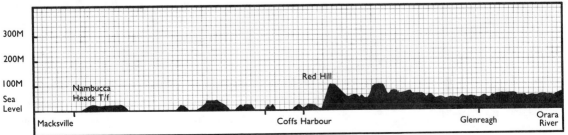

Clarence River Detour

An excellent side tour (122 km) on quiet, secondary, tarred roads. Follow the northern shore of the Clarence River to Lawrence, take the ferry across, then continue through Maclean to Yamba, Angourie (see the Blue Pool) and Yuragir National Park. Rejoin the Sydney to the Gold Coast route through Lawrence (8 km dirt road) which enters the Summerland Way 6 km short of the Stirling Range.

DAY 12: Grafton to Casino

Distance ridden: 101.2 km; Riding time: 4 hrs 45 mins; Average speed: 21.2 kmph; Maximum speed: 56 kmph

Be up early in Grafton, and you'll see rowers slicing through the mirror-like river.

When you reset the bike computer to 0.0 and the road marker says Casino 100 km, it seems a daunting distance. For me, the 21 km mark was a bran muffin break, and 40 km was marked by sharing a cup of percolated coffee with a Dutch couple travelling in a camper. Their memories of biking at home were of riding 120 km for bread during the German occupation of their country in World War II.

As 45 km flash over the bike's odometer, you crest the top of the Stirling Range — all 113 m of it. Whiporie, 50 km, is the only shop on the route and by the 73 km mark, Braemar Forest Park could be an overnight bush camp if you were really tired. But if you decide to continue, Casino hoves into view just as that bewitching 100 km finally comes up on the computer display.

DAY 13: Casino to Nimbin

Distance ridden: 50 km; Riding time: 2 hrs 44 mins; Average speed: 18.2 kmph; Maximum speed: 55 kmph

The height profile shows some good climbs on this section of the route, but the largest marked hill is nicely stepped and rambles through pretty countryside. Providing amusement on the way up is a sign which warns to 'Watch for Fallen Rocks', and at a climbing speed of only 7 to 10 km per hour, falling rocks might still be a hazard. Take care after the top, since the descent is past an interlaced network of wheel-sized potholes and hairpin corners.

Heading towards Nimbin in the afternoon, you travel through remnant pockets of rainforest where whip-birds crack in stereo.

Byron Bay Detour

A **coastal circuit** (120 km) on tarred secondary roads which takes in the spectacularly beautiful Byron Bay, can be included by *not* taking the Nimbin turnoff (see Section 8 Route Slip) but continuing to Lismore, Wardell, Ballina, Lennox Head, Byron Bay, Bangalow, Clunes, The Channon and rejoining the Sydney/Gold Coast Route five km short of Coffee Camp. Be warned however, there are lots of hills to climb.

I refuelled and revived at Coffee Camp and a little tailwind rushed down from the surrounding peaks to hasten me on. Hovering at the back of the breeze were grey-black thunder clouds promoting two or three rain showers. I picked up pace and they picked up pace. It became a race, which I lost. Rain can be very copious around these parts.

Nimbin & Region

New-age lifestyles abound in Nimbin; colourful shops, cafes and meeting places full of alternative products and ways of thinking. Just the place for a relaxed stay at **Granny's Farm Youth Hostel** and a body-rejuvenating massage. A plethora of backroads thread the region and a close study of the map is recommended. **Craft markets** are held at The Channon, Uki and Nimbin on the 2nd, 3rd and 4th Sunday of the month respectively.

Though much of the region is cleared there are pockets of 'big scrub', as rainforest was named

ROUTE SLIP

Directions	R/S km	Ride for	Destination	Cum route km
END OF SECTION 7			**TOTAL FOR ROUTE**	**696.2**
Braemar Forest Park	103.1			696.2
S	80.2	22.9		673.3
Whiporie				
R-T-intersection	31.5	48.7		624.6
L-roundabout	30.5	1		623.6
R-roundabout	29.6	0.9	Casino	622.7
Grafton	29.6			
S-roundabout	27.6	2		620.7
R-stop sign	27.5	0.1		620.6
L-T-intersection	27.3	0.2		620.4
R-T-intersection	21	6.3		614.1
S	0.0	21	Grafton	593.1
Orara River				
BEGIN SECTION 7				

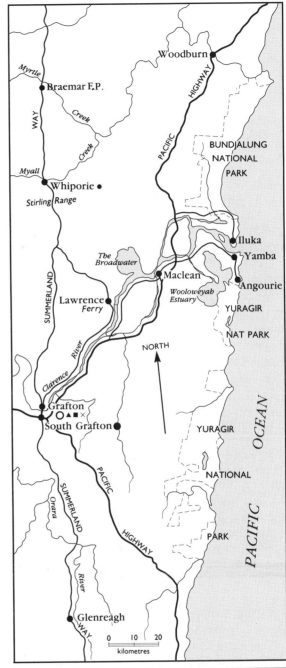

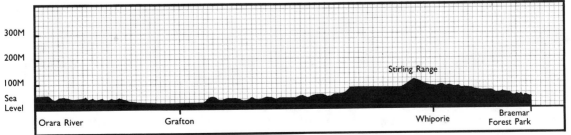

On ride line, each segment = 1 kilometre

here. Nightcap National Park came about after nearly a decade of peaceful protest against the stupidity of felling rainforest. Protesters Falls near Terrania Creek (reached via The Channon) commemorates this long struggle. Mt Nardi (800 + m and 11 km from Nimbin) is a tough climb by bike (if staying at the youth hostel, it is possible to get a lift), but the **rainforest walks** (Pholi's Walk and the Mt Matheson Loop track) are a real delight. Closer to Nimbin and worth a visit are Nimbin Rocks and Hanging Rock Creek.

DAY 14: Nimbin to Murwillumbah

Distance ridden: 51 km; Riding time: 3 hrs 16 mins; Average speed: 15.6 kmph; Maximum speed: 49 kmph

After seeing rainforest in Nightcap National Park, it's a depressing start to the day to be faced with paddocks of buttressed tree stumps. They are like headstones commemorating the vanquished from a hideous battle. Rises become hills and the route travels through an ancient landscape where the reminders of incredible volcanic upheavals are everywhere. Where 22 million years ago all was lava and violence, today the fires are extinguished and the mountains are cloaked in cool green. Just beyond Blue Knob you get a first glimpse of a chain of mountains called the Scenic Rim and the central vent of an old volcano, Mt Warning. They are vestiges of an immense shield volcano which was 100 km in diameter.

Mt Warning Detour

On the way to Murwillumbah, a remnant volcanic plug, Mt Warning, more than 1100 m, dominates the landscape. The national park is reached by turning off 11 km after Terragon (see Section 9 Route Slip) — 12 km return. There is an excellent **caravan/camping area** at Wollumbin Wildlife Refuge just outside the park. An ascent of the mountain takes about four hours return.

Riding through cleared areas, the sun beats down in a sweat-producing, oppressive way, yet within the shaded, tree-lined sections of road, the air seems sweet and clean, cooled to perfection and supercharged with oxygen. Heading towards Murwillumbah, the road gets into step with the Tweed River. The river's long, slow-moving pools are like dragging hill climbs, while the splashy, fast-paced rapids become quick downhill freewheeling plunges for the bike. By the time you encounter the first sugar cane monoculture fields, the river has broadened into a greyer, less interesting character. On the outskirts of Murwillumbah, the little road becomes just a suburban corridor surrounded by houses.

Murwillumbah and District

Murwillumbah (pop[n] 7800) has one of the best-placed **youth hostels** in NSW. It is so close to the Tweed River it seems almost suspended over the water. Sunsets from the back porch are magical — though the electricity authority that placed powerlines across the river showed little aesthetic sensitivity. There are a number of pleasant **half-** and **full-day cycle tours** from Murwillumbah (see the hostel manager for details) which include visiting a large Hare Krishna farm — their free Sunday feasts are legendary.

Information Centre: Cnr Pacific Highway & Alma St, Murwillumbah.

DAY 15: Murwillumbah to The Gold Coast

Distance ridden: 83.2 km; Riding time: 4 hrs 39 mins; Average speed: 17.8 kmph; Maximum speed: 58 kmph

Hit the road early after breakfasting on the porch of the Youth Hostel and watching the sun come up. It is a marvellous way to start the day. The 'road' seems more like a thin channel scratched

ROUTE SLIP

Directions	R/S km	Ride for	Destination	Cum route km
END OF SECTION 8			**TOTAL FOR ROUTE**	**798.3**
Terragon	102.1			798.3
R-T-intersection	91.8	10.3	Murwillumbah	788
BL-X Bridge	79.8	12		772
S	79	0.8	Murwillumbah	775.2
Nimbin				
BR	77.1	1.9		773.3
S	70.1	7		766.3
Coffee Camp Hall				
BL	66.0	4.1		762.2
BR	60.3	5.7		756.5
L-T-intersection	57.3	3	Nimbin	753.5
S-(not left)	53.7	3.6	Nimbin	749.9
L	52.8	0.9	Larnook	749
R-T-intersection	42.6	10.2	Lismore	738.8
BL-top of hill	39.7	2.9	Lismore	735.9
BL-X-train lines	30.7	9	Bentley	726.9
L	29.9	0.8	Naughtons Gap	726.1
R-roundabout	28.9	1	Lismore	725.1
S	27.7	1.2		723.9
Casino				
S	0.0	27.7	Casino	696.2
Braemar Forest Park				
BEGIN SECTION 8				

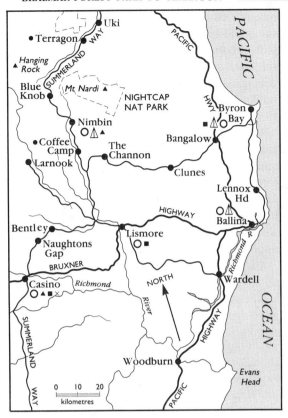

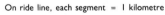
On ride line, each segment = I kilometre

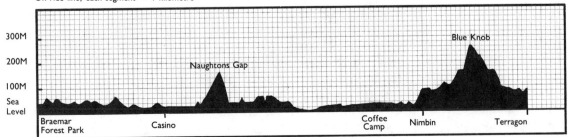

through sweet foliage; sugar cane carpets this valley and its pungent aroma saturates the air. Eons past, the atmosphere would have been thick with sulphur fumes, but today the volcanoes are dormant. However, on some mornings vertical, stacked clouds sitting on top of the surrounding rim of mountains, look uncannily like fumerols.

Although greatly eroded by wind and water, the mountains which form the border between New South Wales and Queensland still present a formidable bicycling challenge. Initially, the road follows the Rous River and steepens gradually. Brightening up my climb was a tempting sign which offered 'Passions: $1 a bucket' — not love potions but purple-skinned passionfruit.

After 17 km of gentle climbs and falls, the terrain induces a few heart-thumping jump-up hills followed by little scooty runs, but the effect is to gain altitude. Then the honest hill climbing begins; down to the lowest gear and off-the-seat pedalling. Thankfully, for part of the climb, the air is cooled by the closeness of massed trees. If you want an excuse to stop, use the sign, 'Bananas 50 cents a kilogram — 100 metres'. Unfortunately for me, it was followed by a deflating 'No Bananas Today'.

Another two hard kilometres and it feels like you're not making much progress, but each time you emerge from the trees, the valley views seem more expansive and the mountain ridges just a little closer. When I did the hill, I found it hard to admire the scenery. With heart rate soaring and sweat pouring after nearly 4 km of climbing, things were starting to get a little desperate. The road steepened a notch and in response my cadence dropped so low that the computer occasionally read zero. When you finally see a sign 'Gate', you'll find a quarantine-inspection gate perched on what feels like the top of the earth.

Having reached the top is reason enough for a small celebration — you'll probably need a long, cold drink. Then the descent into Queensland is a spirit-stirring event, but just prior to turning off at Natural Arch, the road puts on a little rise. This puny hill will show you just how fit you really are (my legs turned to jelly). But the Natural Arch is restorative to body and spirit: a spray of silver water diving into a cave-darkened pool and emerging beneath the muted green world of a rainforest.

It inspires you to tackle 25 km of roadmaker sadism. True, the road has some fabulous sweeping downhill runs through densely-treed landscapes, but virtually all of them are followed by short, steep ascents. Although the overall effect is to gradually lose height, this road seems to make you re-climb the same altitude over and over again.

Binna Burra Detour

For fitness fanatics only. Just before Gilston there is a turn off to Binna Burra (see Section 9 Route Slip). It is virtually 27 km uphill, but the effort is well rewarded. Binna Burra Lodge (and nearby camping area) are on the edge of **Lamington National Park**, a wonderland of ancient, lichen-dripping Antarctic beech forests, awesome waterfalls (that you can abseil) and a network of superb **walking tracks**.

Frustrating as the road is, at least the cars are infrequent. You encounter a different world — the snarling, aggressive, frightening kind of heavy traffic — where this hinterland road crosses the main highway. Thankfully there is an ersatz bike lane marked on the edge of the road and it guides bikers from the leafy jungles of the mountains to a sensuous arc of beach, endless ocean and a forest of concrete towers: the Gold Coast.

Gold Coast and Hinterland

Running from Coolangatta/Tweed Heads to Southport, the pure sand beaches of the Gold Coast (popn 235 000) have attracted tourists since the late 1880s, but today it is a high-rise mecca where some buildings have been built so close to the beach that they block out the sun from mid-afternoon. It is, however, one of the most popular holiday destinations in Australia and a place you will either love or hate.

Accommodation is extensive and broad ranging in available types. You can live in absolute five-star luxury in a hotel like the Gold Coast International or bunk down at the Coolangatta Youth Hostel. You can hire anything (go-carts, sailboards, catamarans, powerboats, canoes or horses), dine at any one of hundreds of restaurants, cafes and takeaways, dance all night or gamble all morning

TOUR 2: Crossing a causeway over the
Mulgrave River near Goldsborough
State Forest Park, Queensland

ROUTE SLIP

Directions	R/S km	Ride for	Destination	Cum route km
END OF TOUR			**TOTAL FOR ROUTE**	**902.8**
Surfers Paradise	104.5			902.8
L-traffic lights	100.5	4	Surfers Paradise	898.8
R-traffic lights	89.6	10.9	Broadbeach	887.9
BL-roundabout	89.3	0.3		887.6
S-roundabout	88	1.3		886.3
BL	84.3	3.7		882.6
BR	81.2	3.1		879.5
L*-Binna Burra t'off				
S	67.5	13.7	Nerang	865.8
L*-Natural Arch t'off	52.3	15.2	Nerang	850.6
S	48.9	3.4		847.2
top of climb				
BR	37.7	11.2	Numinbah	836
BL	28.9	8.8		827.2
L-X bridge	23.4	5.5	Chillingham	821.7
R-roundabout	21.9	1.5		820.2
L	21.4	0.5		819.7
L	20.9	0.5	Nerang	819.2
Murwillumbah				
R-T-intersection	20.1	0.8		818.4
L* Mt Warning t'off	11	9.1		809.3
S	0.0	11	Murwillumbah	798.3
Terragon				
BEGIN SECTION 9				

On ride line, each segment = I kilometre

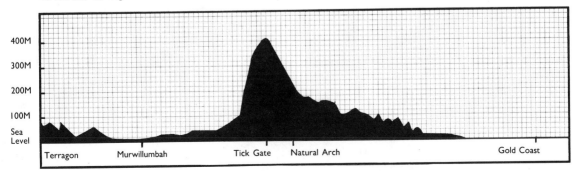

— the list of Gold Coast attractions and activities are so extensive they could fill a book and make it hard to find time to sleep. Away from the coastal madness is a hinterland of exceptional beauty.

Information Centre:
115 Upton Street, Bundall, Gold Coast.

ATHERTON TABLELANDS, NORTH QUEENSLAND

QUEENSLAND

2 • Cairns

2 ATHERTON TABLELANDS, NORTH QUEENSLAND

This is a 415 km camping, hostelling and old Australian pubs tour, best ridden during the dryer, cooler months of May to October. Cycling through the Atherton Tablelands takes you into some of the most beautiful rainforest in Northern Queensland, and past many outstanding waterfalls. The route uses mostly quiet, sealed roads, with some unsealed sections, and is suitable for touring bikes and all-terrain bikes. I rode it in July on my touring bike, with three friends on ATBs, taking 10 leisurely days, (including two rest days) averaging 52 km per day. Though it is possible to do in reverse, the chance to use an historic train trip to gain 500 m is hard to resist.

DAY 1: Palm Cove to Davies Creek National Park

Distance ridden: 51.8 km; Riding time: 2 hrs 59 mins; Average speed: 19.0 kmph; Maximum speed: 61 kmph

At any time of the year, emerging from the cooled interior of a pressurised aircraft, or even an air-conditioned coach or train, Cairns air feels warm and unmistakably tropical. Probably because of the weather, you'll find the locals are unmistakably laconic, speaking in a slow Queensland drawl and exuding an easy-going, laid-back style of living.

Flat-run cycling takes you from Cairns airport to Palm Cove (25 km north), one of the true beach paradises. Settle in for a few days at a lush resort or budget camping ground, stroll the beach and adjust to the slower pace. Then go bicycle touring.

Daintree Detour

For an energetic, all-terrain bike side tour (230 km return), head north on Captain Cook Highway to Port Douglas, Mossman, Daintree National Park and Cape Tribulation. You'll find plenty of crocodiles, mud tracks, steep hills and dense rainforest growing right to the edge of the sea.

Early in the morning take the cycle path south (it runs beside the Captain Cook Highway), and you are likely to enjoy the sight of deep-green forested mountains crowned by white clinging vapour. Rainforests are described by many conservationists as the 'lungs of the world', and in tropical north Queensland, the rainforest breathes in a hot and muggy atmsphere like an outdoor steam bath. An easier atmosphere is close at hand — 500 m higher up on the Atherton Tablelands.

The tough way to the Tablelands involves pumping bike and body up steep grades on the Kennedy Highway. More spiritually uplifting is to pedal to Redlynch station and take the scenic Kuranda train up the Barron Valley gorge. With 15 tunnels and 93 curves, this awesome engineering feat was carved out by 'The United Sons of Toil' with hand tools, dynamite, and buckets over five years, between May 1886 and June 1891. Money, of course, seems to have been the main reason the workers risked life and limb, earning the then heady sum of eight shillings (80 cents) a day.

Bikes (half one adult fare) travel in an ancient van in the front end of the train and are hard to load and unload if you are alone. For the best views on the slow trip up, try to get a seat on the right-hand side of the train. Not too close to the engine though or you will be holding your breath against the mix of diesel fumes whenever the train goes through a tunnel. Alight (or in Queensland railways' lingo 'detrain') at Barron River Falls (the train's second stop) for an excellent picture of the gorge and falls.

From this point onwards you have an easily overlooked bonus of 500 m altitude — the benefit from this comes much later on the tour.

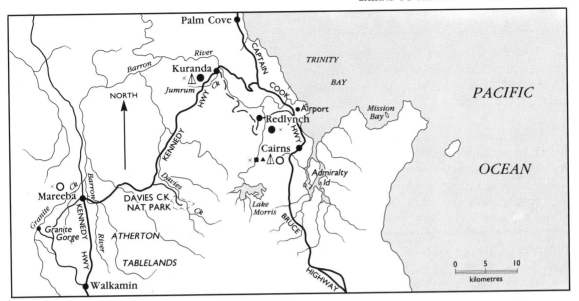

ROUTE SLIP

Directions	R/S km	Ride for	Destination	Cum route km
END OF SECTION 1	94.3		**TOTAL FOR ROUTE**	**94.3**
Mareeba By Pass	94.3			
L-Kennedy Hwy	94.3		Atherton	94.3
BL	93.4	.9	Atherton	93.4
R *-Mareeba			(2 km)	
S-rest area	92.4	1	Mareeba	92.4
L-Kennedy Hwy	80.5	11.9	Mareeba	80.5
R	74.1	6.4	Kennedy Hwy	74.1
Davies Creek NP	74.1			
L	67.7	6.4	Davies Creek	67.7
L	45.1	22.6		45.1
L-Kennedy Hwy	43.9	1.2	Mareeba	43.9
S-**Kuranda**	42.9	1	Mareeba	42.9
Kuranda train				
L-Redlynch	42.9			42.9
R	37.5	5.4	Redlynch	37.5
L-Cpt Cook Hwy	24.5	13	Cairns	24.5
Palm Cove	24.5			
R-Cpt Cook Hwy	3.5	21	Palm Cove	3.5
R-Airport Ave	0.0	3.5		0.0
Cairns Airport				
BEGIN SECTION 1				

KEY

L = left   **R** = right   **S** = straight

BL = bear left   **BR** = bear right

X = cross   * = detour directions

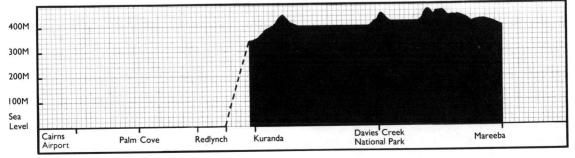

On ride line, each segment = 1 kilometre

Kuranda

This compact little town (pop 300) is a tourist mecca whose attractions include the **Tjapukai Aboriginal Dance Theatre, butterfly sanctuary, local markets** (Wednesday, Friday and Sunday), **canoe hire** on the Barron River and **river boat cruises**. Close to town is the **Jumrum Creek Environmental Park** and a short (400 m) **rainforest circuit walk** takes you through a vine forest with a large population of fruit bats. **Accommodation** in Kuranda includes a youth hostel and rainforest resort.

Bedecked in a jungle of potted plants, Kuranda Railway station must be one of the prettiest in Australia, but carrying a fully-laden touring bike up the steep steps leading from the platform is a real heart-starter. Kuranda can easily delay your bicycling departure for days until you finally head off south-west along the Kennedy Highway.

Some of the national parks in Queensland are often called 'pocket handkerchiefs' since they are incredibly small when compared to this state's vast area. Davies Creek National Park is a case in point. Once you take the national park turn-off from the Kennedy Highway, make sure to turn the lever on your touring bike which converts it to an all-terrain bike. If you haven't one of those, you'll have to gingerly pick your way through the rocks as I did, while my companions gleefully attacked the dirt on their ATBs.

Once you reach the national park amenities block, don't take the first campsite you see, go for a stroll. The better, level, grassy sites (with table and tree cover) aren't immediately evident. With tents erected and bikes locked, you could spend a contemplative afternoon draped over sun-warmed rocks, only occasionally falling into the stream to cool off. Or you might, as we did, like to energetically explore the creek to get nearly within spray distance of its head waterfall. Sure-gripping footware proved to be essential, though we did a little wading and ended the walk with a scramble up to the lookout over the falls. An easier though less scenic route is to walk the road.

DAY 2: Davies Creek National Park to Herberton

Distance ridden: 70.3 km; Riding time: 4 hrs 31 mins; Average speed: 15.4 kmph; Maximum speed: 57 kmph

Atherton Tablelands weather can be just a shade fickle, so an evening spent camping beside Davies Creek might be a wet one. There's an ideally located fruit stall (a few kilometres after rejoining the Kennedy Highway) which can prove irresistible if you like tropical fruits, like sugar bananas and custard apples.

Mareeba

Mareeba (pop 6600) is regarded as the commercial hub of the tablelands and is the site of a popular **rodeo** usually held in July.

Granite Gorge Detour

Avoid much of the Kennedy Highway to Atherton by detouring 15 km south-west. Camp overnight at Granite Gorge where the granite boulders are as high as an eight-storey building. The detour rejoins Kennedy Highway at Walkamin.

Rather than riding into Mareeba, we took the shorter bypass option and kept on pedalling towards Atherton. The cycling from this point gets a little more honest — it's a slight uphill grade (easier than it looks on the height profile) all the way to Atherton and for us there was the additional delight of an enthusiastic headwind. If you are travelling as a group, you can ease the pain by mimicking racing cyclists and ride as the French describe *en echelon* (in close single file drafting off the person in front and rotating the lead after each kilometre).

Just short of Tolga where the soil takes on a rich red volcanic colour, your nostrils may be assailed by a marvellous aroma — roasting peanuts! It is the perfect excuse to take a break (there's a pleasant tree-shaded picnic area beside the peanut/fruit stall).

Beyond Tolga you get a glimpse of Tablelands rainforest, thick and tall enough to eradicate the energy-sapping wind and replace it with rejuvenating shade, renewed muscle power and a multi-voice birdsong serenade which ceases only on entering Atherton.

Atherton

Atherton (pop^n 4600) is a major town by Tablelands standards, and so can make a good stopping place if you are in need of a break. There is a **youth hostel, underground crystal museum** and restored **Chinese joss house**. The most unusual **bike shop** can be found in Albrecht's Nurseryland and Children's Wear, 29 Main St, Atherton.

If your leg muscles are tiring, you could eliminate the Herberton section of the tour by staying on the Kennedy Highway and cycling through to The Crater National Park next day. I decided against that option and pushed on to Herberton.

Pushed is the operative word. Initially it's a fast, scooty road which takes you quickly past Hasties Swamp (a great place for birds — plumed whistling ducks, brolgas, and pied geese). But the road inexorably arrives at the base of a very long, steep hill which is made even harder to ascend by the fact that you are tackling it late in the day. Of course, this means the final run into Herberton is a big gear buzz. However, if you are planning to camp the night, don't get too carried away by the speed since the caravan park and camping area are a couple of kilometres before the town, on the top of a very steep incline with an old log bridge at the bottom. Freewheeling all the way to the bottom could prove exhausting when you find you must turn around and climb back up the hill to the campsite.

DAY 3: Herberton to Ravenshoe

Distance ridden: 47.5 km;   Riding time: 2 hrs 51 mins;   Average speed: 16.4 kmph;   Maximum speed: 56 kmph

Herberton

It's easy to justify a late start from this old tin mining town. If you are cycling through during September there's a **Tin Festival**, but at any time of the year you can slip back in time at the **Herberton Historical Village** (open daily) or devour a few coffee buns at the local bakery. Out of town a few kilometres there's a wonderful example of a newly-built 'old' Queensland style house — with laid-back verandahs all around.

The route through Herberton rejoins the relatively busy Kennedy Highway at the crest of a good-sized hill and from there to The Crater National Park is a magical run. When we travelled it, the fast descents whipped us beside dense foliage flanking the road. The scene was made a wee bit eerie by the tentacles of a will-o'-the-whisp mist. The joyful prospect of this wind-in-the-hair plunge may be tempered by the knowledge that after a walk around the national park you have to reclimb the same hill.

The Crater National Park

The Crater (Mt Hypipamee) is another of those 'blink-and-you'll-miss-it' sized national parks — a tantalising glimpse of what was here before the short-sighted clearfelling commenced.

Once off the bikes, there's a pleasant 400 m walking track leading to a misnamed crater (actually it's a *diatreme*, the explosion vent from a volcano) and another easy 500 m takes you to Dinner Falls.

Be sure to boil the billy and have a bit to eat at one of the tables just near the start of the crater walk. This is not so much for your gluttonous benefit, as for the locals — if you are very fortunate, a fearless little Lewin's Honeyeater (half-moon yellowish-white earspots, curved beak) will fly down and delicately pluck tiny-sized nibbles from between your fingers. Much larger mound-building Australian Brush Turkeys (red head with a bright yellow collar which is inflated by the males during mating season) will also come out of the bush to see what's on offer.

An hour in the Tablelands above 1000 m can produce quite remarkable changes. What was previously a light mist can become a solid dense mass. In such poor visibility situations, it is very comforting to have a brightly-coloured wet weather jacket and reflecting tape on your panniers. Thankfully, once you have done the slow ascent (to the highest point of the whole tour), the route turns off the Kennedy Highway onto a charming little side road to Ravenshoe. This is the sort of soft-sliding descent where the bikes tend to ride themselves and the kilometres click past like power line poles. A lowering of altitude also gives you a good chance of leaving the all-pervading cloud behind.

Our destination for the night was the Tully Falls Hotel which, situated at an altitude of 915 m, is the highest pub in Queensland. Just before town there is an unofficial bush site beside the Millstream if you are looking to camp. By the way, the town is pronounced Ravens-hoe. The locals fall over themselves with laughter if you pronounce it the way it looks, Raven-shoe.

Ravenshoe

Ravenshoe was once a straight forestry town, but with an influx of recent settlers giving the place a new-age feel, it is developing into the 'Nimbin' of the Atherton Tablelands. The dichotomy of views is reflected in seeing alternative medicine practitioners with 'Think Globally, Act Locally' Wilderness Society posters just near a monument of land clearing — the district's first bulldozer (stuffed and mounted). Serious coffee afficionados will be gratified to learn that an espresso machine can be found in Ravenshoe.

DAY 4: Ravenshoe to Millaa Millaa

Distance ridden: 38.5 km;   Riding time: 2 hrs 27 mins;   Average speed: 15.6 kmph;   Maximum speed: 54 kmph

It is a memorable experience to lie in bed having your thoughts drowned out by the din of rain pounding on the tin verandah roof of the Tully Falls Hotel. Knowing that you have to get up and ride in that rain would make the strongest of tourers come down with a severe case of cosy-bed lassitude. This is compounded by the knowledge that, in the tradition of Australian country pubs, the bathroom is at the end of a linoleum corridor

Millstream Falls National Park Detour

The sojourn to Millstream Falls National Park is a chance for pannier-free riding where your bike is transformed into a superbly lithe machine, responsive to the lightest touch. Leave your gear at the hotel and freewheel it down to the falls — bike lock, camera, bathers and morning tea supplies are essential. Track down to the base of the falls, take off your shoes and carefully cross the stream to a tiny island. At the back of this island and partially hidden beyond a tight gap in the rocks, is a secluded **swimming pool** fed by its own waterfall. If you don't mind a few splashes it's possible to slip behind the waterfall into a small cave filled with the charging roar from the tumbling curtain of water. The falls was the site of an army camp in World War II.

about a day's march from your bedroom. It is, however, very inexpensive accommodation — and dry.

Once you have dragged yourself away from Millstream Falls back to Ravenshoe, and are once again a laden bicycle tourer, the route gives you a genuine reward. About 4 km east of Ravenshoe you foresake the Kennedy Highway for a backwoods meander down a road marked on the map as 'not suitable for caravans'. 'Perfect for bicycles' would be a better description of this bitumen pathway through rolling hills, manicured grass and rampant rainforest gulleys.

Extensive signposting is not a feature of the road, but it is still hard to get lost. Keep a lookout on the right for a hillside of flat-topped rainforest trees. According to the words of a laconic local farmer, 'In 1968 that hillside was as bare as a baby's bottom'. Just beyond this little patch of hope for rainforest regeneration, the road crosses Middlebrook Creek. This is a must-see, not only for the happy cascade of water, but for the chance to glimpse a rare Australian very few people have seen in the wild, the platypus.

ROUTE SLIP

Directions	R/S km	Ride for	Destination	Cum route km
END OF SECTION 2	104.6		**TOTAL FOR ROUTE**	**198.9**
Millstream Falls NP	104.6			198.9
L	103.4	1.2		197.7
R	99.6	3.8	Millstream Falls	193.9
R	99	.6	Tully Falls/Mt Garnet	193.3
S	98.1	.9		192.4
Ravenshoe	98.1			
R	78	20.1	Tumoulin & Ravenshoe	172.3
R-Kennedy Hwy	71.2	6.8	Ravenshoe	165.5
S-Crater NP	70.6	.6	Kennedy Hwy	164.9
Crater NP	70.6			
L	70	.6	Crater NP	164.3
L-Kennedy Hwy	65.8	4.2	Crater NP	160.1
S	50.5	15.3	Kennedy Hwy	144.8
Herberton	50.5			
S-Hwy No. 52	31.7	18.8	Herberton	126
Atherton	31.7			
Mareeba By Pass	0.0	31.7	Atherton	94.3
BEGIN SECTION 2				

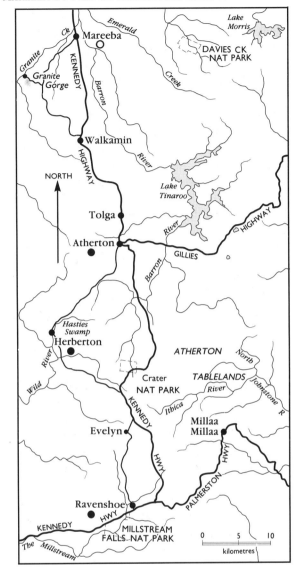

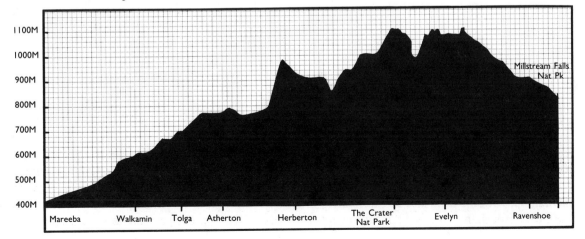

On ride line, each segment = 1 kilometre

The platypus is a web-footed, rudder-tailed monotreme which finds its food with a leathery electro-sensitive duck-like bill, lays eggs and suckles its young. It is very shy, so when you are walking down to the pool underneath the waterfall, move slowly and quietly. If you see a platypus on the surface (there were two when we were there), stop dead still and wait until it dives. Move a metre or so closer then remain stationary again and wait for it to surface. In this way you can get quite close to a platypus without frightening it.

There are still a couple of high ridges and saddles to negotiate between Middlebrook Creek and Millaa Millaa (pronounced *Milla Milla*) and once you leave monotremes behind, about the only animal encounters you may have will be as you round a bend at full tilt and are confronted by a road full of large Friesian cows, queuing to enter their dairy for milking. Millaa Millaa (popn 350) has a nice looking pub (closed for renovations when we were there), and a caravan park with inexpensive cabins.

Millaa Millaa Waterfalls Detour

North-east of Millaa Millaa is a 30 km **waterfalls circuit** which wanders through a selection of rainforest and dairy pastures. Beginning on the Teresa Creek road, there is Millaa Millaa Falls, followed by Zillie Falls, Ellinjaa Falls and Mungalli Falls. There are also great views into North Johnston River gorge.

DAY 5: Millaa Millaa to Malanda

Distance ridden: 22.3 km;   Riding time: 1 hr 13 mins;   Average speed: 17.3 kmph;   Maximum speed: 60 kmph

On any bicycle tour it's remarkable how a burst of morning sunlight lifts everyone's spirits. The Atherton Tablelands can keep up a consistent bout of mist, rain, clouds and generally gloomy weather when it feels like it. But the morning we pulled out from Millaa Millaa, the sun broke through.

This short section of the tour is a cluster of rolling hills where the downs knife into green leafy valleys and the ups are lenient, easy-to-climb slopes. Should you at this point be lucky enough to have your first tailwind of the tour, then the morning vanishes in a smooth blur.

Malanda

Malanda (popn 1000) is roughly the geographic centre of the Atherton Tablelands, and the **Malanda Hotel** (established in 1911) would have to be almost the largest, old pub in Queensland. It's gigantic. And lunching on the verandah amid a congregation of tropical potted plants gives you the feeling that you have wandered onto a set from the movie 'Out of Africa'.

The hotel's internal staircase features examples of Queensland rainforest timbers, but just down the road is a one kilometre walk through **Malanda Falls Environmental Park**, where the rainforest trees are still thriving. Do the walk in the wet and you'll experience this eerie forest at its most primeval. On dusk you may see tortoises.

DAY 6: (Rest Day) Malanda to Lake Eacham

Distance ridden: 11.5 km;   Riding time: 44 mins;   Average speed: 15.0 kmph;   Maximum speed: 56 kmph

The clearing of the big forests that took place in the late 1800s on the Atherton Tablelands was not only a thoughtless loss of ancient trees and animal habitat, but with the trees and the decimation of the local Aboriginal tribes, also went much priceless information on the healing properties of the rainforest plants. The full effect of that fact will be brought home if you get the chance to stay with and talk to John Chambers at Lake Eacham. John has lived on the edge of a rainforest since the early

ROUTE SLIP

Directions	R/S km	Ride for	Destination	Cum route km
END OF SECTION 3	73.3		**TOTAL FOR ROUTE**	**272.2**
Yungaburra	73.3			272.2
L-Gillies Hwy	69.3	4	Yungaburra	268.2
R	68.8	.5	Atherton	267.7
L	66.5	2.3	Atherton	265.4
R*-Wrights Ck t'off	66.5		waterfall walk & Lake Barrine	
S	66.2	.3		265.1
Lake Eacham	66.2			
R	63.2	3	Lake Eacham	262.1
R	55.2	8	Gordonvale	254.1
Malanda	55.2			
L	32.5	22.7	Malanda	231.4
Millaa Millaa	32.5			
S-Souta Falls t'off	24.8	7.7	Millaa Millaa	223.7
R*-Middlebrook Ck	23.7	1.1	platypus pool	222.6
BR	12.4	11.3		211.3
R-Murchison Hwy	7.8	4.6		206.7
S-Tully Falls t'off	5	2.8	Millaa Millaa	203.9
R	1.2	3.8	Ravenshoe	200.1
Millstream Falls NP	0.0	1.2	main road	198.9
BEGIN SECTION 3				

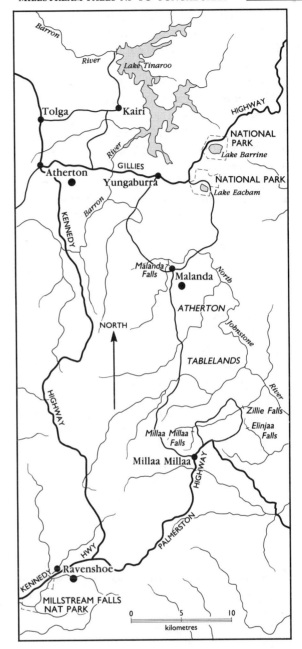

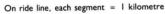

On ride line, each segment = 1 kilometre

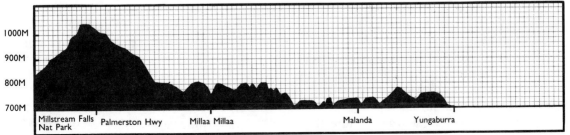

1970s and his knowledge of its flora and fauna is prodigious. We spent our 'rest' day in one of his rainforest apartments, 10 km from Malanda.

A few minutes stroll from the apartment is the start of a 4 km walk which circumnavigates Lake Eacham. Eacham (and nearby Barrine) is a flooded volcanic crater fringed by rainforest. Here you will see some ancient forest giants, the strangler figs, and, if you are lucky, you will be enchanted by a sighting of one of the smallest rainforest dwellers, the Musky Rat-Kangaroo. As you saunter, cat birds less than subtly announce their presence and Honeyeaters do pirouettes on the ends of fresh red blossoms — this is a muscle-soothing stroll beneficial to body and soul.

More animal interaction begins at dusk when John Chambers performs a passable Brush Turkey call and 40 or 50 of them dash out of the bush for a snack. A couple of hours later it is the turn of the red-legged pademelons (a small wallaby) to snack about two metres away while brown and long-nosed bandicoots nibble beside your feet. On the railing outside your unit, where the kookaburras materialise to be hand-fed by day, during the night gentle, big-eyed white-tailed uromys drop by for food.

DAY 7: Lake Eacham to School Point State Forest Park

Distance ridden: 67.5 km; Riding time: 3 hrs 57 mins; Average speed: 16.9 kmph; Maximum speed: not recorded

---

Leaving Lake Eacham on the way to Yungaburra it is worth doing a short detour to Wright Creek. Just before the bridge there's a roughish circuit walk which leads to a delicate lace-like waterfall beside smooth pools which often contain platypus (though they must have been shy when we were there). Back on the route you are biking through a leaf-strewn forested avenue where the sun only penetrates in trifling patches. Emerging to a stark, cleared landscape again can be quite unsettling.

Yungaburra (pop\ 650) is an excellent place to load up with supplies since ahead are three nights of bush camping. After a short detour to view the grand Curtain Fig (it really is immense), the road descends and begins to smooth out. When free-wheeling beside fields of strawberries and potatoes on the way to Lake Tinaroo you are travelling one of the flattest sections of the tour. Given a helpful tailwind (as we had), this can be a very fast ride. If there's room in your panniers, stop in at Kairi — the pottery and wood crafts are excellent.

Lunching beside the waters of Lake Tinaroo you are very likely to be inundated with local birds; black and white magpies, peewees and butcher birds, brown hawks and ebullient king parrots. When we lunched here, I was intrigued by a black bird with an elegantly forked tail and iridescent blue breast, known by the wonderfully evocative name of a spangled drongo.

After a mine-shaft descent to a point directly at the foot of the dam wall, then an equally vertical ascent to regain a height level with the spillway again, the road takes kindly to cycle tourers suffering from after lunch fatigue.

It's also time for all-terrain bikes to enjoy life, as the road is well-formed dirt. How well-formed the surface will be when you encounter it is dependent on two factors: how much rain there has been; and how recently the road has been graded. For us a couple of days of sunshine had dried it out enough to make the going smooth and enjoyable — even with thin tyres. However, when we rode very shaded sections, the suction of still wet clay suggested that during or right after rain you should make a generous time allowance to cover this section of the route.

School Point State Forest Park

There is an ample number of well-established **state forestry campsites** — water, toilets, cold showers, picnic tables and barbecue fireplaces — scattered around the fringes of Lake Tinaroo. A small fee is required (paid on the spot after filling out a form at the entrance of each camping area).

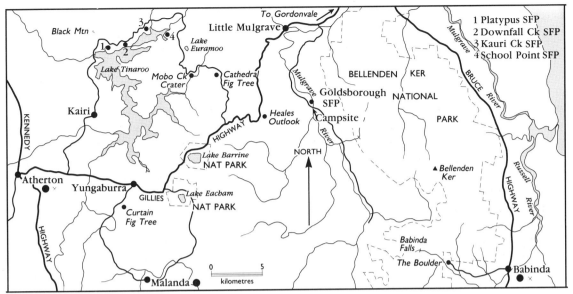

Map labels:
- Black Mtn
- 3
- 4
- Little Mulgrave
- To Gordonvale
- Lake Euramoo
- 1
- 2
- 1 Platypus SFP
- 2 Downfall Ck SFP
- 3 Kauri Ck SFP
- 4 School Point SFP
- Lake Tinaroo
- Mobo Ck Crater
- Cathedral Fig Tree
- BELLENDEN KER
- Mulgrave
- Goldsborough SFP
- NATIONAL
- Mulgrave
- Campsite
- BRUCE
- Russell River
- Kairi
- Heales Outlook
- PARK
- KENNEDY
- HIGHWAY
- River
- NORTH
- Lake Barrine
- NAT PARK
- Bellenden Ker
- Atherton
- Yungaburra
- GILLIES
- Lake Eacham
- NAT PARK
- HIGHWAY
- Curtain Fig Tree
- Babinda Falls
- The Boulder
- Babinda
- Malanda
- 0 5 kilometres

ROUTE SLIP

Directions	R/S km	Ride for	Destination	Cum route km
R*-Kauri Ck SFP	32.7	7.5		304.9
R*-Downfall Ck SFP	30.7	2		302.9
R*-Platypus SFP	27	3.7		299.2
S	23.3	3.7		295.5
end of tar road	23.3			
S	21.3	2	Gordonvale	293.5
Lake Tinaroo	21.3			
L*-scenic lookout	19.9	1.4		292.1
L	14.8	5.1	Tinaroo Dam	287
Kairi	14.8			
BR-	14.2	0.6		286.4
R-(at T-intersection)	10	4.2		282.2
R	7.3	2.7	Tinaroo Dam/Kairi	279.5
L*-Curtain Fig t'off	0.6	6.7		272.8
Yungaburra	0.0	0.6	Atherton	272.2
BEGIN SECTION 4				

Directions	R/S km	Ride for	Destination	Cum route km
END OF SECTION 4	97.7		**TOTAL FOR ROUTE**	**369.9**
Campsite	97.7			369.9
S	86.1	11.6		358.3
end of tar road	86.1			
R	81	5.1	Goldsborough SFP	353.2
S	77.5	3.5		349.7
Little Mulgrave	77.5			
R*-Heales Outlook	63.2	14.3		335.4
L-Gillies Hwy	56.4	6.8	Gordonvale/Cairns	328.6
S	51.9	4.5		324.1
start of tar road	51.9			
R*-Cathedral Fig	50.3	1.6		322.5
R*-Mobo Ck Crater	47	3.3		319.2
L*-Euramoo Craters	41.8	5.2		314
R*-School Pt	40.2	1.6		212.4

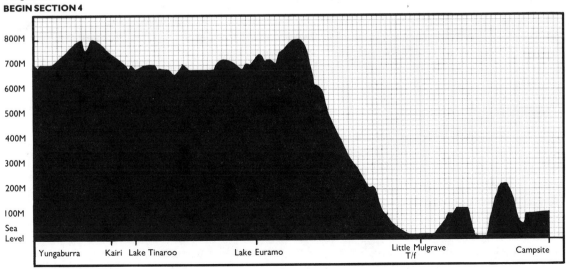

Elevation profile with markers: 800M, 700M, 600M, 500M, 400M, 300M, 200M, 100M, Sea Level.
Labels along base: Yungaburra, Kairi, Lake Tinaroo, Lake Euramo, Little Mulgrave T/f, Campsite

On ride line, each segment = 1 kilometre

DAY 8: School Point State Forest Park to Goldsborough State Forest Park

Distance ridden: 58.5 km; Riding time: 3 hrs 39 mins; Average speed: 15.8 kmph; Maximum speed: 50 kmph

Be up before dawn at School Point to catch the pelicans on a full-wing glide across the water, greater egrets doing perfect imitations of haughty statues, a mist cloaking the forests, and the first sun rays setting Black Mountain alight. Lake Tinaroo is human-created, but Euramoo (3 km past the turnoff to School Point) is a water-filled, twin volcanic crater only 10 000 years young. Be sure to tramp the botanical circuit beside the lake.

There's a heart, lungs and legs testing hill which begins just beyond the forestry depot, but you can catch your breath pausing at Mobo Creek Crater. On this circuit keep an eye out for amazingly bright, orange paperbark trees which seem to almost leap out of rainforest greens, and beware of slippery rocks when crossing the stream. You can pedal right to the base of the Cathedral Fig, yet another larger-than-imaginable tree. A kilometre past the fig don't be surprised if you are hit by a blast of hot air because, not far away, the rainforest ends abruptly and a once magnificent landscape is reduced to little more than green grass.

You hear the Gillies Highway before you reach it. Or at least you hear the traffic on it. After two days of virtually no cars, even the few stray tourists seem a lot. Unfortunately there are also a number of large, fast-moving trucks which use this road, so be aware of them. But bicycle touring here is just too good to be upset by anything. Ahead lies 19 easy kilometres — all downhill! This is where you use up those 500 m that the Kuranda train gained for you on the first day. It's so cool, so easy and so deserved. Take a break at the oddly-named Heales Outlook to savour the Mulgrave Valley (and more downhill to come). As you descend, the temperature begins to ascend, until the Mountain View hotel at the hamlet of Little Mulgrave is virtually impossible to pass. Out the back of the hotel is a charming tree-shaded beer garden with a sparkling (fish-filled) stream running just below. You only have to throw a piece of bread into the water to find out just how many fish are lurking below the surface.

Relaxed and refreshed is the way to tackle the road in to Goldsborough State Forest park. After turning off the Gillies Highway and crossing over the Mulgrave River (beside sugar cane train tracks) the road begins an upward tilt. If the tropical sun is blazing then you'll be sweating by the time you gain the crest and look across a foreground of swaying sugar cane fronds to the dominating mountains of the Atherton Tablelands high above. Almost all this struggled-for height is lost in a series of quick descents and, by the last, a pleasant tarred road has mutated into a chunky rock-strewn skittery slide. At the bottom you meet the Mulgrave River again.

After a section of flat road along an avenue of cane fields and a huge 'beware of the dog' notice (the dog was nowhere in sight when we sneaked past) there is yet another crossing of the Mulgrave, then a rise. It's a good one — the steepest in fact for the whole tour. And it is a hill not improved by the miserable road surface. To climb or walk? I preferred to climb, but down to my lowest gear and going so slowly, and still the computer refused to be moved. I was not confident of making it to the top. Help was at hand in the form of a couple of 'steps' — slightly flatter sections where you can ease back a little and get your second wind. By three-quarters of the way up, I was ragged, steam breathing and self-doubting, but along with eventually gaining the top came a wonderful sense of achievement.

A teeth-jarring plunge leads to the Goldsborough State Forest Park.

Goldsborough State Forest Park

The **campsites** (water, toilets, picnic tables and barbecue fireplaces) here are beside a clear, fast-moving stream punctuated with occasional deep green pools (one has a great rope swing) — the Mulgrave River. This is a great spot for a rest day or two. You can dabble peacefully beside the river or meander up to view Kearney's Falls. Or, you

ROUTE SLIP

Directions	R/S km	Ride for	Destination	Cum route km
END OF TOUR	48		**TOTAL FOR ROUTE**	**417.9**
Cairns	48			417.9
BR	46.9	1.1		416.8
R-Bruce Hwy	25.9	21		395.8
L-Cairns Rd	24.6	1.3	Cairns	394.5
S	24	0.6		393.9
R*-**Gordonvale**	24			
S-Bruce Hwy	23	1		392.9
R-Gillies Hwy	16.7	6.3		386.6
S	11.6	5.1		381.5
start of tar road	11.6			
campsite	0.0	11.6	Gordonvale	369.9
BEGIN SECTION 5				

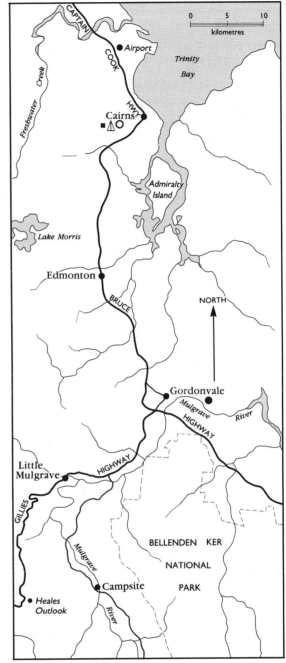

On ride line, each segment = 1 kilometre

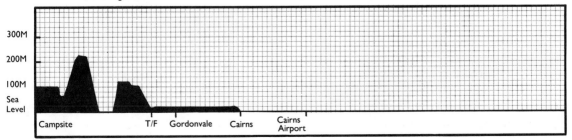

could try our 'rest' day. We tackled 8 km of semi-demolished four-wheel drive track, surfaced in slimy red clay. Then, we force-marched the **Goldfields Track** (10 km of rainforest crossing over a mountain range), took a generous 25 minutes for lunch beside The Boulders, and then did the whole thing all over again in order to get back to camp by dark. Pure madness, but fun.

DAY 10: Goldsborough State Forest Park to Cairns

Distance ridden: 47.7 km;   Riding time: 2 hrs 33 mins;   Average speed: 18.7 kmph;   Maximum speed: 57 kmph

Goldsborough is one of those campsites which comes with a morning alarm — three raucous kookaburras letting fly with the loudest possible laughter. After an overnight break, the hill climb to get out of here is not as dramatic as getting in, though it is still a marvellous relief to get back on the tar.

For us the dog to 'beware of' was still absent, but his neighbours were all ready and primed for their morning exercise. I managed to attract one brown monster who stayed with me till 30 kmph ticked up on the computer.

There's only one hill of note between rejoining the Gillies Highway and Cairns. But in between is the town of Gordonvale where you can order surprisingly cheap hotel counter lunches from 11.30 a.m. Cairns is north of Gordonvale and if you're lucky you'll be pushed into Cairns at the startling speed of 38 kmph by a bustling southerly breeze.

Cairns

Cairns (pop^n 68 000) is the place to meet travellers from all over the globe. It can be the base for a whole range of **reef exploring** (scuba diving and snorkelling), **white-water rafting, canoeing** and **horse riding**. **Accommodation** choice is awesome, ranging from innumerable stars to cheaper than cheap. There are two youth hostels.

Information centre: Sheridan and Aplin Sts.

TOUR 3
RED CENTRE CIRCUIT

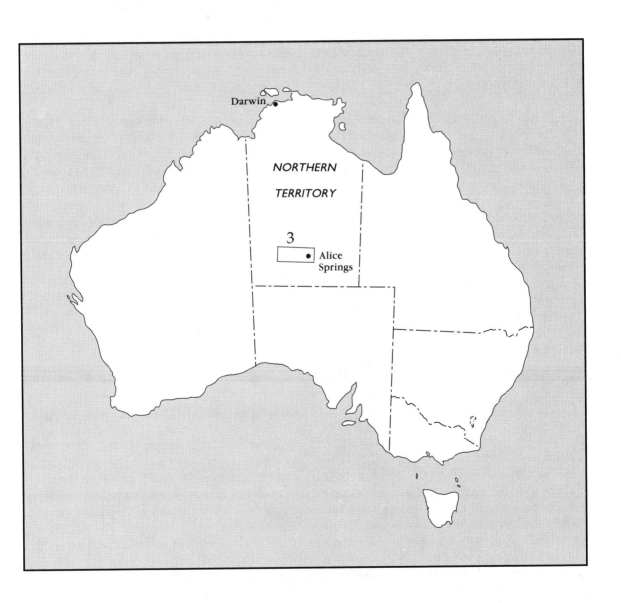

3 RED CENTRE CIRCUIT

This is a two-stage 470 km Central Australian camping tour to be undertaken in the cooler months — from May to September. It requires pre-planning and packaging of meals because shops are few and far between. However, the tour will take you through some of the most stunningly beautiful desert landscapes in Australia. A friend and I rode the tour in August on all-terrain bikes (ATBs), taking nine days (including two rest days) and averaging 68 km per day.

The first half of the tour on sealed road to Glen Helen (133 km west of Alice Springs) is suitable for touring bikes. If you are short of time, you can end your tour at Glen Helen Gorge, hitching a lift back to Alice Springs on one of the day coaches. The second half of the tour is rigorous and suitable only for ATBs. Long stretches of red sand inter-laced with river stones make for a taxing, though ultimately rewarding, tour. The distances covered, especially on the dirt sections of the tour, are less than those covered in the other tours, but necessarily so due to sometimes searing heat.

Sufficient drinking water is essential and carry-ing 7 L (1¾ gallons) for each person is a bare minimum per day. Seven litres (1¾ gallons) can be conveniently carried between two bike bottles, one carrying bottle and a 4 L (7¼ pint) wine cask. To reduce weight, a box of pre-packaged meals can be sent to Hermannsburg Post Office prior to leaving Alice Springs.

Alice Springs

Alice Springs (pop^n 23 000) is at the cutting edge of Australian race relations. 'Alice' as it is abbrevi-ated by locals, was first established in the 1870s (and called Stuart) as a telegraph station for the line which eventually connected Australia to Europe (a message transmitted from Australia took seven hours to arrive in England). At the telegraph station (2 km north of the centre of Alice) rifle slots in the walls of the main building are a reminder of early clashes. The situation has improved, though for many people an us-and-them mentality still breeds hostility and mistrust between whites and local Aborigines.

When the bicycle adventurer Francis Birtles rolled into town in 1908, there were a thousand camels driven by Afghans being loaded up with freight for the Arltunga goldfields. The town he describes in his book, *Battle Fronts of Outback*, as 'a few houses, a store and a pub'. Today, with ritzy hotels, restaurants and a casino, Alice is less a frontier town and more akin to a desert Gold Coast. There are youth hostels, motels, hotels and caravan parks aplenty.

Information Centre: The Mall.

DAY 1: Alice Springs to Ellery Ck Big Hole

Distance ridden: 109 km;   Riding time: 5 hrs 53 mins;   Average speed: 18.5 kmph;   Maximum speed: 55 kmph

Don't rush to get started on your tour if there's a 30-knot westerly raging. Westerlies are an aber-ration in winter, so give it a day and you should manage to find a more benevolent south-easter. Once you are underway Alice Springs doesn't last long in the rear view mirror, even when you're on a bicycle. The town is tucked in against small hills in a dramatic gap in the 300 km long Mac-donnel Ranges. The explorer John McDouall Stuart named the range in 1860. This sedimentary and

volcanic rock range has an estimated age of 2000 million years and is one of the world's most ancient mountain ranges. Today, even though it is an eroded shadow of its former greatness, riding beneath it gives the sense of passing beyond human time scales. In her book *Tracks* (describ-ing her camel journey across central Australia), Robyn Davidson likens the range to a 'petrified prehistoric monster'.

With Alice Springs suburbia gone, all that

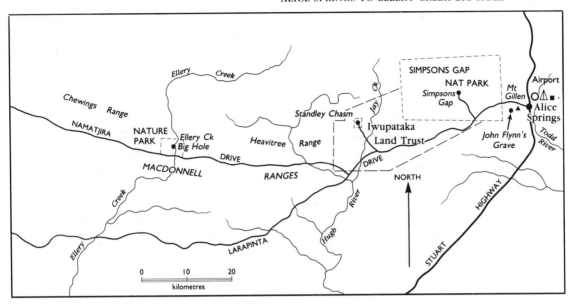

ROUTE SLIP

Directions	R/S km	Ride for	Destination	Cum route km
END OF SECTION 1	104.6		**TOTAL FOR ROUTE**	**104.6**
Ellery Ck Big Hole	104.6			104.6
R-Ellery Ck Big Hole	102.9	1.7		102.9
L* roadside stop	91.5	11.4		91.5
R-Namatjira Drive	59.9	31.6		59.9
R* Standley Chasm	53.6	6.3	9.3 km to Chasm	53.6
L* John Flynn's Grave	19.9	33.7		19.9
L-Larapinta Dr	13.6	6.3	Glen Helen	13.6
Alice Springs	13.6			
Alice Springs Airport	0.0	13.6	Alice Springs	0.0
BEGIN SECTION 1				

KEY

L = left   **R** = right   **S** = straight

BL = bear left   **BR** = bear right

X = cross   * = detour directions

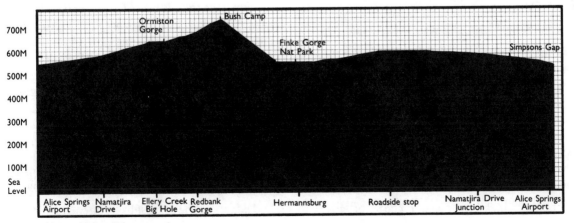

Note — Horizontal is not to scale.
Vertical is an approximation.

remains is you, a shimmering black road and a sky so vast and blue that it is intoxicating. In perfect counterpoint are the ranges; hard-edged rock sentinels which create a vast stony passageway through which you enter the Centre of Australia. Running almost parallel to Larapinta Drive and away to the south is the Heavitree Range which glows orange in both the early morning and late afternoon sun. Astride this range is the tall peak of Mt Gillen, a fitting backdrop for John Flynn's Memorial (he founded the Australian Inland Mission and the Royal Flying Doctor service in 1928). To the north, the Chewings Range dominates the skyline forcing you to redefine the word 'vista'. As you cruise along (aided I hope by the same tailwind we had) the closer, small, unnamed hillocks combine to create a mobile panorama, an effect not unlike those 3-D viewers of last century.

Simpsons Gap

Simpsons Gap (30 950 hectares) is one of the few parks of reasonable size in the Western Macdonnel Ranges. You approach it by taking a turn-off 17 km out of Alice Springs, and the park is open from 8 a.m. to 8 p.m. daily. **Facilities** include tables, gas barbecues, water and toilets. **Natural features** include ghost gums and river red gums.

On a circuit bicycle tour, Simpsons Gap is best left till the last day, otherwise it makes the first day's travel unbearably long. Likewise, whether or not you turn off Larapinta Drive to see Angkale (Standley Chasm) depends on how fit you are feeling and how far you want to cycle on the first day. The minimum distance to a campsite with guaranteed drinking water is 68 km, though you can pick up drinking water at Angkale.

Standley Chasm

Leaving Alice Springs in the morning should put you into the Chasm just prior to the perfect time.

Around noon to 1 p.m., sunlight reaches down into this 9 m gap and lights the 80 m high rock walls. Unfortunately, this is also peak tourist time, so be earlier or stay later if you desire a more peaceful experience. Angkale is owned by the Iwupatak community and a small entry fee is charged (there's a kiosk, water and toilets).

The 9 km road into Angkale is uphill, but so slight that I believed I was stricken by pre-lunch fatigue when cycling it. Heading back out proved to be a reviving, partially freewheeling joy.

Where overgrazing hasn't destroyed the vegetation, the sandy landscape has its own bounty. Aside from numerous spinifex clumps, after good rains there are a multitude of flowering plants including yellow burr daisies and the cotton-like white blooms of the tangled mulla mulla. Between rejoining Larapinta Drive and turning off along Namatjira Drive, the road dips, rises and snakes its way through Heavitree Range and beside stands of stately river red gums dotting the dry bed of Jay Creek (Larapinta is believed to mean snake). Rolling hills begin almost as soon as you turn on to Namatjira Drive (named after Aranda Aboriginal artist Albert Namatjira) and head up Mereeni Valley.

The hills and trees confine the landscape and the perspective from a bike is greatly reduced. It takes a long, slow hill climb, then a hard pump up to a roadside stop before the outback world of orange-tongued ridges and far distant blue-grey ranges is laid out before you. This roadside stop is the first organised place to camp on the route, but it's a pretty barren looking campsite. Twelve km down the track is Ellery Creek Big Hole Nature Park (1766 hectares — also called Udepata), a much nicer place to roll out your swag. Thanks to five weeks of industry from two English cyclist volunteers, just south-west of the waterhole there is a 3 km nature walk which takes in woodlands, rolling spinifex and a lookout.

DAY 2: Ellery Ck Big Hole to Ormiston Gorge

Distance ridden: 56 km;	Riding time: 3 hrs 6 mins;	Average speed: 18 kmph;	Maximum speed: 41 kmph

At Ellery Creek Big Hole, don't be surprised if you find a fine coating of frost has whitened your bike

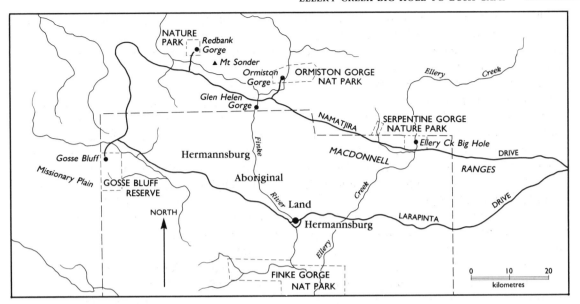

ROUTE SLIP

Directions	R/S km	Ride for	Destination	Cum route km
END OF SECTION 2			**TOTAL FOR ROUTE**	**222.9**
bush camp	118.3			222.9
BL-Telecom Tower	117.8	0.5		222.4
L-T-intersection	109.8	8	Hermannsburg	214.4
R-Namatjira Drive	93	16.8		197.6
exit Redbank	88.2	4.8		192.8
Redbank Gorge	88.2			
R-Redbank Gorge	83.4	4.8		188
start dirt road				
L*-Glen Helen	63.1	20.3	1.5 km to Gorge	167.7
R-Namatjira Drive	59.4	3.7	Glen Helen Gorge	164
exit Gorge	52.1	7.3		156.7
Ormiston Gorge	52.1			
R-Ormiston Gorge	44.8	7.3	Ormiston Gorge	149.4
R*-Ochre Pits	27.1	17.7		131.7
L*-roadside stop	24	3.1		128.6
R*-Serpentine Gorge	16.1	7.9	2.7 km to Gorge	120.7
R-Namatjira Drive	1.7	14.4	Glen Helen	106.3
Ellery Ck Big Hole	0.0	1.7		104.6
BEGIN SECTION 2				

saddle in the morning. This is winter, even if in the middle of the day the temperature soars into the 30s (Celsius). Judging by the gaily coloured tourists, the standard coach tour allows just five minutes to stand and admire Ellery Creek Big Hole before departing. But cycle tourers setting their own schedule can be enticed up a bank to a cave on the left of the rocky outcrop surrounding the pool. A further short climb above the cave affords a fine view across the Alice Valley to the north where the Chewings Range is clad each morning in muted blues and purples.

The rolling hills on Namatjira Drive between Ellery Big Hole and Ormiston Gorge and Pound National Park are probably just as hard as the section you rode the day before, though to us they felt a lot easier because of a good night's sleep, a sunny day and that blessed tailwind still blowing.

The turn off to Serpentine Gorge comes after riding towards a line of dark red parallel ridges, yet more fossilised 'evidence' of an ancient, long extinct creature. The rough, sand strewn track into Serpentine Gorge (518 hectares, picnic area, barbecue and toilets) gives you an indication of how challenging things will become on the second half of the tour, though the 5 km sign seems a little pessimistic since it is actually less than three. Beside the waterhole under the shade of old river gums is the perfect place to lunch, though Chris, my riding companion, reckoned that walking a bike equipped with low rider front panniers over the rocks to get to the waterhole was only for masochists.

The second roadside stop on Namatjira Drive (water, barbecue site and picnic tables) is perched high on the peak of a long hill and even requires you to backtrack — but the views are worth the effort. Riding in this dense tree-packed valley tends to hide the ridges from view, and it's good to be able to see just how far you've come. Between here and the turn off to Ormiston Gorge you ride beside a cluster of roller-coaster hillocks cultivated with tussock grasses in such a uniform pattern that they strongly resemble the dot-dot paintings of the local Aborigines.

It's only 8 km off Namatjira Drive to Ormiston Gorge, but if you have ridden for more than 100 km the day before it may seem a long, slow, hard end to the day. We both found our legs expired on the hill just after crossing the Finke River. At Ormiston Gorge it pays to arrive early. This is the area's most popular camping site and once the campervans and four-wheel drive vehicles have made their late afternoon rush, space can be at a premium.

DAY 3: Rest Day

Ormiston Gorge and Pound National Park

For a cycle tourer, Ormiston Gorge and Pound National Park (4655 hectares) is a magical place — **fresh drinking water** (beside the information centre), **free gas stoves** and cooking area, and, best of all, **solar-powered showers**. The park encompasses some of the catchment of the Finke River, mooted by many to be the oldest river in the world because its general course has not greatly altered since it was cut in the late Palaeozoic period. At the Gorge's southern end is a semi-permanent waterhole just made for swimming on a hot day.

There is a 2.5 km **Ghost Gum Walk** which is very popular with photographers, but just being on the ridge near to the camping area at sundown will provide the opportunity for wonderful evocative landscape photographs. It might also be where you'll meet a brightly coloured spinifex or plumed pigeon (a reddish bronzewing with an upright crest).

Rising very early and walking quietly into the Gorge increases your chances of encountering a shy black-footed rock wallaby. If you are up to a walk on your rest day, do the **Ormiston Pound Walk** (7 km, three to four hours), but remember to wear a hat and carrying drinking water. Meander through Ormiston Gorge as the morning sun slashes down sheer walls of ochre, then head out across the floor of the pound and feel the heat rising from flat plate rock and spinifex. Surrounding this valley is an immense ring of mountain peaks and rock walls which can combine to make you feel an insignificant, temporary speck on the landscape.

Near the half-way point of the walk, with the sun high, take a swim in a sand-fringed pool where the resident fish come over to discover whether or not you are edible. Follow the swim with some unhurried relaxation in the shade of a gum tree (after you have warmed up from the cooler than cool water).

As the afternoon sun begins to throw shadows, saunter up to the highest point of the south ridge (there's a short track running at 90 degrees to the right of the main track). This is the place to view the afternoon light setting the far off red wall aflame. With this awesome display committed to memory (or recorded on film), use the pre-dusk light to stroll back to camp.

For keen, experienced bushwalkers there are **two- to three-day unmarked walks** to Bowman's Gap and Mt Giles, but consult the ranger before attempting them.

DAY 4: Ormiston Gorge to Redbank Gorge

Distance ridden: 37.1 km;   Riding time: 2 hrs 50 mins;   Average speed: 13 kmph;   Maximum speed: 27 kmph

Given a primarily downhill exit and a smooth, sealed road, the run from Ormiston to Glen Helen Gorge is a breeze.

Glen Helen Gorge

At 386 hectares, Glen Helen Gorge is only a small area, but it is an important one for bike tourers. Glen Helen Lodge is based on a station homestead (the original station was established in 1880) and is a **youth hostel**, as well as offering **motel-style accommodation**. The restaurant is a regular award winner and even if you are not staying overnight, try their BLTs (bacon, lettuce and tomato sandwiches) for lunch — delicious!

The earlier you arrive at Glen Helen, the more spectacularly coloured its craggy rock wall will be. And, if you are pushing straight on to Redbank Gorge, then the sooner you can start the struggle with the dirt road ahead, the better. If you are using a touring bike, this is the point at which you should end westward travel and begin heading back to Alice Springs. All-terrain bikers should let down the tyres (ours came down from 60psi to 40psi), take note of the bright red sign WARNING NO SERVICES BEYOND THIS POINT, click down to a lower gear and head towards the geographic centre of Australia. John McDouall Stuart first reached this point on 23 April 1860.

From this point on you become one with the landscape. At least you quickly resemble it. A uniform coating of dust sprayed up from careless cars passing at high speeds turns bikes and bodies mahogany. After the gravel and stones have peppered your body and the dust has cleared enough for the road to become visible again, you emerge from the near-foetal cringe you've adopted over the handlebars and go back to enjoying cycling. Wearing a bandana tied around your face, across your nose (in the style of Australian bushrangers and American cowboys), is highly recommended if you wish to continue breathing.

A more pleasant constant companion on this section of the route, and a major inspiration for artist Albert Namatjira, is 1525 m Mt Sonder (also called Rutjubma — sleeping woman mountain). Even seen as hazy blue in harsh daylight, its huge sway-backed form dominates the landscape, but seeing it radiate crimson in the outback version of Alpenglow is truly breathtaking.

Taking the Redbank Gorge turn-off at least leaves the high speed travellers behind. The condition of the Redbank Gorge track ensures slow passage. The sand is fine enough to rate as 'bull-dust', perfectly camouflaging the pot holes, and the short sharp pinches are sufficiently tough to elicit rasping wheezes. Long-distance cyclist Tom Coleman described what you will find back in 1897 during his Darwin to Adelaide ride: 'Sand,

Sand everywhere . . . It rose in a fine impalpable dust, which made the nostrils and throat feel as if on fire'. (*The Bicycle and the Bush*, see bibliography.)

Redbank Gorge

If you classify a campsite as a level site, with pleasant aspect and encouraging shade, then Redbank Gorge (1295 hectares) doesn't have one. The camping area here is more in the style of heat-baked inclines — even the toilet is perched on sloping ground. Thankfully the Gorge is wonderful, a true oasis reached at the end of a 15 minute stroll along a dry creek bed lined with river gums. However, I defy anyone to last any more than 45 seconds fully submerged in its waters. They are liquid ice, which is a real shame since swimming right into the Gorge, where the water polished scarlet walls come together on either side to within touching distance, is one of the great experiences of this region. A lilo is the perfect way to do it, though sadly few cycle tourers will have one.

DAY 5: Redbank Gorge to Tylers Pass

Distance ridden: 29.9 km;   Riding time: 2 hrs 31 mins;   Average speed: 11.8 kmph;   Maximum speed: 28 kmph

Wallabies moving gently in the bush near camp are pleasant morning sleep-breakers, but crows attempting a demolition job on the 'wildlife proof' rubbish bins are just plain jarring. Aboriginal legend has it that the Australian crow was once pure white and could sing so splendidly that he enticed the eagle's wife to fly away with him. The jealous eagle in hot pursuit dropped a red hot coal down the crow's throat, and the crow became as black as charcoal with a voice like a wood rasp attacking steel plate.

The toughest (though mercifully short) hill on the whole tour is your barrier to exiting from Redbank Gorge. It is a real morning glory. And it's followed by patches of tyre-grabbing sand, after which the memory of the ride over harder packed stones of Namatjira Drive seems like Nirvana. In measured distance it's only a relatively short run from the Redbank turnoff to the Hermannsburg turnoff (our trip was slowed by a disintegrated rear tyre), but on a rapidly decaying road surface you won't be breaking any speed limits.

Once you take the turn towards Hermannsburg the road is transformed into a sand track, interspersed with melon-sized stones. Even in winter it is best to avoid the severe midday heat — we took a break in the middle of a shaded dry river bed. During the wet season, where the track snakes through the western end of the Macdonnell Ranges is probably a raging river, but in winter this is just a heat-baked, bone-jarring, dry creek bed. Every kilometre ridden through this section is well earned.

You are heading for a trig point 800 m above sea level, near Tylers Pass, reached by turning off the main track just as you crest the last ridge and gaze down at the arresting sight of Gosse Bluff. Be thankful you weren't gazing down on Missionary Plain 130 million years ago when the comet which created this amazing formation crash-landed. Today, although a remnant of the original crater, Gosse Bluff is still an extravagant feature of the landscape.

Given its panoramic 360 degree view, the campsite at trig point and communication tower (it 'sings' at night when the wind blows) is perfect for photographers wanting to experience an outback sunset and sunrise. At night it is a fantastic stargazer's paradise (we managed to sight four satellites and seven shooting stars). From a cycle tourer's point of view, however, it is less than ideal. There is no water and it is too close to Redbank Gorge, forcing you to ride an extra long distance the next day. However, because Aboriginal land begins at an unmarked point approximately 25 km from the Hermannsburg turnoff, without an entry permit it is not legally possible to leave the main track before Finke Gorge National Park. Permits are obtainable at the Central Land Council in Alice Springs, but to obtain them sometimes means you become embroiled in local politics. It is thus much simpler to camp outside Aboriginal land, then ride all the way to Finke Gorge the next day.

DAY 6: Tylers Pass to Finke Gorge National Park

Distance ridden: 83.3 km; Riding time: 6 hrs 46 mins; Average speed: 12.3 kmph; Maximum speed: 29 kmph

On paper 83 km may not seem much. But the average speed that we rode it in and the time we actually spent in the saddle, will give you a good indication of just how difficult the conditions can be. This is the sort of country the explorer Giles described last century when he wrote that, 'A day's march wouldn't get you to the horizon'.

Between the trig point campsite and the turnoff to Gosse Bluff (camping is not allowed), the track is pleasant running. If you do this section first thing in the morning, keep a lookout for break-fasting kangaroos. Your tyre pattern will be mingling with a myriad of wildlife tracks, including many dingo tracks.

Beyond the second turnoff to Gosse Bluff and before hitting Larapinta Drive, is the hardest piece of sand-road to ride in all of the routes covered by this book. When it's good, it is like a billiard table, and when bad, it's like a bottomless pit. Sometimes the far, untouched edges of the track are hard enough to allow a bike smooth passage, but it only takes a brumbie hoof print or a four-wheel drive tyre to have cut through the hard crust for the section to become impossible. Unfortunately, at 20 km per hour the reaction time upon finding that the sand has grabbed your front wheel has to be super fast, otherwise three things may happen: 1. you come to a complete dead stop; 2. you execute a demonic cross-track lunge; 3. Splat! you crash. If you had been following our tracks the day we rode this sand hell, even lesser mortals than Sherlock Holmes would have deduced from the bomb craters created that the third of these possibilities was the one we befell most frequently.

Mostly, on being confronted by depressingly long patches of red sand, we dismounted and with agonising slowness hauled the bikes through. Roadside rest stops were usually punctuated by exhausted panting and growing doubts on just how long this would continue and whether we would ever reach Larapinta Drive.

Although it applies to the whole tour, beware of dehydration on this section of the route in particular, even if the sun isn't shining. You may not appear to be sweating (perspiration often evaporates before wetting the skin), but your body, nonetheless, is consuming water at a rapid rate (I drank more than 5 L) that day and was still slightly dehydrated by dusk). Ensure you have enough water, and don't be too proud to ask for a top up from passing four-wheel drive vehicles (they are usually carrying enough food and water to ensure the month-long survival of a football team).

Rejoining Larapinta Drive is cruelly prolonged by the track and road running almost parallel for half a kilometre, but even when you finally hit the established road it is of a very poor standard. There are still depressing patches of sand to be negotiated in the 21 km to Hermannsburg. Much of this is a slow uphill drag, which is made even more painful if, as we did, you also score a headwind.

Hermannsburg

Hermannsburg was first established as a mission station, but in these more enlightened times it is controlled by the local Aborigines. The town's past is on show in the historical precinct (small entry fee). Hermannsburg is only a small place but it takes time to find the post office (marked only as Office). Don't be too surprised if the place is apparently closed for a while during the day, 'normal' office hours seem to be fairly flexible here. There are two supermarkets and a takeaway food shop — I can attest to the delicious nature of the barbecued chicken it sells, even if the video games create an appalling racket.

Although it is less than 20 km from Hermannsburg to the camping area in Finke Gorge National Park, allow at least two hours for the journey. Marked as 'Four-Wheel Drive Only', the track follows, crosses, and is part of, the Finke River as it snakes into a maze of red-banked gorges. We began this journey at 5 p.m., about an hour too late. Late afternoon is the time to ride, bounce, walk, push, stop and admire this section of the route. Even if you are incredibly tired, there is a restorative quality in cooling long shadows and the soul-warming sight of rocks turning flame red. Our 5 p.m. start meant the last three km was cycled with the aid of headlights — not to be recommended — but my dust-streaked body could sense a solar-powered hot shower at the end of the road and drove me unerringly towards the campsite.

DAY 7: Rest Day

Finke Gorge National Park

We made a great mistake in Finke Gorge National Park, in only allocating one rest day. Like Ormiston Gorge, Finke's 46 000 hectares really needs days to explore. In the course of a year, 65 000 visitors enter this place, but most are day visitors (on the coaches from Alice Springs). **Palm Valley** (which the explorer Giles actually named 'Glen of Palms' in 1872) set in the midst of a desert is the most well known feature of this park. The palms, *Livistona mariae*, require a constant source of water to survive and this is provided by water-absorbing sandstone overlaying impermeable rocks which prevent the water from seeping away.

Naturally, this red centre oasis is appreciated by living things other than palms. The extensive list of **fauna** includes birds such as the wonderfully plumed rainbow bee-eaters and Port Lincoln parrots (luminous green with bright yellow necks), mulga parrots (sweet mellow call), budgerigars, and brown falcons; reptiles such as desert death adders, blue-tongued lizards, and thorny devils; and mammals such as rock wallabies and echidnas. **Flora** includes cycads, grevilleas, hibiscus, pea flowers, acacias, river red gums, coolibahs, desert oaks, hakea, ruby saltbush and bloodwood.

There are unmarked **long-distance bushwalks** through the wilderness section of Finke Gorge National Park. Nearer to the campsite are much **shorter walks** including one taking in the Amphitheatre. The large rock in the middle of the Amphitheatre is a perfect spot from which to see a desert dawn, while high up on the rim in the north-east corner you have an immaculate view of sunset.

DAY 8: Finke Gorge National Park to Bush Camp

Distance ridden: 72 km;	Riding time: 5 hrs 59 mins;	Average speed: 12 kmph;	Maximum speed: 28 kmph

On the ride out from Finke Gorge National Park you are slowed not so much by the steepness of the terrain (it's almost all flat), but by the sheer roughness of the riding surface. It seems that 9 km per hour is about the maximum on river stones. At that speed, juddering isn't too tough on the body, though still hard on the bike (Chris's rear carrier, a Blackburn copy, collapsed). The main problem on this track is the daily fleet of coaches — more like bitumen Boeings — from Alice Springs (they arrive around 10 a.m.). Unfortunately some of the drivers seem unwilling to slow down when passing cyclists.

Once back on Larapinta Drive you face a constantly nagging uphill run along a half road-half track. May you not have the same headwind we experienced for it will make this day long and hard. It certainly gave me something in common with the explorer Stuart, who wrote in his diary on 22 April 1861: 'Nipped by the wind's unkindly

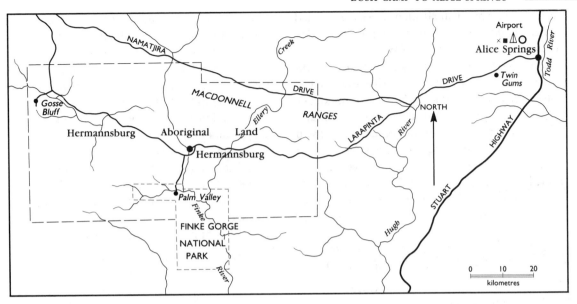

ROUTE SLIP

Directions	R/S km	Ride for	Destination	Cum route km
END OF TOUR			**TOTAL FOR TOUR**	**466.2**
Alice Springs Airport	243.3			466.2
R-traffic lights	229.7	13.6	Airport	452.6
Alice Springs	229.7			
L*-Simpsons Gap NP	213.6	16.1		436.5
S-Namatjira Dr Jnct.	183.1	30.5		406
L*roadside stop	159.8	23.3		382.7
Start bitumen road	137.2	22.6		360.1
R-Larapinta Drive	101	36.2		323.9
Exit Finke Gorge	84.4	16.6	Alice Springs	307.3
Finke Gorge campsite	84.4			
L	67.8	16.6	Palm Valley	290.7
R-Larapinta Drive	66.3	1.5		289.2
exit Hermannsburg	65.3	1		288.2
Hermannsburg	65.3			
L-Hermannsburg	64.3	1		287.2
L-Larapinta Drive	42.5	21.8		265.4
S	13.4	29.1		236.3
S	11.2	2.2	Hermannsburg	234.1
L	0.5	10.7		223.4
exit bush camp	0.0	0.5	Hermannsburg	222.9
BEGIN SECTION 3				

blast, Parched by the sun's more fervent ray'. Had he been pedalling a bicycle, he might have added 'coated by the earth's finest layer of dust'.

The modern day problem with a headwind on a dirt track is that every time a vehicle overtakes you, you get to swallow its dust for a chokingly long time. There is also absolutely never any respite for your legs. You stop pedalling and you stop dead. No coasting. No free running. In an attempt to ease the pain you could, as we did, take a break every 10 km, but at 10 km per hour, ours were hard earned. It's strange how the first 4 km passed by relatively easily, but the last six seem to have doubled.

You get an inkling that the tar road (on the border of Aboriginal land at time of writing) is up ahead when the dust veil being laid down by the last overtaking vehicle suddenly drops. It is so wonderful to see that thin black ribbon disappearing into a far distant point. At least it might have been for us if the wind hadn't taken this as a cue to increase in velocity.

On Namatjira Drive you are given 5 km notice of a roadside stop ahead. For some mystical reason on Larapinta Drive there's a sign only 2 km before a roadside stop. That's one of the reasons we camped out of sight of the road in the shelter of a belt of trees just 4 km short. The other was that after six hours on the bikes we were beyond tired and quite honestly couldn't have ridden any further.

DAY 9: Bush Camp to Alice Springs

Distance ridden: 74.4 km; Riding time: 4 hrs 40 mins; Average speed: 15.8 kmph; Maximum speed: not recorded

---

As it turned out, the roadside stop (57 km from Hermannsburg) is on a barren windswept corner and makes a very exposed, unpleasant place to stop. It does, however, have fresh water. Regrettably for us, that which was a blessed tailwind on the westward journey, continued its persistence as a cursed headwind on the last day of riding towards Alice Springs. Even drafting off each other and rotating the lead every 2 km, it was still energy-sapping riding.

Keeping us going (and it may motivate you under the same trying conditions) was the memory of a sign advertising a restaurant at Twin Gums, just through Honeymoon Gap. The idea of a celebratory lunch to finish the tour forced us down those last painful kilometres and we wheeled up to the restaurant under automatic pilot. However, no matter how wonderful the food, there is still 17 km to go to Alice Springs so beware of a serious post-lunch energy death, especially if you have been exhorted to imbibe a cider or two.

THE SOUTH-WEST OF WESTERN AUSTRALIA

4 THE SOUTH-WEST OF WESTERN AUSTRALIA

This is a 600 km tour in the south-west of Western Australia, from Bunbury to Albany (Westrail train to Bunbury from Perth, returning to Perth by Westrail coach from Albany). The tour features old-growth forests (including living trees that you can walk into), rugged bluewater coastlines (sometimes with gambolling whales), wild caves and bushland bedecked with native wildflowers. You can find accommodation all the way in youth hostels, Bed & Breakfasts and old hotels, or you can camp. I rode it in September with two friends on touring bikes taking 10 days (including two and a half rest days) averaging 70 km per day. The best cycling time is from September to early December when the wildflowers are at their peak. The prevailing winds usually blow from the west quarter, though you can occasionally get a rogue south-easterly. You should also expect some rain as this is Western Australia's soggy section.

Perth

Perth (popn 809 000) was founded in 1829 and is the capital of Western Australia. The city has numerous bike paths and an enthusiastic Cycle Touring Association (see Appendix B).

A pleasant way to tone up on two wheels is to cruise around Kings Park and then take part in the 'Around the River Ride' from Perth to Fremantle.

The Western Australian Department for Youth Sport and Recreation have published a little booklet on the ride. Meander around historic Fremantle and take a high speed catamaran to 'Rotto' — the locals' name for Rottnest Island. Rottnest gained its name from Dutch sea-captain Samuel Volckersen in 1658, who mistakenly believed the quokkas (a little wallaby with small rounded ears and a short tapering tail) running about the island were giant rats (hence, rats nest). The quokkas are still on the island. Take the time to scuba dive over the local coral reef and to cycle around an island free of cars.

Arriving in Perth

If you are arriving by **interstate train**, the East Perth station is ten minutes cycling from the centre of town — you can also use the local train system to get to Perth Central Station (this tour begins there).

Getting from the airports: To get from Perth Airport terminal (international and domestic) to downtown is a much longer ride. A suggested **route** is:

From **International Terminal:** Horrie Miller Dr, X-Tonkin Highway, Into-Kewdale Rd, R-Abernathy St, R-Fairbrother St, L-Belbravia St, Into-Stoneham St, Into-Daly St**

From **Domestic Terminal:** L-at Exit, Into-MacRobertson Dr, Into-Brearley Ave, L-Gt Eastern Hwy, L-Resolution Dr, Into-Daly St**,

Continue from ** X-Garrat Rd Bridge, Into-Garrat Rd, L-Guilford Rd, Into Lord St, R-Wellington St, Perth Central Rly Stn on R after Barrack St.

DAY 1: Perth to Dunsborough

Distance ridden: 78.6 km;   Riding time: 4 hrs 3 mins;   Average speed: 19.2 kmph;   Maximum speed: 29 kmph

A little stainless steel train they call *The Australind* is the painless way to travel between Perth Central Station and Bunbury. In a couple of hours you are at this large (by Western Australian standards) southern city with ample time for a meandering exploration or leisurely dinner (you can lunch on the train). The most restful beginning would be to stay the night in Bunbury before heading off towards Dunsborough via Capel.

Bunbury

This sea port (popn 22 000) has a **youth hostel, motels** and **hotels**. Gourmets will delight in the locally scoop-netted Blue Manna Crabs and steam train buffs will love the **Boyanup Transport Museum**.

ROUTE SLIP

Directions	R/S km	Ride for	Destination	Cum route km
END OF SECTION I	106.9		**TOTAL FOR ROUTE**	**106.9**
R-Dunsborough	106.9			106.9
(return on Cape Nat. Rd)				
Cape Naturaliste Lighthouse	93.4	13.5		93.4
R*-scenic detour	83.9	9.3	Meelup/Eagle Bay	83.9
R-Cape Nat. Rd	79.6	4.3	Cape Naturaliste	79.6
Dunsborough	79.6			79.6
R-Caves Rd	77.8	1.8	Dunsborough	77.8
L	77.4	.4		77.4
R-exit YH	76.9	.5		76.9
Dunsborough YH	76.9			76.9
R	76.4	.5		76.4
R	76	.4	Dunsborough YH	76
L*	54.2	21.8	Dunsborough	54.2
Busselton	54.2			54.2
R*historic detour	44.7	9.5	via Lockville	44.7
Tuart Forest	40	4.7		40
Capel	30	10		30
L*-roadside stop	6.8	23.2		6.8
L-lights	1	5.8	Busselton	1
L-Bunbury railway stn	0.0	1.0	Bunbury	0.0
Perth Central Station			*The Australind* Bunbury	
BEGIN SECTION I				

KEY

L = left   **R** = right   **S** = straight

BL = bear left   **BR** = bear right

X = cross   * = detour directions

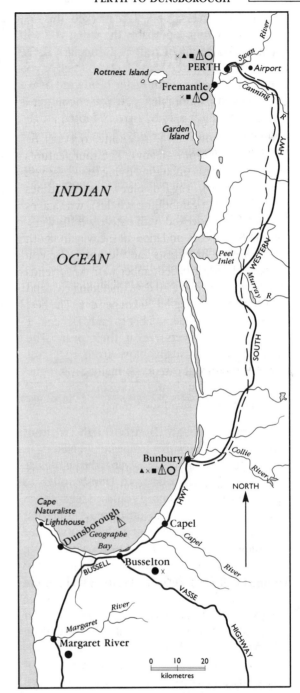

On ride line, each segment = 1 kilometre

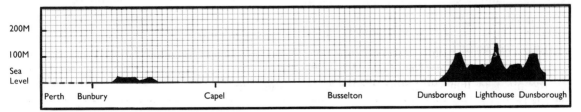

Though it has an ersatz bike lane marked, this first section of the tour is probably the worst you will encounter in terms of traffic, particularly large trucks with uncovered loads. It doesn't help if you also catch a strong south-easter headwind as we did. The first memorable forest you encounter is one of melaleuca standing damp-footed in the middle of a swamp; a true amphibian heaven if the number of Moaning Frogs *(Heleioporus eyrei)* croaking out their lusty love calls is any indication. The Tuart forest, with picnic areas, is more classic-ally beautiful. Here the oldest trees have been living for more than 500 years and stand nearly 40 metres high.

If you are staying at the Dunsborough Youth Hostel, then Busselton is the best place to pick up supplies, since the hostel is a few kilometres short of Dunsborough's township.

Busselton

Busselton (popⁿ 6500) has the usual array of **accommodation** but the town features an amaz-ingly long jetty (2 km), which at one time was the longest in the world. If, as we did, you have taken all afternoon to get to Busselton on the ride towards Dunsborough make sure you are brightly visible. The road runs due west and a long, lazy sunset makes it hard for overtaking motorists to see you. The **Dunsborough Youth Hostel** is set cheek by jowl with an expanse of blue water and white sand called Geographe Bay. Tinkling your toes in the sand at the back of the hostel is marvellous in the soft pink light of pre-dawn. The European influence in place names will carry through for most of the tour, since you are paralleling the travels of exploring sailors from Holland, France and England who surveyed the coastline from 1622 onwards.

DAY 2: Dunsborough to Merribrook

Distance ridden: 72.9 km;   Riding time: 4 hrs 27 mins;   Average speed: 16.1 kmph;   Maximum speed: 61 kmph

Don't ride through Dunsborough without sampling fresh hot wares from the old bakery — it is on your right as you go towards the lighthouse road. By rights, the ride from Dunsborough to Cape Naturaliste lighthouse could be regarded as an adjunct (it makes a great unladen day tour), but I regard it as a must-see. You go not so much for the lighthouse as to make first contact with a string of natural 'pearls' which form the Leeuwin Naturaliste National Park. Leeuwin comes from the Dutch 't Landt van de Leeuwin' (the land of the Lioness) and comprises an 80 km strip of predominantly coastal land from Cape Naturaliste to Cape Leeuwin. There are many walking trails to be explored scattered throughout this place of wildflower-strewn heath (especially between September and December) and unpeopled, unrestrained seascapes. On the way out to Cape Naturaliste, after the first day's flatness, it's good to climb and coast a few hills. Once beyond cleared green fields and grazing sheep you will find the National Park. Turn off onto a dirt track just before the lighthouse for a pleasurable surfside morning tea stop.

Caves Road is a narrow, quiet road disliked by truckers (they tend to use the Bussell Highway direct to Margaret River). As such, it is a fine road to cycle (out of school holidays). The hills seem to take on a rollicking flavour, just enough to induce a feeling that you've climbed and more than enough for an occasional portion of long, fast downhill coasting. Even the cattle are frisky around here, they are just as likely to run beside you — on their side of the fence.

Few places on this wild coastline are more awesome than Canal Rocks. Perched atop the coffee-coloured tors watching wind-driven waves roar and thunder ashore is a sublime way to have lunch. Getting in to Canal Rocks is a good steady climb for 2.25 of the 3 km, but the run back is a blinder — just be sure to grip the brakes before rejoining Caves Road.

TOUR 4: Riding at dawn, south-east of Northcliffe, Western Australia

TOUR 4: Beneath the big trees on
the South Western Highway,
Western Australia

ROUTE SLIP

Directions	R/S km	Ride for	Destination	Cum route km
END OF SECTION 2	101.7		**TOTAL FOR ROUTE**	**208.6**
Augusta	101.7			208.6
R-Bussel Hwy (10)	98.8	2.9		205.7
L*-Jewel Cave	93.7	5.1		200.6
S*Hamelin Bay	85.4	8.3		192.3
L-Caves Rd	85.4			192.3
L*-Tea House/Maze	78.8	6.6		185.7
R-Caves Rd	78.8		Augusta	185.7
R*-camping area	76.4	2.4		183.3
BL	74.9	1.5	sign on L (to Caves Rd)	181.8
S*-lookout	74.9			181.8
R-Boranup Forest Dr	64.5	10.4		171.4
R*-Lake Cave	62.2	2.3		169.1
L*-Mammoth Lake	58.9	3.3		165.8
R*-Wallcliffe Rd	46.8	12.1	3 km to Margaret R. Hds	153.7
L*-info sign	46.8			153.7
L*-Carters Rd	40.4	6.4	7 km to Margaret River	147.3
L*-Cowaramup Rd	33.7	6.7	2.8 km to Merribrook	140.6
R*-Canal Rocks	10.9	22.8	3 km to Rocks	117.8
L-Caves Rd	8.1	2.8		115
S*Yallingup	8.1			
R-Caves Rd	0.3	7.8		107.2
Dunsborough	0.0	0.3	Augusta	106.9
BEGIN SECTION 2				

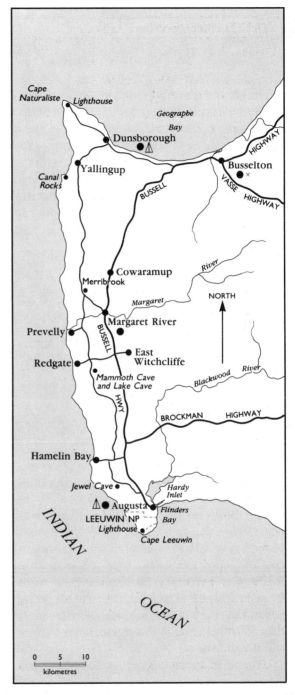

On ride line, each segment = 1 kilometre

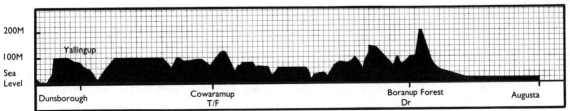

DAY 3: Merribrook to Augusta

Distance ridden: 70.4 km;   Riding time: 4 hrs 3 mins;   Average speed: 17.2 kmph;   Maximum speed: 53 kmph

A night at Merribrook Lodge can easily be stretched to a few if you have the inclination to indulge in a little abseiling, caving, rockclimbing, canoeing or bushwalking. But go to bed early on your last night here, since this is a section of the route where you should be up and away with the sun. There's heaps to do and see. Down a road bordered with wildflowers, it is hard to put in a quick 10 km, though the great downhills do encourage a spot of high speed cycling.

Margaret River Detour

Turn off Caves Rd at Carters Road, then head south on the Bussell Highway to Margaret River. Though this wine-growing region only began in 1967, it has developed an enviable reputation. The town has **extensive accommodation**, excellent **restaurants** and a **bike shop**. Continue down the Bussell Highway to see the marron (freshwater crayfish delicacy) farm at East Witchcliffe, then take Redgate Road back to Caves Road. Margaret River is also known as a top **surfing** location. Catch the action by taking Wallcliffe Road to Prevelly and the river mouth.

An early start from Merribrook gives you enough time to enjoy the wildflowers, so keep a lookout for *Karri hovea*, old man's beard, yellow cone bushes and yellow patersonia. Sharing the sunrise also gives you the option of arriving at both Mammoth Cave and Lake Cave (3 km beyond Mammoth — with a kiosk) at the right time to partake of guided tours. First tour at Mammoth is 9.30 a.m. and each runs for about an hour. Aside from the large caves which are open to the public and lit like fairytale wonderlands, there are more than 300 other caves in this region, many of them still unexplored.

A couple of kilometres beyond Lake Cove you encounter one of the loveliest regrowth karri forests in the south-west. Enhancing the experience for cycle tourers is to turn off Caves Road for a peaceful ride along Boranup Forest Drive, pausing at any one of the picnic areas for a leisurely lunch. Instead of passing traffic, there's only the swish of your own tyres on a hard-packed sandy track and the echoing call of forest birds. Boranup forest lost all of its big trees in an era of exploitive forestry, but the regrowth trees are attractive and, given national park status, should eventually produce forest giants of the future.

The disadvantage of Boranup Road is found towards its end, where a long steep climb will have you working extra hard. At the top is a panoramic lookout — a fine reward (in clear weather) for the hill climbing. And zipping down to Caves Road is a tuck and fly affair. A few hundred metres north from where you rejoin the bitumen, there's the charming Arumvale tea-house and Boranup Maze.

Hamelin Bay Detour

Turn off the Caves Road 3 km south of Bushby Road for the 2 km run to Hamelin Bay. This sleepy location is the site of a pleasant **caravan park**, but towards the end of last century, Hamelin Bay was a bustling timber port serviced by many sailing ships. A surprisingly large number (11 ships since 1882) stayed — permanently. Their skeletons now form the Hamelin Bay Wreck Trail. *The Chaudiere* (43.9 m wooden barque), *Katinka* (59.7 m iron barque) and *The Agincourt*, lie on a sandy bed within snorkel diving depth, only a short distance off the beach. Others can be reached from a boat using scuba equipment.

Jewel Cave is encountered 8 km before Augusta, but since the last guided tour is at 3.30 p.m. it is probably best seen by riding back the next day.

DAY 4: Rest Day

Augusta

Augusta (Youth Hostel, hotels and motels) is an excellent place for a 'rest' day — a day when you can cycle around the town without panniers. Before the breeze gets up, cycle down to the 1895 **Cape Leeuwin Lighthouse** (open Tuesday to

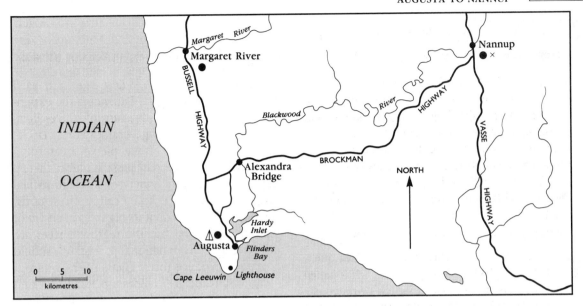

ROUTE SLIP

Directions	R/S km	Ride for	Destination	Cum route km
END OF SECTION 3	88.3		**TOTAL FOR ROUTE**	**296.9**
Nannup	88.3			296.9
S-Vasse Hwy	85.8	2.5	Nannup	294.4
L*-Red Gully	68.5	17.3	water and swimming hole	277.1
R*-Stewart Rd	54.8	13.7	ATB Pemberton short cut	263.4
R*-Cane Brk	54.8		picnic area	263.4
L*-Alexandra Br	22	32.8	2 km to camping area	230.6
R-Brockman Hwy	18.1	3.9	Nannup	226.7
S-Glenarty Rd	6.7	11.4		215.3
R-Molloy Rd	6.5	0.2		215.1
exit **Augusta**	0.0	6.5	Bussell Hwy	208.6
BEGIN SECTION 3				

On ride line, each segment = 1 kilometre

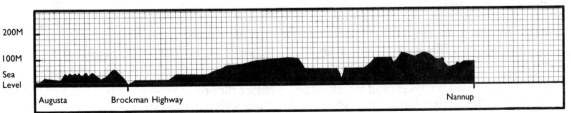

Sunday 9.30 a.m. to 4 p.m.), but go via Albany Terrace and Storm Bay Road, with a swim in a turquoise pond called 'Grannies Pool', a pause at Groper Bay where the navigator Matthew Flinders began charting the Australian Coastline in 1801, and a gaze at the old waterwheel.

For an **afternoon circuit**, take the main road north, then Caves Road, turn left at Greenhill Road, go straight ahead (Diana Street to the left) and enjoy a steep climb through a mixture of karri and marri forest. At the top of the ride (or walk) at Hill View Road, turn right to take in a close up view of grass trees set amidst wattle blossom. Keep a lookout for an ancient, three-headed grass tree. The return to Augusta is down Hill View Road — and *down* is the operative word.

DAY 5: Augusta to Nannup

Distance ridden: 88.8 km;   Riding time: 4 hrs 46 mins;   Average speed: 18.4 kmph;   Maximum speed: 52 kmph

The short cut between the Bussell and Brockman Highways (see Route Slip) is quieter than quiet. That is if you don't count the local white-tailed black cockatoos. They are a bunch of raucously noisy ruffians when vandalising the bark of gum trees looking for grubs. Cycling beneath a mob at work is like riding in a rain storm, only it's raining bits of tree!

Alexandra Bridge, where the Brockman Highway crosses the Blackwood River, makes a good place to boil the billy for morning tea. For most of the year, the Blackwood idles sluggishly past, but occasionally it is whipped into a frenzy powerful enough to demolish, then carry off, the old bridge (the remains can be seen just near the camping area 2 km off the highway). Snow-like tea tree blossom and golden balls of wattle deck the road verges between Alexandra Bridge and a few kilometres beyond Canebreak Picnic Area. If the day is warm, ensure your water bottles are filled at the Blackwood River (boil it first) and keep a lookout for water point signs (see Route Slip).

Although the height profile shows that in the latter portion of this section of the tour you are descending, the road seems reluctant to reflect this. Following downhill runs, as if the land has engaged in a bitter tug of war, a stiff rise thrusts its way up almost to the altitude that you have just lost.

Nannup

After joining the Vasse Highway, it's but a short run to Nannup (pop 550). Named after one of explorer John Forest's Aboriginal guides, this is a timber town settled in a crook of the Blackwood River where acrid wood smoke rises from dinky wooden cottages and fills the air, tree fur carpets the road and the Bunnings mill is surrounded by felled old growth forests.

DAY 6: Nannup to Pimelea Youth Hostel

Distance ridden: 71.7 km;   Riding time: 3 hrs 56 mins;   Average speed: 18 kmph;   Maximum speed: 48 kmph

With smoked trout first course, fillet steak blanketed with sauce and garden fresh vegetables accompanied by damper-like bread, apple strudel for dessert and hot chocolate by the fire, The Lodge at Nannup, is the kind of place a tired cycle tourer could take a few days to waft away the aches and pains. There is also inexpensive accommodation at the local hotel and caravan park. Nannup is a base for Blackwood Expeditions which runs excellent 2–5 day canoeing trips — their home-cooked 'bush' meals are a delight.

If you are intending to stay at Pimelea Youth Hostel (10 km before Pemberton), Nannup is the best place to stock up on supplies (just basics can be purchased at Karri Valley Resort 5 km before the hostel). There are also roadside stalls serving organically grown vegetables, honey and spreads — and even smoked trout!

ROUTE SLIP

Directions	R/S km	Ride for	Destination	Cum route km
END OF SECTION 4	111.6		**TOTAL FOR ROUTE**	**408.5**
Northcliffe	111.6			408.5
R*-Windy Harbour t'off	111.3	.3		408.2
L-Albany	111.3			408.2
R*-Warren NP	88.3	23		385.2
S-Brockman Hwy	83.3	5		380.2
R-Vasse Hwy	81.1	2.2	Northcliffe	378
L*-Pemberton	81.1			378
R	80.9	.2		377.8
S-Stirling Rd	71.7	9.2	Pemberton	368.6
Pimelea YH	71.7			368.6
R	70.3	1.4		367.2
L	61.2	9.1	Youth Hostel	358.1
L*-Beedelup Falls	61	.2	one way road	357.9
R*-Karri Valley Resort	56.6	4.4	general store	353.5
L*-Stewart Rd	35.9	20.7	ATB Pemberton short cut	332.8
L*-Davidson Rd	14.2	21.7	ATB road to Manjimup	311.1
L-Vasse Hwy	2.5	11.7		299.4
exit **Nannup**	0.0	2.5	Pemberton	296.9
BEGIN SECTION 4				

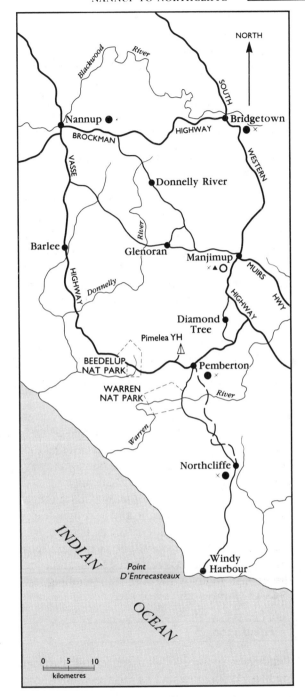

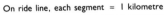

On ride line, each segment = 1 kilometre

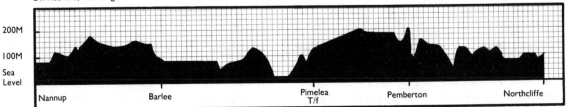

Manjimup Detour

If you have plenty of time, take the Brockman Highway south of Nannup through the Karri Gulley picnic area, and turn right at Sears Road to Donnelly River Mill (holiday centre). All-terrain bikes can take the **scenic dirt route** south to Glenoran Pool picnic area then Graphite Road to Manjimup. **Tar-seekers** can use Sears Road, which becomes Donnelly Road through the Manjimup. Take the South West Highway, turn right at Eastbourne Road, onto Diamond Tree Road, then Pemberton Road North into Pemberton.

Leaving Nannup, the Vasse Highway is initially well-constructed, but is inexplicably transformed into a potholed goat track. Ducking rocks and stones cast up by passing and overtaking vehicles can make this section very unpleasant. Ghostly bare-limbed dead trees and the torn-apart state of the forests only magnify the gloom. This is a die-back hell. Die-back is caused by a root fungus disease, *Pytothera cynamoni*, first diagnosed in the 1970s and now acknowledged to be exacerbated by logging, vehicles and foot traffic. Die-back areas are quarantined but the logging still continues, albeit in 'hygienic' fashion.

Depression is swept away by one of the most gentle and consistent downhill glides of the whole tour. This ends near Carey Bridge and though the road demands some hard work from here on, you will be captivated by a diminutive national park — Beedelup. Entering a section of forest named the Karri Valley, you will be amazed at the size and beauty of the old karri trees. It gives you a tantalising glimpse of what disease-free forests once looked like. There's a charming one-way detour to Beedelup Falls and the Walk-through Tree (76 m high and 2.4 m diameter), but be warned, the unsealed track has some entertaining hills.

DAY 7: Pimelea Youth Hostel to Northcliffe (Light Day)

Distance ridden: 40 km;	Riding time: 2 hrs 5 mins;	Average speed: 19 kmph;	Maximum speed: 54 kmph

Pimelea Youth Hostel is a converted forest township where families (or cycle touring groups) can book little cottages with modern ensuites and cosy pot bellied stoves. Zamia was our home away from home as the rain fell in abundance.

Hope that this section of the tour has a touch of Camelot (rain overnight and sunshine-filled days). That way the tall tree forests fringing the quiet road to Pemberton will be at their glistening best for you. It was enchanting for us and even dry enough to enjoy the adrenalin-pumping last descent into town.

Pemberton

Pemberton (pop^n 900 — hotel, motel, caravan park) is a timber town with a huge sawmill. Climb the Gloucester Tree (61 m fire tower), see Big Brook Arboretum and Warren National Park. From Pemberton to Northcliffe, there is a **no-ride option** using the Pemberton to Northcliffe Tramway, a 40-seat train from the 1900s which meanders through beautiful forests (out of school holidays there is enough room to carry bikes).

Our night at Northcliffe Hotel proved a noisy affair, as boisterous country pubs can sometimes be. Either get into the swing of local life or choose a more serene abode. An alternative for non-campers might be to try the Riverway Chalets. If you have the time, take a ride down to Windy Harbour (caravan park/camping area) for the scenic beauty of Point D'Entrecasteaux.

DAY 8: Northcliffe to Dingo Flat Youth Hostel

Distance ridden: 124 km;	Riding time: 5 hrs 58 mins;	Average speed: 20.7 kmph;	Maximum speed: 52 kmph

On a long distance day, it's always good to get an early start. We managed to be cycling by 6.15 a.m. on a road devoid of traffic. As an added bonus, the landscape was wreathed in leaden mist, which

ROUTE SLIP

Directions	R/S km	Ride for	Destination	Cum route km
END OF SECTION 5	108		**TOTAL FOR ROUTE**	**516.5**
Nornalup	108			
Walpole	98.1	9.9	Nornalup	506.6
R*-Tinglewood Rd	90	8.1	Nuyts Wilderness Area	498.5
R*-Shannon	31.2	58.8	Picnic area	439.7
R-South Western Hwy	28.1	3.1		436.6
R-Middleton Rd	2.2	25.9		410.7
Northcliffe	0.0	2.2		408.5
BEGIN SECTION 5				

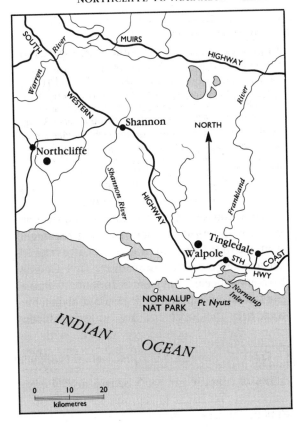

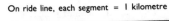
On ride line, each segment = 1 kilometre

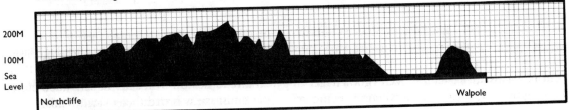

200M
100M
Sea Level

Northcliffe — Walpole

slowly turned gold with the rising sun. Once on to the South Western Highway the volume of traffic does increase, though there are other compensations. A series of rises will encourage you to charge the uphill sections and tuck your body into an aerodynamic torpedo shape to blast down the hills. Comfortingly, the broader road surface keeps most vehicles at a calmer distance. If you are riding in a group, take turns to be *echappee* (breakaway). Stop and look back at your companions in the distance; they will seem miniaturised by the lofty trees forming a canopy over the road.

Shannon, once the site of a township, makes an ideal rest spot (toilets, water, tables). You might even like to try a round of golf if you've packed the inflatable clubs in your panniers. Given a little wind assistance the run from Shannon to Walpole gives plenty of opportunity for big gear flying, but keep your eyes open for large flightless birds, emus. They are blessed (or cursed) with an inordinate amount of curiosity and you can attract one by making weird sounds, wacky arm movements, or virtually any goofy behaviour. The emu will either take to the hills pronto or mosey over to view the strange being.

Wilderness Detours

Beyond Crystal Springs (store and park ranger's residence) is a **side trip** turning down Tinglewood Road then Shedley Drive. If you are set up with food, water and camping equipment, you could take the opportunity to enter **Nuyts Wilderness Area**, one of the few decreed wilderness areas in Western Australia. No vehicles are permitted entry and it is an outstanding place for **backpacking**. Check in with the ranger at Crystal Springs before embarking on an overnight trip.

There's one good hill before Walpole, and at its crest is the John Rate Lookout, giving a marvellous view of Nornalup Inlet and the surrounding forests of Walpole–Nornalup National Park. Or so I'm told. When I came past, little was visible because of a serious rain squall.

If you are intending to stay at Dingo Flat Youth Hostel (primitive but a rare experience), Walpole (motel, caravan park, Che Sara Sara Chalets) is the place to load up with supplies. Riding from the South Coast Highway to Dingo Flat Youth Hostel requires you to slog up a tough little hill on the Valley of the Giants Road (bitumen) then ends the day with 4 km of dirt road. This last section can become very slimy during prolonged wet weather.

DAY 9: Rest Day

Walpole District

Rain and the Walpole district seem to go hand in glove, but the trees like it. When staying in the area, one 'must' is the **walking trail** through the giant red tingle trees in the Valley of the Giants. Walking *inside* the cave-like base of a gigantic

Eucalyptus jacksoni is a unique experience. Bush fires over hundreds of years have eaten away the inside of the tree bases yet left living, thriving trees. Giant karri stumps are museum pieces of a time when ancient forest dwellers were felled with a cross-cut saw and axes.

DAY 10: Dingo Flat Youth Hostel to Denmark Youth Hostel

Distance ridden: 66.7 km;	Riding time: 3 hrs 14 mins;	Average speed: 20.3 kmph;	Maximum speed: 47 kmph

Even after a rest day it is hard to induce yourself to keep on going on a cold, rain-lashed morning. However, given good wet weather gear, it is usually not as bad outside as it seemed when inside looking out. Of course with a tailwind, riding in

the rain takes on a lightfooted feel. It is as if the water angling to earth is keen to push you along the road. The cycling world on the way to Denmark flattens and, as the big trees are left behind, opens out onto broad valleys with huge sand

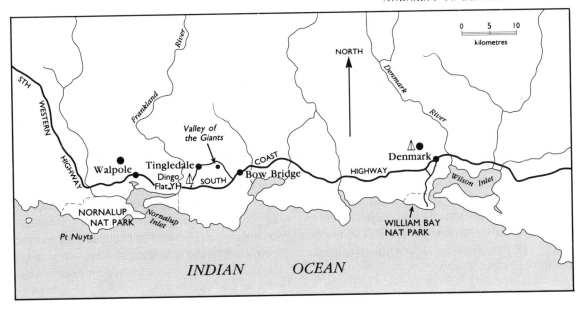

ROUTE SLIP

Directions	R/S km	Ride for	Destination	Cum route km
END OF SECTION 6	55.3		**TOTAL FOR ROUTE**	**588.1**
Denmark	55.3	17.2	Albany	588.1
R*-Wilson Inlet	54.9	.4	youth hostel	587.7
R*-William Bay NP	41	13.9	4 km to Greens Pool	573.8
L*-Meadery	39.6	1.4		572.4
L*-Bow Bridge	12.6	27	shop	545.4
L-South Coast Hwy	12.6			545.4
L-Valley of Giants Rd	4.1	8.5		536.9
R-Dingo Flat Rd	1.3	2.8		534.1
Dingo Flat YH	16.3	1.3		522.9
L-youth hostel	15	1.3		521.6
L-Dingo Flat Rd	12.2	2.8		518.8
L-Valley of Grants Rd	3.9	8.3		510.5
Nornalup	0.0	3.9		506.6
BEGIN SECTION 6				

On ride line, each segment = 1 kilometre

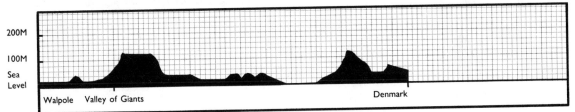

dunes set in the far distance.

Out of school holiday times this is a quiet stretch of highway where cars appear rarely and the day's tally of trucks can be counted on one hand. Even if it isn't a cold day, you won't need too much incentive to stop and sample the mead wine at Bartholomew's Meadery. Their literature mentions that Nordic, Hindu, Celtic, Roman and Greek cultures all used mead as a love potion. Sex aside, the mead will warm you on an essential detour down to Green's Pool in William Bay National Park (see Route Slip). The pool is swimming perfection with an emerald luminosity that is so often seen on the Western Australian coastline. Out to sea, you might be lucky enough to spot a group of passing whales.

Denmark

The only large hill of the day guards Denmark (youth hostel, motel, hotel, caravan park). Denmark is a medium-sized south-coast town with a good range of **supplies** and a healthy interest in conservation. It also has an interesting, if slightly tortuous, **bike route** skirting the mouth of the Denmark River which is an optional way to the youth hostel/caravan park on the shores of Wilson Inlet (Holling Road, Inlet Drive, S-bike path). On a still night you can hear the roar of ocean surf skipping across the surface of the inlet. If you are staying a couple of days in Denmark, try out the Scotsdale/Mt Shadforth Scenic roads — you can get a map from the helpful people at Wilson Inlet Holiday Park.

DAY 10: Denmark Youth Hostel to Albany Youth Hostel
Distance ridden: 62.9 km;   Riding time: 2 hrs 52 mins;   Average speed: 21.5 kmph;   Maximum speed: 47 kmph

Back on the South Coast Highway and cresting the slight hill east of Denmark, you gain an appreciable view of Wilson Inlet and tantalising glimpses of secluded sandy beaches. Leaving the highway on the Torbay road reduces the passing traffic to almost nil and leads you through a valley of green where the road verges are lined by old tea trees and melaleucas. These stunted forests are lit by brilliant banksia cones the colour of wind-fanned coals in a campfire. Western Australia has a startling array of the country's banksias which seem to compete in their brilliant floral displays. When you cycle into Albany on the completion of the tour, consider yourself lucky if it is not raining. A fine day here is greeted with some surprise — even by the locals!

Albany

Albany (popⁿ 15 000 — motels, hotels, youth hostel). The major commercial centre of the south-west and the oldest city in Western Australia, having been established in 1826. There are **five museums**, including one devoted to whaling

(Whaleworld) — that destructive industry ceased in Albany in 1978 and the only whale spotting done nowadays is to wonder at these marvellous creatures. Torndirrup National Park features a spectacular section of coastline and is reached by taking Frenchman Bay Road then turning off to see Natural Bridge and Gap, Blow Holes, Newell's Harbour and the Salmon Holes.

Stirling Ranges Add-on Tour

Though Tour 4 ends in Albany, if you have additional time, head on up to the **Stirling Ranges** (115 600 hectares) and **Porongurup** (2400 hectares) **National Parks** (camping/caravan park and Stirling Range Youth Hostel — bookings for the hostel are essential). North on the Albany Highway, right on Chester Pass Road, then tar road all the way to the caravan park/youth hostel (86 km). All-terrain bikers will discover an excellent dirt road, Stirling Range Drive, which via Red Gum Road can take you to Mt Barker where you can connect with coaches back to Perth. Stirling Range features five peaks over 1000 m and both parks contain a network of walks which will take you beside some of the most beautiful displays of wildflowers in the south-west.

ROUTE SLIP

Directions	R/S km	Ride for	Destination	Cum route km
END OF TOUR	112.3		**TOTAL FOR ROUTE**	**645.1**
Albany	112.3			645.1
R-town centre	112	.3		644.8
L-town centre	111.8	.2		644.6
R	109.6	2.2		642.4
L-town centre	109.5	.1		642.3
R-Lower Denmark Rd	72.5	37	Albany via Torbay	605.3
Denmark	0.0	17.2		588.1
BEGIN SECTION 7				

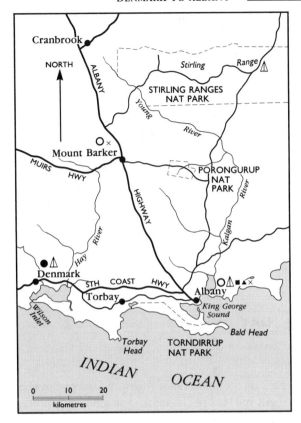

On ride line, each segment = 1 kilometre

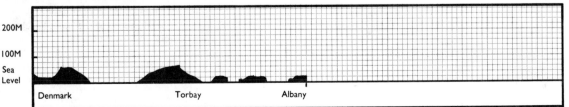

TOUR 5
SOUTH AUSTRALIA

5 SOUTH AUSTRALIA

This is a 630 km tour which begins in Adelaide, the capital of South Australia, and then curves up through the Adelaide Hills, across the Barossa Valley wine country, down the Murray River, over the flatlands of the Coorong and into the Southern fishing ports, before terminating at the site of an extinct volcano, now Mt Gambier. I rode it in October with two friends on touring bikes taking 12 days (including four rest days) averaging 70 km per day. A wide variety of accommodation can be used en route including camping, youth hostels, bed and breakfasts and revamped country hotels. The best cycling time of the year is in spring (September to November) when the prevailing breezes will give more than a fair share of tailwinds, with only the odd day of perverse tough head winds.

DAY 1: Adelaide Airport to Kersbrook Youth Hostel

Distance ridden: 53.3 km;	Riding time: 3 hrs 24 mins;	Average speed: 15.5 kmph;	Maximum speed: 58 kmph

Ah! — that every Australian city was as bike friendly as Adelaide. There's even iced water to fill water bottles at the airport terminal. After a short back street sojourn, once on to the joint walking/bike path of the River Torrens Linear Park you encounter walkers, cyclists, strollers, couples and family groups, instead of trucks and cars. It's a warm, welcoming way to begin a long bike tour.

From the airport to the city is a slow, almost imperceptible climb, but it is interspersed with plenty of zigs and zags as the bike path keeps in step with the river. Occasionally you pass under traffic-snarled roads, but they are someone else's problem. You can ignore them and enjoy the rowers churning across the river's surface and the ducks dabbling in the shallows. Spring blossoms and young vigorous trees form a pleasant canopy through which to cycle.

Adelaide

Some unkind creatures have suggested that Adelaide (pop^n 1 003 000) is the only cemetery in Australia with neon lights. Dead it is not, but it is fairly relaxed. The city is well laid out with a small core of tall buildings, giving it a refined ambience which was planned by Captain Light, Adelaide's founder. Light arranged the city on a square patterned grid and generous allocation of parklands. His vision has since been blurred a little by the encroachment of a multitude of buildings onto the parks.

Beyond the city centre, the bike path forsakes the Torrens River and instead links passage with the O-Bahn busway where buses are guided on concrete tracks, to meander through this still-developing parkland — more than 40 000 trees are being planted. You leave this peaceful life at Grand Junction Road, are joined by some traffic and begin a more serious climb up the Lower North East Road. It is a nice hill, one that brings quick rewards of views over Adelaide. The little unofficial lookout on the right, part way up the climb, is probably the first chance you have to appreciate just how much height you have gained since leaving the airport terminal.

Adelaide Hills Detour

It is easy to find the Adelaide Hills and lose days in the process. Quaint villages, cosy bed and breakfasts, tempting restaurants, cafes and coffee lounges, almost continuous craft shops and galleries are all set against a backdrop of remnant native forests and recreated European forests. If there is one place in Australia where it is possible to gain weight on a cycle tour, the Adelaide Hills is it. There are too many options to detail here but a great **side tour** could be built around Crafers, Stirling, Aldgate, Hahndorf, Onkaparinga and Mt Lofty — see local tourist offices for guide brochures/maps. **Warrawong Sanctuary** (Mylor) is the place to see native animals, including some endangered nocturnal

ROUTE SLIP

Directions	R/S km	Ride for	Destination	Cum route km
END OF SECTION 1			**TOTAL FOR ROUTE**	**102.4**
Marananga	102.4			102.4
L	97.8	4.6	Marananga	97.8
BL-after X rail	96.5	1.3		96.5
R*-Mengler Hill	96.5		3 km to view	96.5
Tanunda	93.4	3.1		93.4
L	92.7	.7	Tanunda	92.7
R*-Crayfors	92.7			92.7
tar road begins	91.3	1.4		91.3
S-(don't go left)	84.4	6.9	boggy when wet	84.4
dirt road begins	83.3	1.1		83.3
L	81.1	2.2	Gomersal	81.1
S*-Lyndoch	81.1		2 km to town	81.1
L*-info board	80.5	.6		80.5
R	75.6	4.9	Tanunda	75.6
BL-give way sign	71.2	4.4	Gawler	71.2
L*-Whispering Wall	70.2	1.0	Steep downhill	70.2
L-(cycleway)	64.8	5.4	Korringal	64.8
L-Williamstown	64.5	.3	Gawler	64.5
L*Kersbrook YH	53.3	11.2		53.3
L-Kersbrook	45	8.3	Williamstown	45
BL-Birdwood	44.6	.4		44.6
R	36.7	7.9	Inglewood/Chn of Ponds	37.7
Houghton	36	.7		36
S-Range Rd	33.9	2.1		33.9
S-Lower North East Rd	30.4	3.5		30.4
R-Grand Junction Rd	28.5	1.9	where bike path forks	28.5
follow bike path	15.9	12.6		15.9
L-Holton Cr	15.7	.2		15.7
R-Eleventh Ave	15.6	.1		15.6
L-Winchester St	15.5	.1		15.5
R-Tenth Ave	15	.5		15.0
L-River St	14.8	.2		14.8
R-Eighth St	14.4	.4	see blue bike signs	14.4
L-Goss Ct	14.3	.1		14.3
L-Richmond St	14	.3		14
R*-cultural centre	11.4	2.6	Downtown Adelaide	11.4
follow bike path	3.7	7.7		3.7
R-Torrens R. Bpath	3.7		X bridge	3.7
L-Rowells Rd	2.3	1.4		2.3
R-traffic lights	2.2	.1		2.2
S-May Tce	1.6	.6	X Burbridge Rd	1.6
R-Frank Collopy Ct	1.4	.2		1.4
L-James Schofield Dr	0.9	.5		0.9
exit **Adelaide** Airport	0.0	.9	one way road	0.0
BEGIN SECTION 1				

KEY

BL = bear left   BR = bear right

L = left   R = right   S = straight   X = cross   * = detour directions

On ride line, each segment = 1 kilometre

103

forest dwellers. All-terrain bikes can also utilise part of the **Mawson Trail** which stretches from Adelaide to Blinman, in the Flinders Ranges, some 800 km of adventure. **Bike Moves** of Adelaide hires bikes and both they and **Freewheelin' Cycle Tours** run touring holidays.

Once you move into the hills above Adelaide, there are plenty of bends to whip around and lots of swooping descents. Even the climbs seem fun. You will probably encounter local racing cyclists out for a fast afternoon — some might even return your wave. Motorcyclists also treat the place as a hill-climbing race circuit, so keep an eye open for them. Enjoy these hills, for they are the only real climbing that you'll do for the whole tour.

With a plethora of forests and lakes, Millbrook Reserve and Chain of Ponds have a Scandinavian feel to them. There are numerous old stone houses dotted like gems through the landscape, but keep a lookout for a particularly lovely building on the left-hand side as you enter Chain of Ponds.

Beyond the hamlet of Kersbrook it is easy running. Our destination was the Kersbrook Youth Hostel and after a chat with the keyholder we coasted down to the entrance track. The entry gate is not biker-friendly. We entered by taking panniers off and slinging the bikes over the fence, then walking them down a steep gully strewn with sheep droppings.

Kersbrook Youth Hostel

Kersbrook Hostel is leased from the National Trust, but a less likely National Trust building I cannot imagine. Perhaps, in years to come, tacked on, mismatched building styles so often seen in the Australian countryside, will attain a level of quaintness — or perhaps not. However, the hostel is cosy and dry, with basic facilities and hot showers.

Be sure to stroll south of the hostel to the **Roachdale Nature Trail**. It is obvious where the nature reserve starts: that's where the wildflowers amass and the trees abound. The eucalypts dominate here, messmate stringybarks, South Australian blue gums, pink gums and long-leaved boxes. Seen in soft, misty conditions they are beautiful.

Only a short distance from Kersbrook is Section 2 of the long-distance **Heysen Trail**. This writhing track was named after the late Sir Hans Heysen, whose paintings of eucalypts first made the gum tree famous — 'There is something immensely exhilarating when tall white gums tower in the blue heavens — the subtle quality of the edges where they meet the sky . . .'.

DAY 2: Kersbrook Youth Hostel to Kapunda

Distance ridden: 74.5 km;   Riding time: 4 hrs 11 mins;   Average speed: 17.6 kmph;   Maximum speed: 57 kmph

To begin the morning there's a welcome descent through groves of trees and small clumps of wild-flowers. The downhill section is real enough, but the trees left are unfortunately just a sad reminder of what must have been alluring forests. If you are away early or, as it was for us, the day is grey and misty, then kangaroos will probably still be out breakfasting.

Williamstown seems to arrive quickly, but don't blink or you will miss the turn off to Barossa Reservoir. A drop like a mineshaft bullets you down to the edge of the Whispering Wall. This is eavesdropper's paradise where you can stand on one

Barossa Valley Detours

With the first Europeans settling in 1842, much of the Barossa Valley native vegetation has since been cleared, but to see what was there, have a look at **three conservation parks**, The Hale (2 km south of Williamstown), Sandy Creek (3 km west of Lyndoch) and Kaiserstuhl (8 km south-east of Tanunda). From Williamstown to Nuriootpa, Tour 5 takes in part of the **Barossa Valley Cycle Route**, which can be followed by using a map and information sheet produced by the South Australian Department of Recreation and Sport (available in Adelaide). The Barossa Valley Cycle Route takes in Angaston, Keyneton, Eden Valley and Springton. Wine buffs could take many long, pleasant days to circle this route.

TOUR 5: Beginning
a flowing 16 km
descent towards the
Murray River, South
Australia

TOUR 5: Pushing bikes across the hard-packed sand at Nora Creina Bay, South Australia

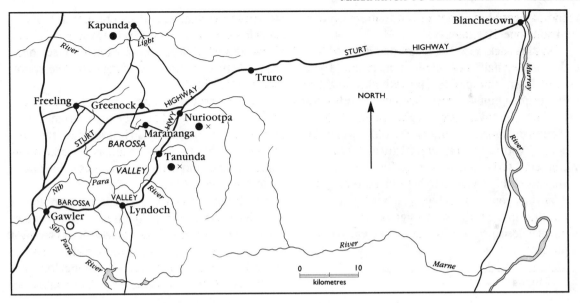

ROUTE SLIP

Directions	R/S km	Ride for	Destination	Cum route km
R	22.5	1.9	Truro	124.9
Kapunda	22.1	.4		124.5
L*-info board	20.7	1.4		123.1
BR	18.1	2.6		120.5
Greenock	7	11.1	Kapunda	109.4
S-(under bridge)	6.3	0.7	Greenock	108.7
BR	3.5	2.8		105.9
R	2.5	1		104.9
L	1.9	.6		104.3
R	1.3	.6		103.7
L	.7	.6	Avenue of Palms	103.1
Marananga	0.0	0.7		102.4
BEGIN SECTION 2				

Directions	R/S km	Ride for	Destination	Cum route km
END OF SECTION 2	117.7		**TOTAL FOR ROUTE**	**220.1**
Blanchetown	117.7			220.1
R	116.8	.9		219.2
L*-lookout	79.8	37		182.2
L*-picnic area	58	21.8		160.4
Truro	57	1		159.4
R*-Nuriootpa	41.2	15.8		143.6
L-Hwy 20	40.6	0.6	Blanchetown	143
BR-(Y intersection)	36.9	3.7	golf course on L	139.3
BL-(3 way intersection)	31.9	5		134.3
dirt road begins	29.9	2		132.3
R-(L-sign Rockbrock)	29.9			132.3
R	24.4	5.5	Nuriootpa	126.8

On ride line, each segment = 1 kilometre

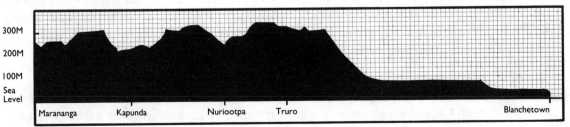

end of a very long dam wall and whisper secrets to someone 100 m away.

Getting back up to the main road is a stand-on-the-pedals affair, but this is soon replaced by a head-down run past a sign which remains a favourite of mine — 'Steep Descent'. **Watch out for the 'Give Way' sign at the bottom**. A short section of more heavily trafficked road is left behind with a sharply angled turn off towards Gomersal. Along with the traffic, the tar disappears and is replaced by a black soil road with a slightly ominous 'Boggy When Wet' sign. Pushing up the hill past this sign reveals a woven green landscape, its weft and warp created by the plough.

Tanunda

Tanunda is unashamedly a tourist town, but a prettier one is hard to find. Venerable stone buildings, from minuscule one-bedroom cottages to grandiose civic monuments, sit shoulder to shoulder down the main street — along with a few newer stone creations. This most enlightened of towns actually has two bakeries and an enticing shop — Tanunda Wurst Haus — where you can choose from locally produced German Mettwurst and a staggering array of cheeses.

Beyond Tanunda, there are 4 km of heavily trafficked road to negotiate before you peel off towards Seppeltsfield. Camera-toting hill lovers should not go past the turn off to Mengler Hill. The views from the Hill are reported to be outstanding, though I must confess to turning down the opportunity to climb it.

Along this route you are immersed in wine, well the vines at least. They seem to stretch away towards infinity as the road just squeezes through. In some places the road's route is determined by the vineyards, forcing it to take a series of inexplicable right-angled bends.

On the Barossa Valley Cycle Route map there's a triple-arrowed hill (denoting a steep climb) beyond Seppeltsfield, but it is so short, you just seem to be getting into the ascent when it ends. From Greenock to Kapunda is fast going, long loping descents through broad open fields and the occasional pleasurable uphill.

Kapunda

This town was the site of the first successful metal mine in Australia in 1842, thanks to Francis Dutton finding green copper ore instead of the sheep he was supposed to be looking for. Today the town retains some of its old character, though the surrounds no longer resemble the aftermath of an atomic blast. 'Map, The Miner' (a statue 7 metres tall and weighing 3 tons) is a reminder of the Cornish miners who established the first copper mine.

DAY 3: Kapunda to Blanchetown

Distance ridden: 83.8 km;   Riding time: 3 hrs 51 mins;   Average speed: 21.5 kmph;   Maximum speed: 60 kmph

For cycle tourers, Ford House, a Bed and Breakfast on the main road, has combined the best of two eras: modern plumbing and generous, traditional English breakfasts. The fast well and truly broken, if not completely destroyed, we discovered that weather in this part of the Barossa is a tad fickle: dawn fog, breakfast sunshine, riding rain! But for the second time it is a freewheeling start and the kilometres click past swiftly.

Getting my companions to turn off the tar and take the quiet back route to Nuriootpa took a little convincing. About 1 km along the road I was unsure that it had been a good move. The freshly dampened dirt had transformed into a gummy black mud track with a particular attraction for bike tyres. This is not the place to have close fitting side pull brakes and no mudguards. Take heart if it is the same for you, after 4 km the road changes colour, and becomes harder and smoother.

Nuriootpa

Called 'Nuri' by the locals, it is seen by ordinary travellers as just another pretty Barossa town, but

I regard it as an essential detour. Starving tourers can hardly pass up the chance to partake of Bee Sting Cake! This honey/nut/sponge/yeast/bread concoction is perfect cyclist's food.

The semitrailers that use Highway 20, The Sturt, are the cause of constant, thunderous noise all the way to Blanchetown. At about one-minute intervals you hear them coming, the noise grows louder and louder, the ground trembles, and then ROOOOAAAARRRR!! — another interstate semitrailer parts the air beside you. To give them credit, the great majority give you a wide berth, but even so it is a welcome respite to pull off at the lookout 22.8 km from Truro.

Savour the view and the downhill to come. Ahead, below you, is the Riverland where broad flat plains radiate out from Australia's greatest river, the Murray. The Murray River is the fourth-largest river in the world, draining about one seventh of Australia's total area. It was first navigated in 1830 by explorer Captain Charles Sturt and his long boat crew. River steamers and barges followed European settlement and they thrived until the arrival of the railway.

Away from the river, the landscape has a dry, slightly parched feel to it and though you won't see it on the ground, before Blanchetown you cross Goyder's line. This line was placed on a map of South Australia by the then surveyor-general, to denote drought-affected country. To get down from the edge of the Barossa escarpment is almost a dead straight run. Now, admittedly, I did have a tailwind, but after selecting top gear and winding up to speed, I didn't have to push the pedals again for 16 km!

At Blanchetown you can bid a not-so-fond farewell to the truck-laden Sturt Highway and take a break from the bike seat. Blanchetown is an upriver pickup point for the *P.S. Proud Mary*, a modern shallow draught vessel, built in the style of river boats of an earlier age.

DAYS 4 & 5: Rest

From a deckchair the sun beams down. The *Proud Mary* glides down a river the colour of molten earth. The cockatoos call from perches high on red sandstone walls. Houseboats huddle against the shore shaded by ancient river red gums. Then an announcement: 'breakfast/morning tea/lunch/afternoon tea/dinner/supper is ready'. Life on a Murray River boat is pure restful, restorative bliss.

DAY 6 (pm): Murray Bridge to Wellington

Distance ridden: 36.1 km;   Riding time: 2 hrs 16 mins;   Average speed: 15.8 kmph;   Maximum speed: 38 kmph

The last banquet on board the *Proud Mary* will probably give cause for an easy start to the afternoon ride — it certainly did for us.

Murray Bridge

Murray Bridge (popn 14 000) is a major town with full facilities. Be sure to check out Mary, the Blacksmith (weekends and public holidays). Your fare on board the *Proud Mary* includes a visit to the Butterfly House, but it's best to cycle there rather than taking the coach.

After being captivated by gentle butterflies you can just continue on down the road towards Wellington. The road is really a country lane, put in place to connect the farms. This image is reinforced by the occasional cow pat one has to avoid in the middle of the road. The landscape through which you ride is one of cattle dogs and cockies (farmers), milking machines and bellowing jersey cows. If you get the chance, stop and chat. That way you'll experience dry Australian humour at its most parched and perhaps get a few surprises. The dairy farmer with whom we passed the time of day turned out to be an ex-bike rider. As a young man he raced an Australian-made Malvern Star bike with French *wooden* rims.

He didn't have much helpful advice about coping with headwinds, so we slogged painfully up the invisible wind-created hill all the way to the caravan park at Wellington. There, a small A-frame cabin and hot shower awaited. If you are there before 4 p.m. check out the old courthouse.

DAY 7: Wellington to Tea Tree Crossing

Distance ridden: 108.3 km;   Riding time: 5 hrs;   Average speed: 21.6 kmph;   Maximum speed: 49 kmph

While local maps and tourist blurb state that the punt at Wellington runs 24 hours a day, the punt's driver has been known to ignore three cycle tourers who have arisen specially early. Of course, as soon as a car pulled up, the punt sprang into action.

For once it's great to have a side-angled head-wind first up. Then, when you make the 90 degree turn on rejoining the alternative Highway One, it becomes a tailwind. The road is a series of flat sections punctuated by small sand ridges; ancient vegetated sand dunes full of shells. Deeper gullies contain shallow lakes fringed by tea trees. In the reclining desert-like landscape there are a few 'hills'. The largest of these monoliths, called Mount Misery, is all of 30 m! Beyond it you may be forgiven if you don't believe your eyes. After all, pink lakes are a little unusual. In this case it is caused by a certain species of algae which favours the salty water of the lakes.

Poltalloch Detour

For dirt road lovers only: take the Poltalloch turnoff at Ashville. Poltalloch is an historic property (**accommodation** is available) on the shores of Lake Alexandrina. Beyond it is the smallest inland lighthouse in Australia. A punt takes you across to Narrung and you rejoin the alternative Highway One south of Meningie.

Just before Meningie, you travel parallel to Lake Albert, a large body of normal coloured water. This massive lake is often a mass of birds, particularly huge colonies of black swans and pelicans. There's a pleasant picnic area for your morning tea on the right in Meningie where yellow-cheeked honeyeaters make a feast of golden wattle blossom.

It takes a while before you sight Coorong National Park. First sighting is really near Magrath Flat, but if the day is hot and windy, use the sheltering trees there as a lunch spot. Between the Park and Policeman's Point there are few places to escape from the sun. Though the shell-packed beaches on the shores of the lake do look inviting, the water is shallow and fringed with a strange white spongy substance, which looks like rock.

Coorong National Park

Coorong National Park (43 500 hectares) is today a home to the birds, but it was once home to the Ngarrindgeri (Tanganekald) Aborigines. They lived in semi-permanent dome-shaped dwellings called wurlies on the shores of the lakes and hunted using rafts made from bundles of reeds. Today, **accommodation** is available at Policeman's Point and Gemini Downs, but it would be a shame not to camp in the Coorong. Drop in to the national park information centre at Salt Creek to purchase a **camping permit** and have a chat with the friendly rangers. Each year Coorong water levels can change dramatically. By October you would normally be able to get across the lakes to the sea at Tea Tree Crossing, but when we rode the tour this crossing was expected to be closed until December.

Salt Creek also has an unusual monument, a replica of an oil rig. It commemorates this country's first oil rush in 1866. The 'oil' turned out to be an algae, coorongite, and if you ever have to wade through this black goo you will understand why they believed it was oil.

ROUTE SLIP

Directions	R/S km	Ride for	Destination	Cum route km
END OF SECTION 3	227.9		**TOTAL FOR ROUTE**	**448**
Kingston	227.9			
S	227.7	.2	Robe	447.8
L*-42 Mile Crossing	161.5	66.2	3 km to campsite	381.6
R*-Tea Tree Crossing	143.3	18.2	1.5 km to campsites	363.4
Salt Creek	142.8	.5		362.9
Policeman's Pt	133.3	9.5	Salt Creek	353.4
Meningie	81.3	52	Policeman's Pt	301.4
R-Hwy One	38.4	42.9	Meningie	258.5
ferry	36.3	2.1		256.4
Wellington	36.1	.2		256.2
L	36.1			256.2
BR	25.2	10.9		245.3
L-traffic lights	1.1	24.1	Wellington	221.2
L-Murray Bridge	.9	.2	at traffic lights	221
R-*Proud Mary* Dock	0.0	.9		220.1
Blanchetown	0.0		Board *Proud Mary*	220.1
BEGIN SECTION 3				

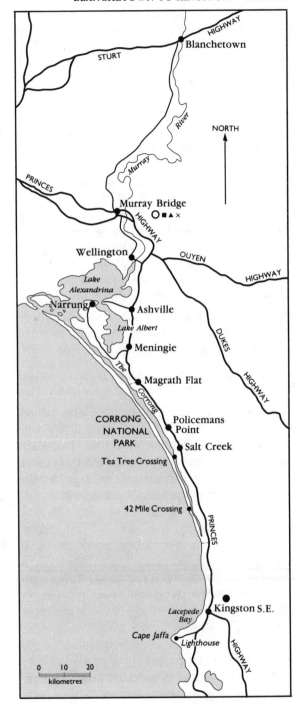

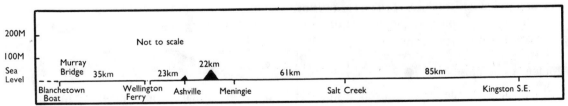

DAY 8: Tea Tree Crossing to 42 Mile Crossing (Light Day)

Distance ridden: 22.5 km;   Riding time: 1 hr 7 mins;   Average speed: 20 kmph;   Maximum speed: 36 kmph

Primitive campsites (no facilities) are found all along the Tea Tree Crossing road — be warned though, it is soft sand in patches. Also Coorong mosquitoes are unlikely to ever be placed on the endangered list. I found a biker-style campsite just opposite The Lakes Walk (3 km self-guided) which takes in Pipeclay (one of the carbonate lakes) and Salt Lakes. Strolling at first light I came across a mallee fowl on a mound. It walked off huffily and blended into the dappled shade of mallee trees. Mallee fowl are unique birds, just recently beginning to rebuild their numbers from the edge of extinction. In a complicated schedule lasting 11 months, a mound is constructed then manipulated so that the laid eggs (5–35) are incubated at near to 33°C. Chicks dig themselves out of the mound, and can quickly run and fly on their first day.

Unable to traverse to the sea at Tea Tree Crossing, I moved south to the 42 Mile crossing (my companions had chosen to stay in a cabin at Gemini Downs). Between the campsite and the sea is a sandhills walk through swaying grasses and flitting honeyeaters. The beach itself is a wild affair scalloped in cusps. There are shells enough to delight the most jaded observer and mysterious balls rolling freely down the sand which are formed by fibre ball plant *(Posidoniaceae posidonia)*. Unfortunately this beach is frequented by four-wheel drive vehicles (see the rogues gallery of rolled and bogged vehicles in the national park information centre). Pedestrians at least can move out of the way, but this is not so easy for dotterels whose nesting sites share these 'highways'.

DAY 9: 42 Mile Crossing to Kingston

Distance ridden: 69.5 km;   Riding time: 2 hrs 25 mins;   Average speed: 28.6 kmph;   Maximum speed: 48 kmph

As the old song goes 'some days are diamonds, some days are stone'. A glance at the day log above will show this was a sparkler. To average 28.6 km per hour with full panniers on a dead flat road requires something special. For us it was a 30-knot tailwind! Big gears, blue sky and fast riding. Huddling in protective clusters beside the road, woolly sheep seemed to mimic the clumps of tea trees — the wind ruffled fleece and leaves with equal carelessness. We pedalled on, revelling in the speed. You travel through broad flatlands as far as vision allows. To the west, yellow sand dunes are the only glimmering indication that the ocean is still not far away.

A cluster of gums can provide a brief morning-tea respite from the wind. Revived by the break, one of my companions decided to go for a sprint.

I acted as pace rider up to 48 km per hour, then he broke away and pumped up to 59 km per hour — on a dead flat road. Some days to ride 70 km takes from dawn to dusk. On this day it took us until 11.10 a.m.!

Kingston

On entering Kingston it is hard to miss Larry, the 17 m high lobster which weighs four tonnes. Slightly less weighty specimens (for eating, not viewing) can be purchased just near the town's long jetty; in 1876 this jetty was 1200 m (4000 feet) long, though it has stunted with age. Nearby is the Cape Jaffa Lighthouse, re-erected on the foreshore.

DAY 10: Kingston to Robe

Distance ridden: 44.1 km;   Riding time: 2 hrs 47 mins;   Average speed: 15.8 kmph;   Maximum speed: 31 kmph

The trouble with gale force winds in this part of the world is that as the fronts move through, the

ROUTE SLIP

Directions	R/S km	Ride for	Destination	Cum route km
END OF TOUR			**TOTAL FOR ROUTE**	**633.5**
Mount Gambier	185.5			633.5
L*Tantanoola Caves	156.9	28.6		604.9
Millicent	136.3	20.6		584.3
R-town centre	136.3			584.3
L	134.5	1.8		582.5
BL	133.1	1.4		581.1
R	100.9	32.2		548.9
exit Beachport	100.7	.2	Millicent	548.7
Beachport	100.7			548.7
L	100.5	.2		548.5
R	98.8	1.7		546.8
R	94.8	4		542.8
R-Alt Hwy (One)	71.2	23.6	Beachport	519.2
tar road begins	71.2			519.2
L-Powell's Rd	65.5	5.7		513.5
R*-Nora Creina Bay	65.5		2.6 km to bay	513.5
L*-Lake St Clair	64.8	.7		512.8
R*-Little Dip	57.8	7		505.8
R*-info sign	57.1	.7	Little Dip NP	505.1
dirt road begins	54	3.1		502
R*-	51.4	2.6	Lake Robe	499.4
R	47.1	4.3		495.1
R-(Route 69)	45.8	1.3	Nora Creina Scenic Dr	493.8
exit Robe	44.1	1.7		492.1
Robe	44.1			492.1
R	41.2	2.9	Robe	489.2
R*-Cape Jaffa	8	33.2		456
Kingston	0.0	8	Robe	448
BEGIN SECTION 4				

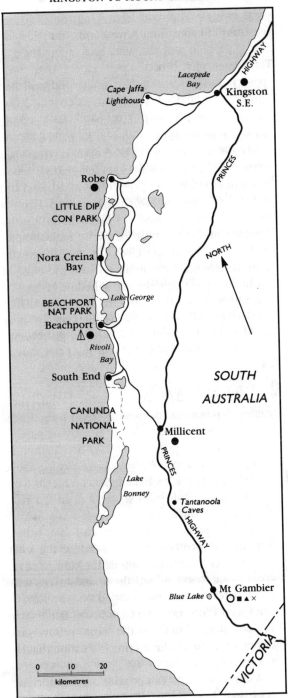

On ride line, each segment = 1 kilometre

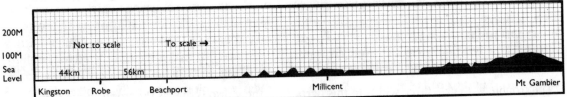

wind swings. The road from Kingston to Robe runs south to south-south-west and, you guessed it, that's which way the wind had swung for us. The beautifully broad, open aspect that you appreciate with no wind or a tailwind will be roundly cursed in a head and sidewind. You quickly grow to love trees and hate open paddocks. In the protection of the former, life is gentle and quiet. In the latter, some sort of giant, invisible hand takes random swipes at your bike. Riding a metre or so inside the edge of tar can mean either being forced off the road by strong gusts or, when big trucks rumble beside you, nearly being sucked into the path of oncoming traffic. One way to counter the breeze when cycling in a group is to ride spaced across the left-hand side of the road, at an angle which corresponds with the wind direction. That way, there is some relief for the second rider and considerable relief for the third rider. Care is of course needed in any such action. Make sure you don't ride more than two abreast and be ready to peel off back to single file on hearing approaching traffic.

If you strike a gale force side- to headwind, take heart — the worst of it generally lasts for the first third of the way to Robe. There is a saving patch of pine forest large enough to dampen the strongest of winds and it is followed by small rolling hillocks. Since white-tailed black cockatoos have learnt to adapt to pine trees, you might even come across a flock of these fun flyers gambolling about the place. They are guaranteed to take your mind off headwind horrors.

Robe

We cycled in to the Caledonian Inn, which though now a pub, was once a parsonage. Robe (proclaimed in 1847) has a history that is just a little on the seedy side. It was used as a landing point for thousands of Chinese gold diggers who were seeking to evade a tax placed on them by the Victorian government. These hardy people simply walked overland, from Robe, to the gold fields.

Today, the town retains many fine old buildings and is a delight to stroll around (get a heritage audio cassette from the Historic Interpretative Centre). Also, drop in to the local National Parks and Wildlife Service office for a chat with the ranger and to pick up helpful information on the nearby national parks.

DAY 10: Robe to Beachport

Distance ridden: 61.8 km;   Riding time: 3 hrs 33 mins;   Average speed: 17.1 kmph;   Maximum speed: 41 kmph

Alternative Highway One feels pretty quiet, but when you turn off that and onto Nora Creina Scenic Drive it seems like you are on a deserted country lane. This country lane takes on a slightly wilder aspect when smooth tar becomes sandy dirt and riding becomes a little more adventurous. Soft patches are hard to avoid even when running so close to the road edges that your panniers are being brushed by waving grasses.

The road fringes Little Dip National Park, a tiny vestige of coastal dunes and delicate tree-fringed lakes. If luck is on your side you may encounter an echidna perambulating its way along the road verges. These little anteaters are lovely creatures who will, if threatened, dig themselves into the ground or roll into a ball of spikes. Take care in handling them for they do have venomous spines on their legs. Echidnas lay one egg, then after it hatches, they carry the baby in their pouch.

If you are keen-eyed and the day is warm, this is probably one place where you will almost certainly see a snake. Being a small creature, a snake is easily frightened, particularly if you are cutting off its avenue of escape. Given the option of retreat, almost every snake that you meet will move away from you. Being bitten by a snake is usually the result of trying to pick it up, trying to hit it with a stick, or treading on it. An inveterate bike tourer of the early 1900s, Francis Birtles, reckoned that snakes were attracted by the shiny, sparkling parts of his bike. Perhaps the snakes today are a bit more worldly, or bikes are dirtier, but none of the many snakes I've encountered seemed the slightest bit interested in me or my bike.

Be sure to take the 2.6 km detour to Nora Creina Bay. In fact, if you have the time, it would make a great place to stop for a day or two. The bay is a real jewel, with close diminutive islands serving as rookeries for a variety of sea birds. There is also a nude bathing beach nearby. Where track becomes beach, you can push your bike across hard-packed sand south to a finger of rocks. It makes a sheltered lunch spot.

You rejoin the tar and alternative Highway One just prior to skirting an immense body of water, Lake George. The road conforms to the wishes of the lake and curves around to end up in Beachport. The youth hostel at Beachport is sited in a charming old building within the caressing sounds of waves sliding ashore.

DAY 11: Rest Day

Beachport

Today it is a quiet little spot, but in the 1830s Beachport was a whaling station, then a thriving port. In 1878, a railway line from Mt Gambier established it as a relaxing holiday spot. Thankfully, today the fishermen chase lobster not whales. Visit the **Old Wool and Grain Store** (a National Trust museum). Close to town is the **Beachport Conservation Park**. Stroll out to, then around Wooleys Lake, before cutting across the sand hills to a wild windswept beach with intricate rock formations and ancient Aboriginal shell middens.

DAY 12: Beachport to Mount Gambier

The Beachport to Millicent road skirts Rivoli Bay which on a sunlit, balmy day would be a delight to explore by little side roads. However, when we rode it, the rain was teeming down, reducing visibility to a few hundred metres either side of the road. In this subdued manner I was loathe to see South End and the Canunda National Park, one of the only reasonably sized parks in the southeast of South Australia, which, because it's on the coast, would offer no shelter from the conditions.

Millicent

Millicent is a large commercial centre and features one of the best National Trust Museums in regional South Australia and an excellent shell garden (Williams Rd). Unfortunately, the weather was so wet and miserably cold when we cycled in to town, my riding partners decided to stop here and catch the bus from Mt Gambier to Adelaide. I pushed on towards Mt Gambier hoping that the forecast hail was not going to dump on me. Just at 20.6 km out of Millicent the road runs beneath ancient marine cliffs. Within these is the **Tantanoola Caves Conservation Park** (tours are run in the single chamber cave seven days a week).

By the time I pedalled into Mt Gambier to complete this tour, the combination of icy winds and continual rain had zapped my legs and feet. Mt Gambier's maximum temperature that day in October was 12°C — the hot shower in Jen's Hotel was never appreciated more.

Mt Gambier

To discover the delights of this town (pop[n] 23 000) cycle out to 'The Lady Nelson' at the information centre (on the Jubilee Highway). The helpful people there will show you that the town has far more to offer than the Blue Lake, which turns cobalt blue during November to March.

TOUR 6
VICTORIAN COASTAL TOUR

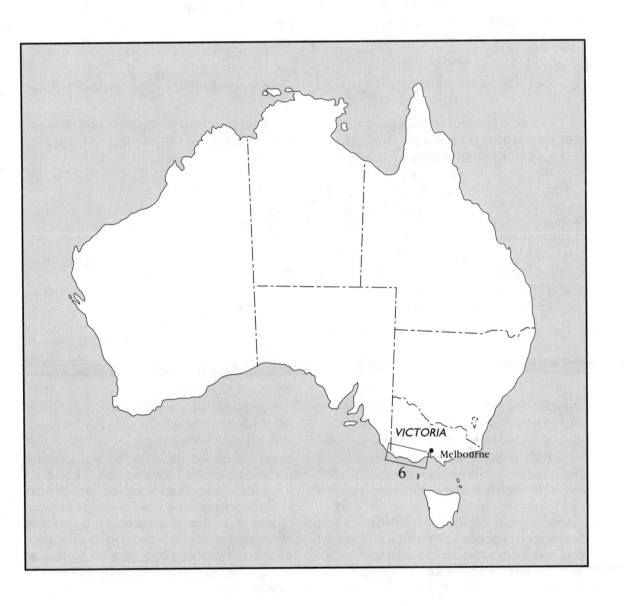

6 VICTORIAN COASTAL TOUR

This 530 km tour of Victorian coastline actually begins at Mt Gambier, in South Australia's far south-east. It heads across to Dingley Dell, home of famous Australian poet Adam Lindsay Gordon, then slips over the Victorian state border at Nelson into the beauty of Lower Glenelg National Park. From Portland almost to Geelong the sea-loving route hugs some of the most spectacular coastline in Australia. Highlights along this section include the Great Ocean Road and some startling limestone formations called the Twelve Apostles. The only inland deviation takes you up through the Otways old growth forests with plenty of hill climbing and fabulous freewheeling descents. I travelled the route solo in late October taking nine days (including one rest day) averaging 66 km per day. Best times are from September to December. You could camp all the way, though I chose to ride a little more lightly laden and utilised youth hostels, hotels and motels.

DAY 1: Mt Gambier to Nelson

Distance ridden: 65.3 km;   Riding time: 3 hrs 27 mins;   Average speed: 18.8 kmph;   Maximum speed: 53 kmph

At 7.30 a.m. on a blustery Sunday morning, Mt Gambier is as quiet as a graveyard. (See Tour 5 for details on Mt Gambier.) Heading towards Allendale, the stiff hill which begins at the end of Mt Gambier's main street ensures you are quickly started into this tour. On that morning, the drowned volcano beneath the Blue Lake seemed alive as the wind ruffled its dark surface.

'Country' begins very soon after leaving Mt Gambier. Originally this was a densely forested land of heady wattles and casuarinas, described by the Australian poet, Adam Lindsay Gordon:

Lightly the breath of the Spring wind blows
  through, laden with faint perfume
'Tis fragrance rare that the bushman knows,
  the scent of the wattle bloom

But the land was cleared and although the contractors were required to leave 10 trees to the acre, many of the surviving trees died leaving a bald and windswept landscape through which to cycle. The poet's words take on a truly ironic quality when instead of a spring fragrance, the wind is tainted by meatworks.

Another extinct volcano, Mt Schank, is a sentinel marking the route. It makes an interesting detour and can provide a challenging climb. At Allendale East the road inexplicably breaks into a divided section. If you stop and walk over to the cluster of trees between the two roads, you will find the entrance to Allendale sink hole. The earth beneath your path is riddled with wild caves. This area is very popular with scuba divers, but cave diving is not something to try unless you are very experienced and have obtained the necessary paperwork from the relevant authorities.

Just before reaching Port Macdonnell is the turn-off to Adam Lindsay Gordon's house in Dingley Dell Conservation Park. It is a 2 km diversion, but even if you face the same blasting headwind I found, the effort is worthwhile. The little house, Dingley Dell, is a dinky white-washed classic, and inside the museum (small entrance fee charged) Gordon's personal belongings and other mementos give you a glimpse of an earlier age — there is even a cycling tourist pictured in 1908. Pick up a guide sheet from the friendly caretakers and stroll along the self-guided walk. Take your time, the black-trunked golden wattles in full bloom and plethora of twittering bush birds are a relaxing interlude for both mind and body.

Leaving Dingley Dell and turning down Springs Road you are travelling beside Germein Reserve, a public woodland. In its own way it, too, is an outdoor museum, recording a landscape since modified. If you are riding on a Wednesday or Thursday afternoon, take the short detour up to Cape Northumberland Lighthouse — built in 1882.

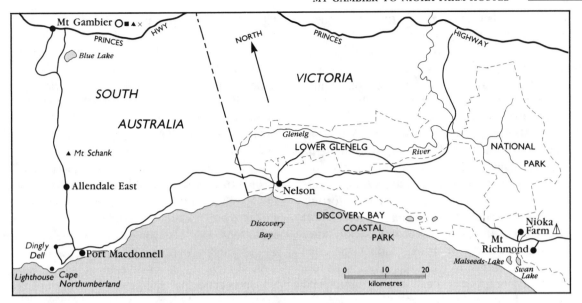

ROUTE SLIP

Directions	R/S km	Ride for	Destination	Cum route km
R-Mt G/Nelson Rd	55.3	2		55.3
R	48.2	7.1		48.2
BR	33.5	14.7	Nelson	33.5
Port MacDonnell	32.4	1.1		32.4
L-(tar)	30.6	1.8		30.6
R*-to lighthouse	30.6		Cape Northumberland	30.6
L-Springs Rd (dirt)	28.8	1.8	Port Macdonnell	28.8
R*-Dingly Dell	28.8			28.8
R	26.9	1.9	Dingly Dell	26.9
Allendale East	22.3	4.6		22.3
L*	15	7.3	Mt Schank	15
S-roundabout	2.2	12.8		2.2
BL	1.2	1		1.2
Mt Gambier	0.0	1.2	Port Macdonnell	0.0
BEGIN SECTION 1				

Directions	R/S km	Ride for	Destination	Cum route km
END OF SECTION 1			**TOTAL FOR ROUTE**	**102.2**
L*-Nioka Farm Hostel	102.2			102.2
R*-scenic lookout	101.3	.9		101.3
L*	83.3	18	camping area	83.3
L-Portland Nelson Hwy (tar)	81.6	1.7	Portland	81.6
L	81.4	.2		81.4
R-Bulley Ranges Rd	78.2	3.2		78.2
L*-Forest Camp	78.2		camping area	78.2
L*-Sapling Ck	74.7	3.5	picnic area	74.7
R-Forest Rd (Dirt)	66.5	8.2		66.5
L*-info centre	66.5			66.5
R	65.6	0.9	information centre	65.6
L	64.3	1.3	Lower Glenelg NP	64.3
Nelson	64.3			64.3
R*	57.3	7	Piccannii Ponds CP	57.3

KEY

L = left   **R** = right   **S** = straight

BL = bear left   **BR** = bear right

X = cross   * = detour directions

On ride line, each segment = 1 kilometre

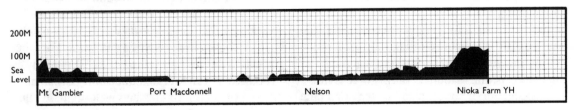

The coastline beneath it is reef-strewn and rugged, having claimed many ships, and since this is the southernmost point of South Australia, it seems to attract any rain showers that are about. In gigantic grandiose displays, the cloud masses come whirling in from the sea to dump grey-walled swathes of water across the landscape.

Port MacDonnell's (pop^n 700) past glories as a major port are reflected in the maritime museum which contains artifacts from 25 shipwrecks, contrasting with its present day image of a quiet fishing port. If you have suffered the misfortune of a buffeting south-west gale on the way to Port MacDonnell, things improve dramatically after dipping down to the town. Riding the road towards Nelson turns what was a side blast to a tail wind, but it can be a challenging, high speed game of tag and dodge. Win and you escape those almost inevitable downpours; lose and you get well and truly dumped on. Even big-gear rolling at 40 km per hour I was in a soggy state on rejoining the main highway to Nelson.

Nelson

The last short section to Nelson is not made particularly pleasant by the increase in cars and trucks. But on arrival in Nelson you're likely to agree comletely with the town's slogan — 'A good place to relax'. I certainly collapsed at Pinehaven Chalet. If time is a friend rather than a nagging companion, Nelson can be an excellent base for some off-bike exploration. Instead of riding to Portland, you could trek through **Discovery Bay Coastal Park** (8530 hectares), part of the 250 km Great South West Walk. You need to be fully self-sufficient, but there are established bush campsites along the way. The whole walk is a circuit comprising 16 campsites, and October to December and March to June are the best times to tackle it. Rather than trekking the complete circuit, you could send your bike to Portland by bus or with a local transport company.

Another leisurely pursuit to be taken from Nelson is canoeing. Sited near the mouth of the Glenelg River, Nelson provides a base for two canoe hire businesses. After buying supplies, your group (and hired canoes) can be transported to one of the up-river camping sites in Lower Glenelg National Park. Over a few relaxing days you paddle downstream, returning to Nelson on a waterway described in 1836 by the Surveyor General Major Thomas Mitchell as '. . . the finest body of fresh water I had seen in Australia'. Be sure to pack a fishing line for the odd moments when you're not wielding a paddle.

DAY 2: Nelson to Mt Richmond Youth Hostel

Distance ridden: 41.9 km;   Riding time: 2 hrs 24 mins;   Average speed: 17.4 kmph;   Maximum speed: 53 kmph

This little segment of Tour 6 is short on kilometres but long on distractions since it traverses a section of Lower Glenelg National Park (27 300 hectares). Those disciplined souls who enjoy an early start will be well rewarded for their effort. With the morning mists still draped over the handlebars, a ride down meandering Forest Drive can feature wild animal encounters. Provided your panniers don't jangle, being onboard a bike means you can glide silently up to a multitude of browsing native animals. Lucky cyclists might even spot an emu and a clutch of chicks scuttling along the track.

Indulge yourself with extra time when exploring Lower Glenelg National Park — there are over 700 species of native plants to see. Camping cyclists can experience idyllic sites hidden along the shores of a gently moving stream which begins high in the Grampian ranges and travels 400 km to the sea. When you do take the tiny track detours to secluded campsites, there are some sand patches to negotiate — get off and walk if it gets too bad, the destinations are generally worth a struggle.

Once you do get back onto the Portland–Nelson road, cycle touring can become a little more serious. The road is used by a fleet of wood-chip trucks. In the forest, portable chippers quickly reduce chosen trees to wood chips which are then loaded into tall trucks and trailers. On my visit, it seemed that an average of one every five minutes set out on a dash to Portland — more trips equal more money. Most drivers are courteous enough to give a touring cyclist a wide berth (and the odd shower of wood chips thanks to uncovered loads) but every once in a while, an inbound truck meets an outbound truck exactly at the point you are travelling. If you hear the cry of truck brakes followed by tyre squeals, don't wait to argue the point — get off the road, pronto!

Nioka Farm Hostel

Country hospitality is one of those things often talked about but not so frequently encountered. It certainly will be offered by Ruth and Terry Stanley at Nioka Farm Home Hostel (Mt Richmond). Their cosy little retreat is the kind of place where your original plans to stay just one night can easily change, and a week later you find yourself still there, feeling like one of the family. The hostel is really a 481 hectare working sheep property and in whatever season you are travelling, there are always a host of things to see and do. Be sure to check out the nearby forest walk for spring blossoms and just down the road a short ride away is the turn off to pretty Swan Lake and Malseeds Lake. Negotiating your way over this sandy road isn't easy, but between the lakes and coast are some of the most impressive sand dunes to be seen.

DAY 3: Mt Richmond Youth Hostel to Port Fairy

Distance ridden: 102.6 km; Riding time: 4 hrs 41 mins; Average speed: 21.8 kmph; Maximum speed: 46 kmph

Just as sun piercing the grey cloak of cloud cover gives a cycle tourer hope for a good day of riding, so too do the little pockets of forest give native wildlife a chance for long-term survival. On this route section, excessive clearing has decreased the local fauna's seclusion. However, there certainly seem to be no shortage of sheep running about the paddocks.

One prolific native, the black and white magpie, perches malevolently on property fences. During the lustful months of spring, Australian magpies regard cycle tourers as either a rival or the enemy. This devious bird waits till you have passed, then takes off for a divebombing attack from the rear. In the manner of Second World War fighter pilots, it gains height then comes in with the sun behind it. If you are cruising along you may see your shadow on the road joined by a smaller one above it. A swoop, a rattle of wings and a squark as the bird tries to take a piece out of your helmet — or your head if you are so foolish as to ride (now illegally) without a helmet. In your effort to wave the menace away, beware of wobbling off line and into the path of an oncoming truck.

Unfortunately, between Mt Richmond Youth Hostel and the turnoff before Portland, there's no need to check your watch on the passing minutes as every five or so you'll be monstered by one of the mobile woodchip convey. In between the passing of trucks keep an eye open for black/brown wedgetailed eagles, not that they are the slightest bit interested in cycle tourers. They are Australia's largest bird of prey and, with a characteristic wedge-shaped tail, are easy to recognise in silhouette. If not soaring at great height they are often seen being hassled by fearless pairs of birds often no larger than the eagle's talons.

Mt Richmond National Park Detour

Mt Richmond National Park (east of the Portland–Nelson Road) is reached via Hanns Rd, Stephens Rd and Mt Richmond Rd. Since there is no camping allowed in the park (closest campsite is Tarragal Camp to the south-east) it is very difficult for a cycle tourer to get a good appreciation of the park's spectacular spring wildflowers. This is another location where you might see an emu and chicks.

If you decide to go into the city of Portland (pop[n] 12 000), after enjoying the sights of Bridgewater Bay, the wharf area and, perhaps, the aluminium smelter, be sure to pick Dutton Way as a more pleasant exit from town. Eventually you will find that you have rejoined the Princess Highway from Portland to Port Fairy, a frustrating

121

road since it manages to keep the beach just out of sight. Unfortunately there is no option but to ride it. Worse still, you may, as I did, strike a prevalent south-east breeze. This wind is a real nag. Local cycling legend has it that a south-east breeze is so constant that it blows through tree trunks. I can agree with that. After 85 km of relentless grind I was so tired that, quite honestly, over the next 15 km I reached the lowest mental point of any tour in this book. Thank heavens for the charm of Port Fairy and a friendly welcome at the youth hostel.

DAY 4: A Well-earned Rest Day

Port Fairy

This town (pop^n 2400), began life in the early 1800s as a sheltering place for whalers and sealers seeking to escape from wild gales. Today the only whalers are hand-rolled, flour-dusted loaves of bread so-called, and the wildlife are much better cared for. With periods of boom (it was once Victoria's second largest port) and bust (workers downed tools and left during the gold rushes), the town was left with a legacy of many fine old buildings. Intelligent planning has kept over fifty 19th-century structures worthy of classification by the National Trust.

Once you have sated your appetite for history, take a late afternoon stroll to Griffiths Island (carry warm clothing if there's an onshore breeze blowing). Circumnavigate the island anticlockwise, arriving at the viewing platform on the west side just on dusk. As night falls, short-tailed shearwaters (mutton birds) fly in from the sea in their thousands, to return to their burrows. Though the sky is filled with fast-moving birds all is virtually silent, save for the whirr of wings. Incredibly, these birds migrate each year to Alaska with the first usually arriving back on Griffith island on the 22nd of September each year!

Port Fairy is home for Graham Woodrup, who at time of writing is the current winner of the Perth-to-Sydney (4380 km) Cycling Record. Graham rode the distance in 10 days, 17 hours and 56 minutes. He runs Cycles Woodrup at 5 Uebergang St, Port Fairy.

DAY 5: Port Fairy to Warrnambool

Distance ridden: 41.5 km; Riding time: 2 hrs 8 mins; Average speed: 19.5 kmph; Maximum speed: 54 kmph

There's something special about a broad curve of yellow-white sand being lapped by lazy blue and white waves. No matter how early you leave Port Fairy, it's hard to make good time along this section — beach exploring on Port Fairy Bay is too tempting. Though it can look peaceful and inviting at times, this is a wild and unforgiving coastline — there are four major ships lying wrecked just off the beach. Never letting truth get in the way of a good yarn, further east is reputed to be the resting place for the mysterious Mahogany ship. Ask the locals about this one over a glass of amber fluid, but beware — the tails get taller with the amount of beer consumed.

Detouring off the main highway towards Koroit gives an immediate easing in traffic. This is Irish country. Rich brown earth attracted the Irish to this district in the 1800s and they have lost none of their sense of the blarney. Nearby Killarney Beach is regarded as the most beautiful in the world by the locals. If you can afford the time for a weekend in Koroit, be sure to spend it at the Micky Rourke's Koroit Hotel — and be doubly sure to book the fourposter bed. Leeroy the hotel dog has a particular trick of showing patrons to the loo, not a bad idea if you are wandering the upstairs hall at night and suddenly come across the eerie sight of an old dressmaker's model.

TOUR 6: The last hundred metres of the climb up to Cape Paton, Victoria

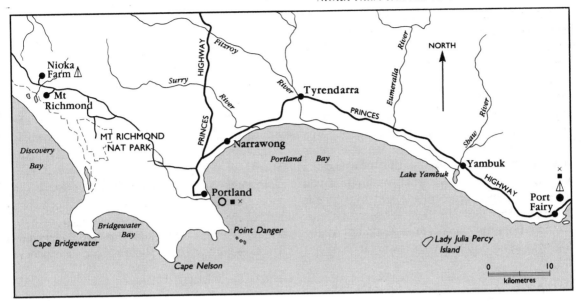

ROUTE SLIP

Directions	R/S km	Ride for	Destination	Cum route km
END OF SECTION 2			**TOTAL FOR ROUTE**	**204.8**
Port Fairy	102.6		information centre	204.8
R	102	0.6	town centre	204.2
Yambuk	83	19		185.2
Tyrendarra	55	28		157.2
Narrawong	46	9		148.2
R *-Keller's Bch Rd	38.8	7.2		141
R *-scenic lookout	36.7	2.1		138.9
R	35	1.7	Warrnambool	137.2
L-divided road	34.3	0.7		136.5
L-West Lakes Rd	30.9	3.4	Warrnambool	133.1
BR *	30.9		Portland 10 km	133.1
R *	18.3	12.6	Mt Richmond NP	120.5
R *-soft sand track	5	13.3	Swan Lake	107.2
Nioka Farm Hostel	0.0	5		102.2
BEGIN SECTION 2				

On ride line, each segment = 1 kilometre

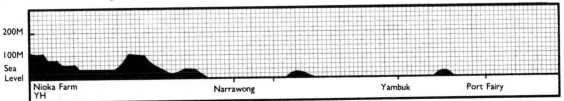

On the way back to the Princess Highway, Tour 6 skirts Tower Hill Reserve, which is the location of a fascinating restoration project begun in 1961. The landscape is being revegetated, using as a blueprint a precise painting by Eugene von Guerard showing Tower Hill as it was before being denuded by rabbits and clearing. To ride in means you must back-track to find the one-way entrance road, then follow a wild, wheel-spinning descent into the bowels of this now extinct volcano. Emus will share lunch with you if you are not diligent in protecting it, and grey fantails belie their tiny size with their ear-piercing calls. Getting from the picnic area back up to the highway again will test your low gears.

Warrnambool

Arrive in Warrnambool (pop^n 22 900) early enough in the afternoon to stroll to the adjacent **surfing beach** on Warrnambool Bay and catch a wave or three. It's a great salty end to a day's cycling. While in Warrnambool drop into the information centre to discover the city's many attractions. Be sure to visit **Flagstaff Hill Maritime Village**, an historic recreation of Port Warrnambool. One of the exhibitions details the most famous wreck on the coast, the Loch Ard, a three-masted clipper which foundered in 1878, losing 52 lives. Miraculously two teenagers survived, as did a priceless Minton porcelain peacock.

DAY 6: Warrnambool to Macka's Farm

Distance ridden: 89.2 km;   Riding time: 4 hrs 9 mins;   Average speed: 21.4 kmph;   Maximum speed: 52 kmph

If you can manage a dawn start on only one day on this tour, let it be when you leave Warrnambool. The first section prior to reaching the Great Ocean Road may seem a little wandery but it eliminates virtually all traffic. Once on the Great Ocean Road there are more than enough distractions to counteract the traffic — though there are few trucks. Childers Cove is the first of what will become a bewildering array of caves and grottos, gorges and beaches, each one astounding and quite different from the others.

With 142 recorded wrecks between Barwon Heads and Cape Otway (1836 to 1958) it is little wonder this is called the shipwreck coastline. Going 'on the hard' featured heavily in the nightmares of sailing boat captains of the last century. Many of them lived and died their worst nightmares as the lumbering ships were driven ashore by relentless gales and pounding seas of the great Southern Ocean. Evidence of the Ocean's all encompassing violence are the sentinel-like pillars of soft limestone out in the water, eroded mementos of the shore cliffs.

Port Campbell National Park

Port Campbell National Park (1750 hectares) is a long thin stretch of coastline which takes in virtually all the public land between Peterborough and Princetown. The large camping area is located near the beach in Port Campbell township. Dotted along the shore of the national park are the Bay of Islands, The Grotto, The 'New' (meaning collapsed) London Bridge, Loch Ard Gorge and the most famous, the Twelve Apostles (only eight are visible). If you visited Flagstaff Hill in Warrnambool, actually seeing Loch Ard Gorge makes the story of the pottery peacock's survival even more astounding. Another miraculous survivor from the region's early history is the southern right whale. Hunted almost to extinction, they are now returning to calve from June to October and they can often be seen along the coast.

Turning off the Great Ocean Road up to Macka's Farm means leaving the tourist coaches behind for the mellow mooing of dairy cows and sundry noises of an Old Macdonald's variety of farmyard animals. Carey and Denise Mackieson, who are the friendly hosts at Macka's, will also run you back down to the beach near the Twelve Apostles to see fairy penguins coming ashore just on dark.

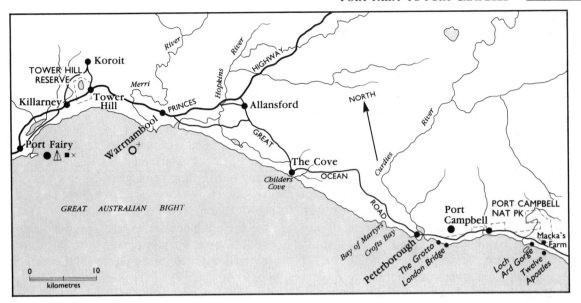

ROUTE SLIP

Directions	R/S km	Ride for	Destination	Cum route km
S-(dirt road)	54.1	1.4		258.9
R-Burkes Rd	51.8	2.3	Lake Gillear	256.6
L	44.6	7.2	Allansford	249.4
R-Hopkins Rd	44.1	0.5		248.9
R-Flaxman St	43.3	0.8	Logans Beach	248.1
R-Nicholson St	43.1	0.2		247.9
L-Merri St (roundabout)	40.9	2.2		245.7
R-Liebig St **Warrnambool**	40	0.9		244.8
L-Hwy One	27.3	12.7	Warrnambool	232.1
R-at hill top	26.9	0.4		231.7
L*-info centre	25	1.9	picnic area	229.8
R-one-way road	23.4	1.6	Tower Hill Reserve	228.2
R-Hwy One	22.8	0.6	Port Fairy	227.6
L-Lake View Rd	20.4	2.4		225.2
R	18.4	2	Tower Hill	223.2
Koroit	18	.4		222.8
R	13.1	4.9		217.9
BL	10.1	3	Koroit	214.9
R-Hwy One	6.8	3.3		211.6
L*-Woodbine	5.4	1.4	National Trust house	210.2
R*-beach access	4.3	1.1	Belfast Coast Reserve	209.1
L-East Beach	.3	4	X bridge	205.1
Port Fairy	0.0	.3	from info centre	204.8
BEGIN SECTION 3				

Directions	R/S km	Ride for	Destination	Cum route km
END OF SECTION 3			**TOTAL FOR ROUTE**	**314.5**
Port Campbell	109.7			314.5
R	108.5	1.2		313.3
R*-Two Mile Bay	106	2.5	Port Campbell	310.8
R*-The Arch	104	2		308.8
R*-London Bridge	102	2		306.8
R*-The Grotto	100	2		304.8
R	96.8	3.2		301.6
L-Irvine St	96.6	0.2		301.4
Peterborough	96.4	0.2		301.2
R	95.8	0.6	town centre	300.6
R*-Bay of Martyrs	94.3	1.5		299.1
R*-Crofts Bay	91.2	3.1		296
R*-Bay of Islands	90.7	0.5		295.5
R	88.2	2.5	Bay of Islands	293
BR-Delaneys Cnr	80.3	7.9		285.1
S-Great Ocean Rd	75.4	4.9		280.2
R	71.6	3.8		276.4
R	69.4	2.2	Peterborough	274.2
BR*-Childers Cove	67.8	1.6		272.6
R-Childers Rd	61.3	6.5	Childers Cove	266.1
R-Great Ocean Rd (tar)	57.8	3.5	Port Campbell	262.6
R	56.2	1.6		261
R-Richies Rd	55.5	0.7		260.3

On ride line, each segment = 1 kilometre

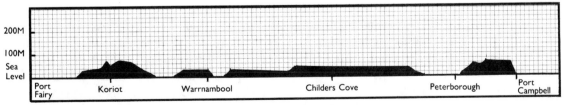

DAY 7: Macka's Farm to Laver's Hill

Distance ridden: 39.3 km;   Riding time: 2 hrs 40 mins;   Average speed: 14.7 kmph;   Maximum speed: 65 kmph

Keen readers of the day logs will notice the one above has a good maximum speed but a very low average speed. This is a bad omen for cycle tourers who dislike long severe hills. In fact, I clocked the 65 kmph in the first 4 km, but by Princetown I was averaging 22.7 km per hour. From then on the average slid backwards. Achieving the ascent of Laver's Hill and the hills before it, is the reason for a diving average. Out of a total riding time of two hours 40 minutes, most of that was spent in the lowest gear climbing, ever climbing.

To break the slog there are continually improving views (particularly across to Cape Otway) and a fantastic flying descent to the Gellibrand River but beyond it comes the real crunch. Down into the lowest gear and grind, over and over again. The super steep bits encouraged me off the saddle to stand on the pedals (see Riding Technique in Touring chapter section for tips) just to give a new set of muscles a bit of a run in. It may seem strange but, though the day was hazy, when I was climbing Laver's Hill from every scenic lookout there was a possible photo opportunity. It is nice to justify a breather stop.

Laver's Hill and District

A few kilometres short of Laver's Hill township (top of the climb) is the turn off to **Melba Gully State Park**. An annual rainfall of more than 2 m means outstanding plant growth, especially of myrtle beech, blackwood and tree ferns. This little oasis of rainforest (48 hectares) is worth two visits. Obtain a self-guide leaflet and cover **Masdens Track Nature Walk** in the daylight, but as you are strolling, try to paint a picture of the track in your mind. Go up to Laver's Hill, organise your accommodation or campsite, have dinner, then unladen, come back at night. Once walking, use your torch only to light the way to the start of the track, then let moonlight and your night vision guide you. The bushland will become filled with twinkling jewels; glow worms. They are actually the larvae of a small fly which creates sticky glowing threads to capture tiny insects, but the effect is magical.

DAY 8: Laver's Hill to Anglesea

Distance ridden: 123 km;   Riding time: 5 hrs 43 mins;   Average speed: 21.3 kmph;   Maximum speed: 79 kmph

There are few more wonderful ways to begin a day's cycle touring than coasting down a big hill. Leaving Laver's Hill you are bound for a crisp air descent on a road where the only noise is newly fallen leaves crackling under your tyres. Strong early cross light on surrounding hills makes them grow in stature and the sheep's purest white fleece seems etched onto green pastures. Though initially the hills seem a little reticent to give way, the height gained on the way up Lavers Hill towards Glenorie really lets go with complete abandon. The last sweeping left-hand bend to the valley floor is a full test of one's nerve and faith in the staying power of your tyres.

From here to Horden Vale turnoff the road skirts a flat valley devoid of trees but full of grazing cattle — you might even surprise a fox gambolling home from a night of mischief. Don't drift off to sleep with the peacefulness of it all — at the entrance to Otway National Park this road goes from flat to semi-vertical. You are climbing 200 of the toughest metres on the whole tour. I was certainly not unhappy to make it to the top.

The actual summit is deceptive. I decided I had found it prematurely, at least three times, only to skirt round the next bend and see the road soaring upwards again. Though not marked on the road, you are actually conquering a place the map

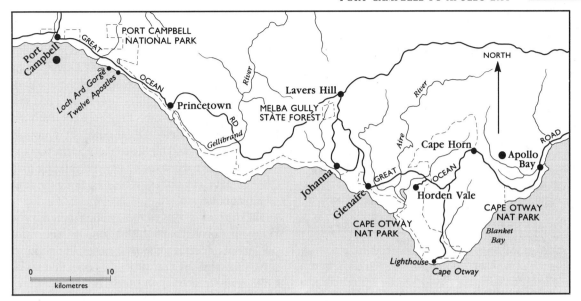

ROUTE SLIP

Directions	R/S km	Ride for	Destination	Cum route km
END OF SECTION 4			**TOTAL FOR ROUTE**	**412.8**
Apollo Bay	98.3			412.8
L*-Beech Forest	84.9	13.4		399.4
R*-Cape Otway	77.6	7.3		392.1
R*-Horden Vale	74.3	3.3		488.8
R*-Red Johanna Rd	59.5	14.8		374
R*-Blue Johanna Rd	53.6	5.9		368.1
R	50.2	3.4	Apollo Bay	364.7
Lavers Hill	49.5	0.7		364
R*-Melba Gully	47.4	2.1		361.9
R*-scenic lookout	36.6	10.8		351.1
R*-Princetown	18.2	18.4	Lavers Hill	332.7
L*-Macka's Farm	14.1	4.1	4 km to farm	328.6
R*-Twelve Apostles	11.9	2.2		326.4
R*-Loch Ard Gorge	8.2	3.7		322.7
Port Campbell	0.0	8.2		314.5
BEGIN SECTION 4				

On ride line, each segment = 1 kilometre

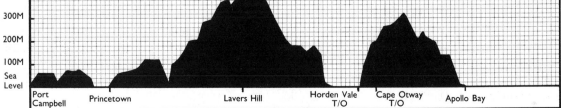

calls Cape Horn. On reaching the down side you will probably feel an enlivened kick equalling the lift the mariners of old must have felt on successfully rounding that other Cape Horn.

Detours: Johanna, Aire River, Cape Otway and Blanket Bay

If you are camping and don't mind a few extra climbs, there are three excellent places to explore between Lavers Hill and Apollo Bay. About 4 km from Lavers Hill, take Johanna Blue Road to Johanna camping area, then come back up on the Red Road. At Horden Vale take the right turn to Aire River Camping area, coming back up the same road. Just prior to the summit of the climb up from Horden Vale, take Lighthouse Rd down to Cape Otway Lighthouse (open Tuesdays to Thursdays). There is a very rough (and at times very muddy) track down to the Blanket Bay camping area on the eastern side of Otway National Park.

On the Great Ocean Road, beyond Cape Horn, is a superior downhill where you freewheel out of the mountains and into the sea — from the sweet elixir of eucalyptus to the heady aroma of the ocean. Once you inhale a blast of that ozone rich air you'll be riding into Apollo Bay on a natural high. Apollo Bay (pop^n 920) is a little fishing and tourist town which certainly has a high opinion of itself, judging from the sign on entering the town, but this is well justified. The location is quite beautiful and you are now beginning a section of cycle touring along one of the most spectacular roads in Australia. Though you have been travelling the Great Ocean Road since Warrnambool, it doesn't really cling to the cliffs until you reach Apollo Bay and ride it through to Lorne. Completed in 1932, the Great Ocean Road was built over six long hard years by returned

soldiers as a works project during the Great Depression and it remains today as an engineering achievement.

On the run from Apollo Bay to Lorne, to be given a tailwind you would really feel that the gods of cycle touring were smiling upon you. I had that smug belief. Even climbing up to Cape Paton, a tough little hill, felt exhilarating. It is doubly exhilarating to stand on the lookout at the top and gaze back down the coast to see this amazing road that you have just ridden, wriggling along the edge of a turquoise sea.

The memory of this view is enough to pump you along to Lorne (pop^n 1000), one of the most popular playcentres for Melbournites. For popular, read 'crowded'. If you strike this on a Sunday as I did, then your bike will feel the slip-stream of the would-be Formula-one motorbike riders trying out their skills on the continuous sets of S-bends.

Angahook-Lorne State Park Detour

Rising up from the sea between Kennet River and Aireys Inlet, this 22 500 hectare park takes in some fine Victorian coastal and timbered hill country. Walking tracks abound through the spectacular bush. Some work their way beside, in and out of the creeks and rivers, amidst tree ferns and past beautiful waterfalls. Some of the tracks follow the old timber-getting tramways with easy gradients, while others zigzag up and down hillsides.

Between Lorne and Anglesea the traffic really increases, but there is one memorable hill with a mineshaft descent where you are more than likely to be much faster than the impatient Sunday drivers. After riding over 120 km on this day I was pleased to slip into a motel pool at Anglesea (pop^n 1500).

DAY 9: Anglesea to Melbourne

Distance ridden: 42.1 km;	Riding time: 2 hrs	Average speed: 21 kmph;	Maximum speed: 48 kmph

After the ride from Laver's Hill to Anglesea the last 42 km of the route is an anti-climax, though a worthwhile detour is to ride via Bells Beach, the location for an international surfing competition each year. Torquay (pop^n 5000) is pleasant, but the coastline has lost its wild character, subdued

and dampened by the brooding presence of a large city through the haze. Geelong (pop^n 150 000) is a major city in its own right, but thankfully the train station is easy to find and there are frequent trains to Melbourne — they arrive at Spencer Street Station.

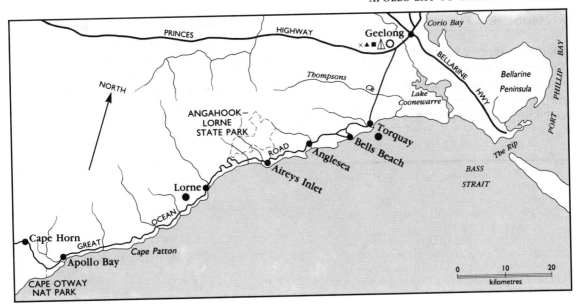

ROUTE SLIP

Directions	R/S km	Ride for	Destination	Cum route km
END OF TOUR			**TOTAL FOR ROUTE**	**529.4**
Geelong PO	116.6			529.4
R-traffic lights	116.2	.4		529
R-traffic lights	111.8	4.4		524.6
R-Geelong Rd	95.8	16	Geelong	508.6
L	94.8	1		507.6
L-The Esplande	93	1.8		505.8
R-Torquay	92.4	0.6	surfing beach	505.2
R	87.4	5	Torquay	500.2
S*	87.4		Geelong 26 km	500.2
R*-Bell's Beach	83.5	3.9		496.3
Anglesea	75.1	8.4		487.9
Lorne	45.2	29.9		458
R*-Cape Patton lookout	17.9	27.3		430.7
Apollo Bay	0.0	17.9		412.8
BEGIN SECTION 5				

On ride line, each segment = 1 kilometre

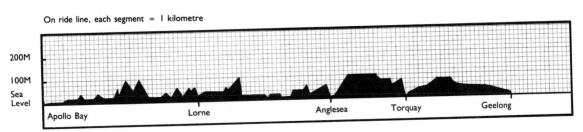

131

Melbourne

Melbourne (pop^n 2 900 000) is the capital city of Victoria. There are more than 750 km of **bicycle paths** in the Melbourne area, including those along the Yarra River, Yarra Bend Park, Albert Park Lake and edges of Port Phillip Bay — see *Melbourne Bikeways Book* and Melbourne Bikeplan route maps (contact Bicycle Victoria, 31 Somerset Place, Melbourne for details). If you are planning to ride Tour 8 in Western Tasmania and are flying to Devonport, you can get a bus from Geelong direct to Melbourne Airport.

TOUR 7
THE WEST COAST OF TASMANIA

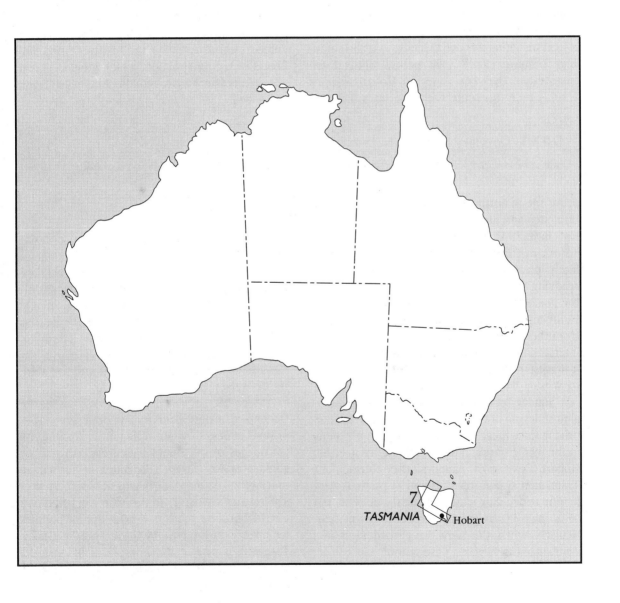

7

TASMANIA · Hobart

7 THE WEST COAST OF TASMANIA

Tasmania is Australia's most mountainous state — a fact you will become intimately familiar with on this 540 km hill-lovers' tour. The big hills, little hills and inbetween roller-coasters are all included. Beginning at sea level in Devonport in the state's far north, you ascend to an altitude of 860 m in Cradle Mountain country, slide down to the Southern Ocean at Strahan via the historic mining village of Zeehan, then climb again to more than 830 m travelling through Queenstown and stunningly beautiful Lake St Clair, before rolling down picturesque Derwent Valley to Hobart and sea level. I rode this route with two friends during December, taking 13 days (including three rest days) averaging 58 km per day. Tasmania's low density motor traffic, closely spaced villages and friendly people make it a pleasant destination for cycle touring. Although the weather is very fickle, to the extent that even during the best cycle touring months of late November to February it can turn wintery, the changing moods of the countryside which accompany a change in weather are a bonus. I chose to enjoy the luxury of Bed and Breakfast accommodation, which I find is a great way to meet the locals, but you can also camp and use hostels.

DAY 1: Devonport Airport to Latrobe

Distance ridden: 12.8 km;	Riding time: 43 mins;	Average speed: 17.8 kmph;	Maximum speed: 48 kmph

From the mainland to Tasmania seems a quick hop, step and jump, either by air or on the new fast Bass Strait ferries. If you have flown to Tasmania, Devonport airport is probably the most likely place to encounter other cycle tourers readying their bikes (and expressing wonder that the machines are still straight and in one piece). In the mystical ways of Tasmanians, to exit right from the terminal you go left, then at the first T intersection there is the silliest sign. At first glance it suggests both left and right is road number C701 to Wesley Vale — but you turn left.

A Sunday on a road coded 'C' in Tasmania is almost devoid of traffic. This shouldn't be too surprising since there are only 450 000 people living in the whole state and most of them live in either Hobart, Devonport, Launceston or Burnie. The Tasmanian system of A, B and C roads is very helpful in deciding which will be the quietest, but of no help in navigating to specific towns, particularly when the signs have road class and number but divulge no destination!

Devonport

In 1823, the Devonport (pop 25 000) region was described as 'extremely barren and totally unfit for habitation'. That may have been harsh, and certainly today the town has many friendly people and a good range of shopping facilities. Sited at the mouth of the Mersey River, it is the landing point for water-based transport across Bass Strait. Visit the **Maritime Museum** and Tiagarra, the **Tasmanian Aboriginal Cultural and Art Centre** at Mersey Bluff.

Devonport airport seems to have been scraped out of sand dunes, so when riding away from it you get images of old dunes backdropped by a last glimpse of Bass Strait. Like much of Tasmanian touring, the countryside begins very swiftly after leaving any township. In this case you roll down a road bordered with colourful opium poppies which are farmed to be processed at Glaxo. Tasmania is one of the few places in Australia where opiates are grown legally and even on a grey day they are a startling sight.

ROUTE SLIP

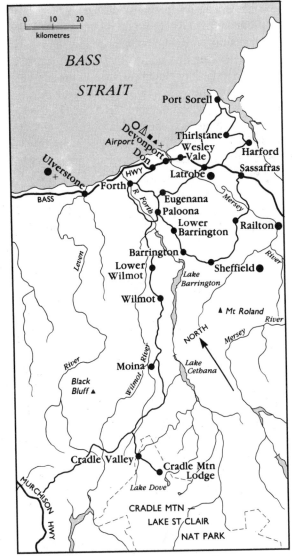

Directions	R/S km	Ride for	Destination	Cum route km
END OF SECTION 1			**TOTAL FOR ROUTE**	125.2
Murchison Hwy jnct	125.2			125.2
L-A10	125.2		Tullah	125.2
R*-Black Bluff lookout	107.9	17.3		107.9
L-C132	99.3	8.6	Waratah	99.3
exit Cradle Min	94	5.3		94
Cradle Mtn Lodge	94			94
R*	91.8	2.2	campsites	91.8
L	88.7	3.1	Cradle Mtn	88.7
L*-Post Office tree	78.3	10.4		78.3
Moina	67.5	10.8		67.5
BR	57.2	10.3		57.2
Wilmot	53.0	4.2	Cradle Mtn	53
L*-scenic lookout	48.6	4.4	Mt Roland	48.6
L*-Alma Reserve	35.4	13.2	picnic area	35.4
L-C132	33.1	2.3	Wilmot/Cradle Mtn	33.1
S-C144	32.6	0.5	X bridge	32.6
S	29.8	2.8		29.8
R-C147	27.1	2.7		27.1
Melrose	26.9	0.2	Wilmot	26.9
L-C145	26.0	0.9	Melrose	26
Eugenana	24.2	1.8		24.2
BR-C146	21.7	2.5		21.7
R-C146	20.3	1.4	Eugenana	20.3
BL-B14	20.2	0.1	Sheffield	20.2
L-C146	16.8	3.4	Eugenana	16.8
BR	15	1.8	Burnie	15
Latrobe	13	2		13
R-B19	13		Spreyton	13
S-(at roundabout)	12	1		12
R-C702	9.6	2.4		9.6
S-C701	7.3	2.3		7.3
R-C701	5.2	2.1	Latrobe	5.2
L-B74	5.1	0.1	Pt Sorrell	5.1
L-C701	0.6	4.5	Wesley Vale	4.5
Devonport Airport	0.0	0.6	exit	0.6
BEGIN SECTION 1				

On ride line, each segment = 1 kilometre

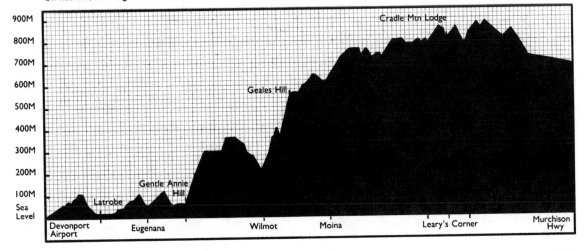

135

With expansive gardens and an air of old-fashioned charm, Lucinda Guest House in Latrobe has a comfortable, welcoming quality. For us it made a relaxing first night. On a Sunday, Latrobe is worth a stroll to find a treasure in the market, or lose your heart in the Mistletoe Gallery to a teddy bear in a top hat and tartan scarf riding a penny farthing. Latrobe is also home to George and David Forster, World Sawing Champions — recognising their home with its sign posts of cross-cut saws and axes is a breeze.

Lucinda Guest House is run by Michael Wilson, a successful professional bicycle rider rated in the world's top 70. He suggested the following detours:

The Hills and Dales Circuit

This is a challenging 85-90 km tour from Latrobe to Devonport, then B19 to Don and Forth, C132 to Lower Barrington (via Paloona), Barrington, then C143 to Sheffield, Railton, Mersey, then C153 to Sassafras and back to Latrobe. Be sure to see the **Sheffield murals** depicting the history of the area and **Lake Barrington**, setting of the 1990 World Rowing Championships.

Sun and Sand Circuit

This is an easy 55-60 km tour from Latrobe to Thurlstone, Exeter Highway to Squeezy Point, Port Sorrell, Hawley Beach (vineyard), Harford and back to Latrobe.

DAY 2: Latrobe to Wilmot

Distance ridden: 40.3 km; Riding time: 2 hrs 39 mins; Average speed: 15.2 kmph; Maximum speed: 67 kmph; Vertical metres climbed: 420

Once away from Latrobe and the main road, you are on a quiet tree-lined avenue where goats are tethered outside small acreages near their own little A-frame houses for the chilly nights. Green country pastures, miniature valleys and clusters of dwellings ensure even the steep climbs are fun. We had morning tea on the top of the hill before Eugenana (pronounced you-g-nana) looking down into a valley where the juxtaposition of native forests and cultivated pastures creates what seems like a dozen hues of green. Eugenana has a unique park of native and exotic species — The Tasmanian Arboretum.

After crossing a rippling, black, swirling mass called the Forth River, you begin to slowly work your way up the valley, beside the river. There's a lovely picnic site at Alma Reserve, but we ignored it, since it is sited before the first real climb of the tour — a sweet rise called Gentle Annie. It climbs through a dense cover of timber where golden leaves scattered across black tar crunch beneath the tread of your tyres. The Australian who named this hill did it with typical dry humour, for there is little gentleness about it. On a warm day this is a sweat-maker, 7 kmph of pumping the pedals where it's essential that you keep as far on the outside of the steeply-banked curves as safety will allow. Staying tall in the saddle to allow maximum oxygen intake and staying calm, also helps in a successful ascent of Gentle Annie. We lunched with relief on the penultimate peak.

Well-fuelled with carbohydrates you can easily tackle the last 80 m vertical rise, even if it is that dreaded first hill after lunch. The top brings you face to face with a strikingly rugged peak, Mt Roland. It's hard to know where to pause to get the best view, though the official scenic lookout is as good as any. Roland and its companions seem to fade off into infinity and are the first of many 'real', head-in-the-clouds mountains that you will encounter on this tour. It also marks the first of the big downhills, in this case Chinaman's Bends. Be sure to check for oncoming traffic before taking a fast line through the suggested 35 kmph corners.

Wilmot

We rolled into a comfortable night in Wilmot's Antill Apartments, just on the edge of town. They are attached to Antill Antiques and craft shop. One perfect purchase here is a little sachet of boronia bath salts to ease the aches and pains. Wilmot, which is actually lower in altitude than Lower

Wilmot, is an unpretentious town. It's only claim to fame is that the now Australia-wide major food chain Coles–New World began here with the Wilmot GJ Coles general store.

DAY 3: Wilmot to Cradle Mountain Lodge

Distance ridden: 41 km;   Riding time: 3 hrs;   Average speed: 13.3 kmph;   Maximum speed: 64 kmph; Vertical metres climbed: 900

If you are after supplies, the general store in Wilmot opens on the dot of 7.30 a.m., give or take 45 minutes. Beyond Wilmot, the day's hill climbing however is guaranteed to begin after a leisurely 20 m of flat running. This is a 3 km primer to get your legs, heart and lungs working. You don't want to be cold for Geales Hill (pronounced *gales*). Geales is one of those fortunate, or unfortunate, hills where from the bottom you can see just how far it is to the top. Not a positive psychological factor to help you up the climb. There's no pretence about Geales being gentle, this is a heart-stopper of a hill. For my companions, this was the first Tasmanian hill which forced them to walk the last few hundred metres.

Doleful, big-eyed cattle don't seem to appreciate just what a wonderful part of Tasmania they inhabit. To a cycle tourer, the surrounding peaks give the illusion of travelling in a rare, heady place if not on top of, certainly near, the crest of the world. Occasional glimpses of sharp summits breaking through the cloud cover enhance this feeling of being on a higher plane.

Moina

At Moina, where the Sheffield road joins C132, take time out to visit the Cheyne Purdue Gallery. Aside from the original art which the proprietors may package and post for overladen cycle tourers and the reviving Gold Mine teahouse, take a look at the **Cradle Country Experience Audio-Visual** (small charge), just in case the mountain is hiding behind an Antarctic-like blizzard when you arrive. Moina was where Boags beer (a popular Tasmanian ale) was first brewed.

Riding between Moina and Cradle Mountain can be like moving through a world of mists and soft greens. But when cycling through sharp road cuttings, the intensity of bright red mosses can make it seem as if the rocks have caught fire. Ascending to near 800 m altitude, vegetation takes on a hardy sub-alpine quality and extravagant displays of white blossoms create the illusion of summer snow.

Sadly, the landscape then changes to sub-wasteland of wantonly killed trees. Vandals were a race of people which invaded Western Europe in the 4th and 5th centuries, and perhaps their ancestors came to the edge of Cradle Mountain country to carry on the practice. Thankfully, there was foresight from some of the area's other inhabitants, otherwise the jewel which is Cradle Mountain — Lake St Clair National Park might have been smashed to dust. Rolling into a self-contained cabin at Cradle Mountain Lodge topped off a great day's high country cycling.

DAY 4: Rest

Cradle Mountain - Lake St Clair National Park

This area (161 000 hectares) is part of Tasmania's World Heritage Area and its existence is owed to an Austrian, Gustav Weindorfer. In 1909 he climbed Cradle Mountain, then spent the remainder of his life working towards a dream which he first expressed on the summit of the mountain: 'This must be a national park for the people for all time. It is magnificent, and people must know about it and enjoy it.'

137

At the Cradle Valley end of the park today, cycle tourers have an excellent choice of **accommodation**: from the campground and bunkhouse, to Cradle Mountain Lodge (all outside the park) and Waldheim Huts (inside the park). There are also overnight huts within a day's walk of Dove Lake. **Day walks** in the Park are a real joy, taking you to ascend Cradle Mountain and to within toe-dabbling reach of alpine tarns. Some of the tarns are fringed with dwarfed ancient alpine pine trees and others feature clusters of pandani, a strange spiky, curly-leafed Tasmanian plant which is the world's tallest heath. Be warned, however, even on day walks take good wet weather gear and warm clothing, as the weather can dramatically change for the worse.

If you have the time and inclination for a long-distance walk, tackle the **Overland Track**. It is an 80 km mountain path winding a north–south route through dense rainforests and glacial valleys, skirting alpine tarns, whilst all the time in the company of wilderness peaks. Fit backpackers can load up with equipment and supplies for up to 10 days and slog through, rewarded by the solitude and beauty of the forests and surrounding sentinel peaks. If your bike load doesn't allow you the joy of carrying trekking gear, or you just want an unladen amble to remind your backside what it is like not to be moulded to your bike saddle, take an easier alternative by joining a **commercial trip** through the area. Equipment is generally supplied as part of the package or can be hired. Experienced guides carry most of the heavy items. Bushwalker transport buses can take you back to your starting point in Cradle Mountain. See the **NPWS information centre** for further information.

DAY 5: Cradle Mountain Lodge to Rosebery

Distance ridden: 71 km;   Riding time: 3 hrs 53 mins;   Average speed: 18 kmph;   Maximum speed: 72 kmph; Vertical metres climbed: 640

The benefit of a grey misty morning at Cradle Mountain Lodge is that you just might see a wombat waddle past on its way home to the burrow from a night of foraging. Wombats are probably much quieter now than they were in the 1800s when they were on the menu of European explorers.

If the clouds have descended as you leave Cradle Valley, you will be riding in a strange, slightly eerie world where the trees are black irregular shapes which seem to loom out of nowhere. Being in the Tasmania highlands, as like as not, 10 minutes after you have decided grey is the colour of the day, a blast of sunlight hurtles down through a breach in the fog.

This image is appropriate since this is a day of hurtling down hills (and climbing too). As you will notice in the day log, this was the first day I cracked more than 70 kmph — on a broad sweep of newly made road just after struggling up a dead straight pull to Black Bluff. While the road across to the Murchison Highway is an excellent engineering achievement, it is a shame more effort has not gone into rehabilitation of the verges. The Tasmanian Department of Roads and Transport should consider implementing schemes such as the roadside rehabilitation program which has been in operation in Western Australia's south-west for some time.

Even after you turn onto the A-class highway towards Tullah, fast car and heavy truck traffic is light by mainland standards. There are a few frustrating ups and downs before a bullet-pockmarked sign announces the highest point on the Murchison Highway. What follows is 20 km of wind-in-the-hair freewheeling.

Tullah

Tullah is a dot on the map. For cyclists, the dot is enlarged by the presence of The Bush Nook. Ostensibly tea rooms, this nook is in fact an under-cover haven for cycle tourers; especially those tired, cold, wet and emotional souls who have had the misfortune to be struck down by a case of West Coast Woeful Weather Blues. Ones like the Belgian around-the-world tourer who wrote in the visitors book '... I have never cycled in such dreadful weather ... strong winds, a lot of rain ... hail (and) a thunderstorm'. Owner Veronika Smith

ROUTE SLIP

Directions	R/S km	Ride for	Destination	Cum route km
END OF SECTION 2			**TOTAL FOR ROUTE**	**236.2**
Strahan	111			236.2
R*-Henty Dunes	96.9	14.1		222.1
BL-B27	67	29.9	Strahan	192.2
BR*-Zeehan	67		1.6 km to Zeehan	192.2
R-B27	62.3	4.7	Zeehan	187.5
Rosebery	38.9	23.4		164.1
Tullah	23.9	15.0	Rosebery	149.1
highest point	6	17.9		131.2
Murchison Hwy jnct	0.0	6	Tullah	125.2
BEGIN SECTION 2				

KEY

L = left **R** = right **S** = straight
BL = bear left **BR** = bear right
X = cross ***** = detour directions

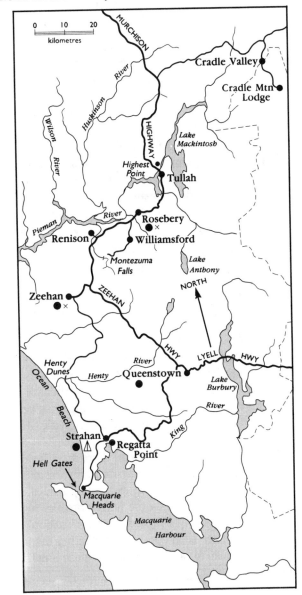

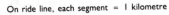
On ride line, each segment = 1 kilometre

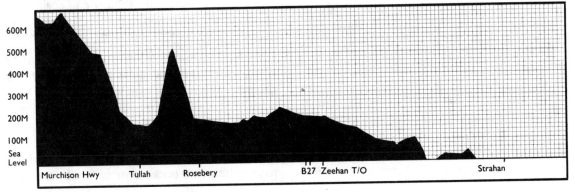

reports that tourers have also been known to pull in to quell the hunger pangs, then proceed to eat their way through the entire menu.

Between Tullah and Rosebery is a blip — a 360 m blip. The highway seems to run straight at a tall haughty mountain, before spinning off to writhe upwards for four long hard kilometres. It is a climb punctuated with roadside waterfalls (gratefully enjoyed on a stinking hot day) and culminating with a deceptive apex. You are into the descent before you realise the long-awaited crest has come and gone. Bulleting into Rosebery is adrenalin-powered joy.

Rosebery

The mining township of Rosebery (popⁿ 2700) has one special feature for cycle tourers, the Mess House — a place where you can get a well cooked, inexpensive four-course meal, then come back for 2nds and 3rds! Ask a local for directions and meal times. Rosebery is part of the 'wild' west, so don't be too surprised if you see guns 'n 'ammo available at the supermarket. Rock drilling — by hand — is a local sport.

DAY 6: Rosebery to Strahan

Distance ridden: 75.2 km; Riding time: 3 hrs 42 mins; Average speed: 20.2 kmph; Maximum speed: 71 kmph; Vertical metres climbed: 120

Staying in Australian pubs, you always seem to have a hundred stairs to carry your bike down in the morning. The Plandome Hotel at Rosebery is no exception. Typical of West Coast weather we were greeted by a gale warning, but since it was sliding in over the rear panniers we made it welcome.

Between Rosebery and Zeehan there are a few doozy little downhill dashes into densely forested gulleys, followed inevitably by exhausting uphills, few of which show up on the height profile. In drawing the profiles for this book I was occasionally forced to use 40 m contour maps rather than the standard 20 m, and they can disguise small hills.

Montezuma Falls Detour

This 11 km (return) ride/walk detour begins at Williamsford, south of Rosebery and takes you through a rainforest canopy of leatherwood, myrtle and sassafras trees to one of the **tallest falls** in Tasmania. This is the site of an old tramway, constructed last century.

The luxuriant regrowth forests beside the Murchison Highway tend to hide the mining activity, but your nose knows. Renison Tin Mine is however out on display in all its grey and noisy magnificence. If you can look beyond the mine,

there are rings of peaks and high places softly muted by blue gum tree haze. This is such a beautiful landscape, it is sad to see unrehabilitated mine dumps and an incredible number of bottles and cans littering the road verges.

Zeehan

If the West Coast Pioneers' Memorial Mining **Museum** at Zeehan (popⁿ 2000) is any guide, the landscape was really hammered in the early days of west-coast mining. Take special note of Mt Lyell smelters (Queenstown) shown in 1899 with 11 furnaces at full blast. This free museum is excellent, particularly Renison Ltd's Mihajlowits mineral collection. Zeehan was named after one of Abel Tasman's ships — he discovered Tasmania in 1642. During the summer Gallery Z in Zeehan has an annual art exhibition — paintings are for sale.

Between Zeehan and Strahan you are riding a road of smooth curves and slight gradients — it was originally the route of a mine railway. On a fine, warm day this section is quite pretty, particularly strolling across the Henty Dunes to dabble a toe in the Great Southern Ocean. Keep a look out for pumice, the porous, floating rock which made its passage across the ocean from the South Sandwich

TOUR 7: Heading towards
Mt Roland on the road to
Cradle Mountain, Tasmania

TOUR 7: Legacy of the Mt Lyell copper mine at Queenstown, Tasmania

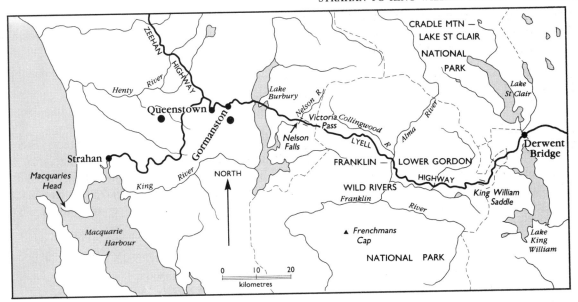

ROUTE SLIP

Directions	R/S km	Ride for	Destination	Cum route km
END OF SECTION 3			**TOTAL FOR ROUTE**	**342.8**
King William Saddle	106.6			342.8
R*-scenic lookout	104.1	2.5		340.3
Franklin River	96.8	7.3		333
R*-Donaghy's Hill	87.3	9.5	40-minute return walk	323.5
Collingwood River	83.4	3.9		319.6
Victoria Pass	67.2	16.2		303.4
L*-Nelson Falls	63.1	4.1	20-minute return walk	299.3
R*-King River	53	10.1	picnic area	289.2
Queenstown	40.9	12.1	Derwent Bge/Hobart	277.1
BR-A10	37.5	3.4		273.7
BR	0.2	37.3		236.4
Exit **Strahan**-B24	0.0	.2	Queenstown	236.2
BEGIN SECTION 3				

On ride line, each segment = 1 kilometre

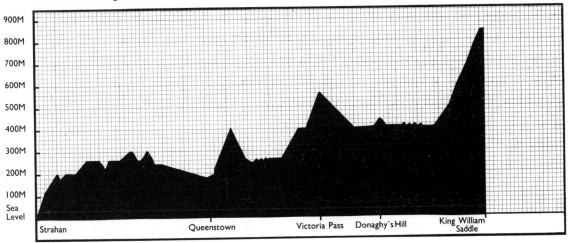

143

Islands after a volcanic eruption in 1962. To us, the surrounds were grey and wet since we rode it in a classic west-coast downpour: a roaring deluge which cuts into your face like hail. A half-hour soaking in bath salts at the Strahan Inn erased the worst of the memories.

DAY 7: Rest

Strahan

Strahan (pop^n 400) is the access point for **Gordon River cruises**. The cruise boats generally travel up Bathurst Harbour, into the Gordon River, stop at Heritage Landing and return via Hell's Gates (the narrow harbour entrance). There is also a **seaplane flight** into the same area. A couple of interesting 30 + km **detours** (mostly dirt roads) are to cycle to Macquarie Heads via Ocean Beach, or to King River and the old ABT railway via Regatta Point.

DAY 8: Strahan to Queenstown

Distance ridden: 40.9 km; Riding time: 2 hrs 32 mins; Average speed: 16.1 kmph; Maximum speed: 54 kmph; Vertical metres climbed: 400

When a south-wester blows in Strahan, the whole place feels like it has slipped 1000 km towards Antarctica. Leaving Strahan for Queenstown is an ascent. Hills followed by more hills, through a green corridor which quite often shelters under a damp grey canopy. Cresting the 260 m altitude mark on a fine day would be a wonderful feeling; there's an uninhibited wild openness to the outlook. On a day fit only for penguins on the other hand, this is where your feet finally lose all sense of feeling and it seems not the most exciting place on earth.

Queenstown

Losing altitude usually means gaining a little warmth, but as we descended into Queenstown it seemed to get colder! Queenstown (pop^n 4300) is a bleak and barren place. The violence wreaked on nature here is awesome to behold. From the 1890s Mt Lyell Mine **copper mine** pumped out sulphurous fumes from its pyritic smelters. You can visit the mine to view the workings and the mine's **museum**.

DAY 9: Queenstown to Derwent Bridge

Distance ridden: 81.6 km; Riding time: 5 hrs 26 mins; Average speed: 14.8 kmph; Maximum speed: 55 kmph; Vertical metres climbed: 990

Leaving Queenstown is an awesome experience: riding at funereal speed up a black road switch-blading into ochre hills. Bare hills except for the occasional headstone-like tree stump. It feels like and looks like some future earth laid to ruins. Reaching the top is a relief and the descent through Gormanston down to Lake Burbury is short and fast — mind out for the twin-jinker trucks.

The Nelson River is one of those black-as-coals, tannin-stained streams, but a 20 minute return walk to its falls is one of the 'musts' on this section of the route. The second serious climb of the day — Victoria Pass — begins just after the waterfall walk detour.

Franklin–Lower Gordon Wild Rivers National Park

Beyond Victoria Pass you enter Franklin-Lower Gordon Wild Rivers National Park (440 000 hectares), the central core of the World Heritage area. Contained within it is the Franklin River, which provides experienced, well-equipped adventurers with one of the great rafting trips in Australia. Donaghys Hill Wilderness Walk is a 40 minute return trip (see Route Slip) giving excellent views of the Franklin River.

When you are pedalling towards a big climb, it always seems there are a few false starts. Getting onto the King William Saddle climb is no exception. It finally begins after crossing the Collingwood and Franklin Rivers. This 9 km, 430 m lift is not a hill to be rushed. Don't pass up the opportunity to stop at the scenic lookout a couple of kilometres from the top, if only to see the classic lines of Frenchman's Cap. As like as not it will still have snow clinging to its southern face.

The type of landscape over which you gaze was described by government geologist Charles Gould in 1860 as 'a confused mass of mountain summits of the wildest and most rugged character'. It is the same today.

King William Saddle marks the watershed for the westward-flowing Gordon–Franklin system and the eastward-flowing Derwent (ending in Hobart). It is not a place to be caught unprepared in a rainstorm. This is a sharp-edged, sub-alpine landscape where the wind-chill factor can make for dangerously cold conditions. Unfortunately, the annual rainfall of 2.5 m means it rains on average 300 days each year! With an ogre-like storm charging down on us, we finished a quick lunch and scooted towards the Derwent Bridge Wilderness Resort.

DAY 10: Derwent Bridge to Lake St Clair return (light day)

Distance ridden: 10.8 km; Riding time: 35 mins; Average speed: 18 kmph; Maximum speed: 26 kmph

Lake St Clair

Lake St Clair is at the southern end of the Cradle Mountain–Lake St Clair National Park and was known to the Aborigines as *Leeawuleena* — the sleeping water. In-park **accommodation** includes a camping area and self-contained huts. There are numerous **day walks** from Cynthia Bay (visit the information centre) but if you have the inclination, do the **overnight walk** to Narcissus River Hut. Go up on the inside of Mt Olympus and over Byron Gap (Cuvier Valley Track), then come back along the shores of Lake St Clair (Overland Track). There is a **passenger launch service** on the lake if your feet are overwalked. Hope that it rains since beech forests, which are a feature of the walk, take on a peculiar Tolkien-like, eerie quality when dripping wet and caressed in mist.

DAY 11: Derwent Bridge to Bronte Park

Distance ridden: 29.9 km; Riding time: 1 hr 24 mins; Average speed: 21.3 kmph; Maximum speed: 53 kmph;
Vertical metres climbed: 150

Diversity is the spice of life they say. So don't be too surprised, as I was, if you hear that the top temperature in Perth is a scorching 38°C (100°F) and you look outside to see light snow falling! Tasmania in late December is one place in Australia where you might just crack a white Christmas. Or then again, the temperature might be in the high 30s.

Packing for a summer tour in the highlands of Tasmania means anticipating the best and worst. Riding from Derwent Bridge to Bronte Park I was wearing gloves, woollen socks, long silk pants over my riding shorts, silk T-shirt, long cotton top, wind jacket and a wet weather jacket over that with the hood up over my helmet. I had a tailwind and I was still iced by the falling snow.

Even if you do strike summer snow, it is a lovely ride; sunlight sparkles through the trees and the road verges shimmer with summer wildflowers. Strong winds are frequently encountered in this part of Tasmania. The cold air can be a bit scythe-like and side gusts make fast descents even more interesting. However, once you are cosily warm in front of a raging fire at the Bronte Park Highland Village Lodge, sit by the window and watch bundles of clouds bustling across the sky.

The central highlands of Tasmania contain a series of lagoons organised and managed by the Hydro Electricity Commission, and to the delight of trout anglers. If you are fishing, then this is the place to take a few days off touring and try your hand at catching trout. Trout fishing does seem to have a mystique about it and conjures up visions of a quiet stretch of water with a solitary angler in waders. Talk to the friendly people at Bronte Park about the necessary equipment, fishing licence and where the trout are biting.

DAY 12: Bronte Park to Ellendale

Distance ridden: 85.3 km; Riding time: 4 hrs 46 mins; Average speed: 19.2 kmph; Maximum speed: 72 kmph; Vertical metres climbed: 900

A good highland wind will stop you in your tracks, try to sweep you off the road or throw you down it. It can turn the prettiest most inviting lake into hectares of ominous chopped froth.

In attacking the first good downhill of this section you are mimicking the path of highland water. The sparkling water of Lake Binney which looks so inviting when glimpsed through a stand of young eucalypts, is the same liquid which comes hurtling down massive surge pipes to spin the turbines of Tungatinah Power Station at 600 rpm. Standing in the visitors gallery of the station you can feel the earth vibrate.

Though it is just on the other side of the Nive River (after a lovely picnic area), Tarraleah Power Station gets its water from the Derwent River and Lake St Clair. The two power stations are at the bottom of a steep gully and riding out of it requires considerable effort. At the crest of this big hill take a breather and look for a lightning fast little bird with a breast of molten red — the flame robin.

Initially, the road is a bit of a roller-coaster, tracking beside an open canal and crossing over a pick-a-plank bridge (it has a warning sign) before entering a forest of pines. Just beyond the pines arguably the best downhill of the whole tour begins. This is a 300 + m drop over 5 km on a road that is smooth, winding around corners that are not too sharp, with light traffic. In other words, a no-brake, tuck-and-go hill!

To bring you back to reality, there are a couple of hundred metres to ascend before you begin more than 15 km of rolling descent all the way to Ouse (pronounced *ooze*). This is the upper Derwent Valley and after all the wild tree-covered mountains of the high country, emerging on cleared pastures is quite a shock.

Another shock is the last hill of the day. After crossing the Derwent River on the causeway-like Dunrobbin Bridge, the road lifts 200 m in one short sharp hike. Urging the bike upward may feel murderous to muscles late in the afternoon after you have already had a day of good climbs. Once you have attained the top and your rasping breath returns to near normal, there's a pretty valley to be ridden. It's dotted with strange looking wooden buildings called 'oast houses' — hop kilns. The many beautiful groves of poplar trees in the valley were planted in the 1860s to protect wind-sensitive hops. Lower down the Derwent Valley at Bushy Park, take a short detour to the Text Kilns — biblical texts are set into their walls. Also take time to view the Oast House Museum at New Norfolk to learn about this fascinating segment of Derwent Valley history.

Before you enter Ellendale, gaze skyward. High above the village there are distant, snow-dusted views of Mt Field National Park. Hopfield Cottages, in the tiny village of Ellendale, made a pleasurable end to the day's cycling.

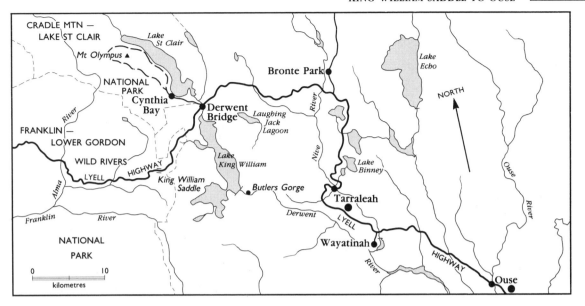

ROUTE SLIP

Directions	R/S km	Ride for	Destination	Cum route km
END OF SECTION 4			**TOTAL FOR ROUTE**	**442.3**
Ouse	99.5			442.3
R*-Wayatinah	76	23.5		418.8
L-A10	65.3	10.7	Hobart	408.1
R*-C603	65.3		Butlers Gorge	408.1
R*-C601	64.1	1.2	Laughing Jack Lagoon	406.9
L*-Tarraleah	61.6	2.5		404.4
Tungatinah P Stn	58.1	3.5	picnic area	400.9
L*-Lake Binney	50	8.1	campsite	392.8
BR-A10	43.9	6.1	Hobart	386.7
R*	43.5	0.4	shelter shed	386.3
L*-B11	41.8	1.7	4 km to Bronte Park	384.6
R*-C601	35.8	6.0	Laughing Jack Lagoon	378.6
L*-Lake St Clair	15.9	19.9	5 km to Cynthia Bay	358.7
Derwent Bridge	15.9			358.7
King William Saddle	0.0	15.9		342.8
BEGIN SECTION 4				

On ride line, each segment = 1 kilometre

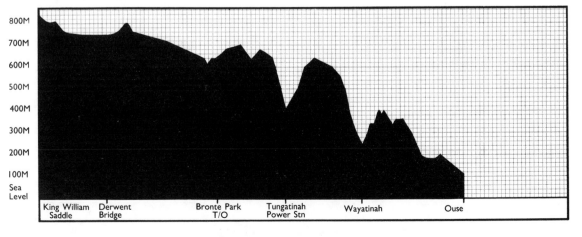

DAY 13: Ellendale to Hobart

Distance ridden: 75.6 km;   Riding time: 3 hrs 26 mins;   Average speed: 21.8 kmph;   Maximum speed: 62 kmph;
Vertical metres climbed: 320

Derwent Valley

It could take a week to bicycle from Ellendale to Hobart, or a day. The Derwent Valley has a tremendous variety of features to explore, including a wonderful array of old buildings. To track down the best and where to see them, consult an excellent book *From Black Snake to Bronte — Heritage Buildings of the Derwent Valley* by Holiday and Trigg. There is also a swag of charming little villages, like Fentonbury and Bushy Park, with an array of farm, home-host and colonial **accommodation** — check out the quiet elegance of Hawthorne at Bushy Park. Never fear, just to replace the lost kilojoules there are more Devonshire tea outlets than in Devon.

Mt Field National Park Detour

At Westerway, turn right and head up the Gordon River Road towards Mt Field (8 km). Mt Field became Tasmania's first national park in the days of steam trains and horse-drawn drays. Even today, the silken white veils of Russell Falls (close to the park entrance) have an old-world charm about them. Below the falls is a likely place to spy a platypus. If you are very keen about **hill climbing**, then tackle the 16 km drive past Russell Falls to Lake Dobson. Call in to the Ranger's centre for advice on road conditions and a free pamphlet on the park. It is a tough climb but immensely rewarding as it passes through a thriving rainforest of lustrous treeferns, backdropped by some of the tallest, straightest gum trees in Australia, *Eucalyptus regnans*. There are also russet hues and tones, colours from the deciduous beech and Tasmanian myrtle. To make the effort of climbing worthwhile, stay a time in the primitive huts which offer pot-bellied stoves, running cold water, and nearby toilets but no lighting (bookings with the Ranger). **Day walks** can be made onto the Tarn Shelf overlooking glacier-carved valleys, lakes and alpine tarns (in winter some freeze over).

Just beyond the diminutive village of Plenty are the Salmon Ponds (see Route Slip) where the first of Tasmania's imported rainbow and brown trout were bred in the 1860s. About the only place to pick up a bit of traffic is on the approach to Hobart. But by following the preferred bike route (signposted with blue bike symbols) you can avoid most of it and make a relaxed end to the tour.

Hobart

Hobart (pop^n 180 000) is a hilly, but enjoyable capital city where it is easy to find your way around. Meandering the waterfront is pleasing at any time but more so in the first week of January as **Constitution Dock** will be full of yachts and yachties celebrating their arrival in the annual Sydney-to-Hobart race. Summer Saturdays get down to **Salamanca Place** for the morning market, and for a real climb and fantastic downhill run tackle the mountain which overlooks Hobart, **Mt Wellington** (1270 m). Other attractions include **Battery Point**, the **casino** and the **Maritime Museum**.

You could complete the rounding of Tasmania with an east-coast tour (much gentler than the west coast). Be sure to include the Tasman Peninsula, Maria Island, Freycinet, Bicheno, St Helens and Launceston.

Getting to the Airport

Beginning at the major downtown roundabout, follow the plane symbol signs to Tasman Bridge (cross the bridge on the footpath). After 16 km, turn right down Holyman Ave, 3.9 km to the terminal.

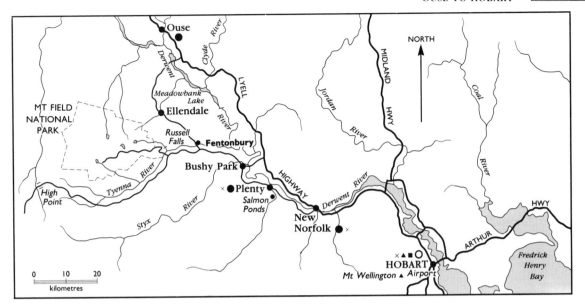

ROUTE SLIP

Directions	R/S km	Ride for	Destination	Cum route km
END OF TOUR			**TOTAL FOR ROUTE**	**537.9**
Hobart	95.7			537.9
L*-info centre	86.5	9.2		528.7
L	82.9	3.6	Glenorchy	525.1
L	77.2	5.7	Blue Bike Route	519.4
L	76.9	0.3	Granton	519.1
R-A10	76.7	0.2	Hobart	518.9
L*-Oast House	61.1	15.6		503.3
New Norfolk	59.7	1.4		501.9
S-A10	59.7		Hobart	501.9
R*-Salmon Ponds	51.2	8.5		493.4
Plenty	49	2.1		491.3
L*-laneway	41.7	7.3	Text Kilns	484
R-B62	41	.7	Salmon Ponds	483.3
Bushy Park	41			483.3
R*-B61	29.8	11.2	Mt Field NP	472.1
Fentonbury	26.2	3.6		468.5
Ellendale	20.2	6.0	Hobart	462.5
R-C608	6.9	13.3	Ellendale	449.2
Ouse	0.0	6.9		442.3
BEGIN SECTION 5				

On ride line, each segment = 1 kilometre

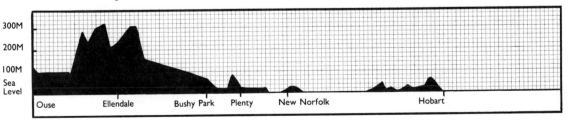

THE HIGH COUNTRY

8 ● Canberra
ACT

8 THE HIGH COUNTRY

This is a tough but rewarding 515 km tour through sub-alpine landscapes surrounding Australia's highest peaks. It begins in the planned elegance of Australia's national capital, Canberra, taking the bike paths around Lake Burley Griffin, then heads out through undulating country to Cotter Dam. The climbs begin, firstly over the Brindabellas (on dirt), then up rough, steep tracks to Long Plain in Kosciusko National Park. Tar road (interspersed with minimal dirt) takes you to the old gold-mining area of Kiandra, past Cabramurra (the highest town in Australia), down a magnificent descent to Tumut Ponds and up a long ascent to Round Mountain. From the Mountain to Khancoban is the longest road descent in Australia. The tour then tackles Scammels Spur and Dead Horse Gap (sustained hard climbing on a dirt road), before the ski resort village of Thredbo hoves into view within walking or riding distance of Mt Kosciusko, Australia's highest mountain. Completing the circuit you head back to Canberra via Lake Eucumbene and Namadgi National Park.

I rode this tour with my partner in December/January taking 11 days (including three rest days), averaging 69 km per day. The tour is best ridden between November and March. We camped for the majority of the tour but also used Thredbo Youth Hostel, and a couple of hotels. Towards the end of summer water becomes scarce in the area and total fire bans may be imposed. When camping, you need to carry sufficient drinking water, a fuel stove and food. On the route there are no stores between Canberra and Cabramurra, or from Adaminaby to Tharwa.

Canberra

Founded in 1913, Canberra (pop^n 225 000) is a planned city. American architect Walter Burley Griffin won a world-wide competition to design the city and the lake which bears his name is its focal point. As Australia's capital, it houses the Australian National Gallery, Academy of Science, Institute of Sport, War Memorial, High Court, Mint, Federal Parliament House and National Library — all well worth visiting. You will be travelling in the region which spawned a national legend, The Man From Snowy River, so when visiting the National Library listen to the Jindabyne Tapes — oral history of the 'real' Man. Canberra has developed bike paths as a natural part of its transport systems — upwards of 150 km of them. Highly recommended reading includes *Riding Canberra's Bike Paths* by Graeme Barrow, a map called 'Canberra Cycleways' and, for a bunch of day tours, *Forty Bicycle Rides around Canberra and Southern NSW* by Pedal Power, Australian Capital Territory (ACT) Inc.

DAY 1: Canberra to Brindabella

Distance ridden: 65.5 km;   Riding time: 4 hrs 59 mins;   Average speed: 13 kmph;   Maximum speed: 62 kmph;
Vertical metres climbed: 1100

The bicycle path trunk route (which is characterised by a white line dividing the path down the middle) provides a car-free exit from downtown Canberra (there may be no cars but there are lots of other cyclists). The path skirts the west basin of Lake Burley Griffin, slipping in and out of young forests but always keeping to gentle contours. High above is the stark dominance of Black Mountain and its communication tower.

Even the light traffic on Cotter Road is hard to take after the pleasure of riding a well designed bike path, though you do get a first glimpse of the real mountains to come; powder blue peaks in the far, far distance. Stargazers would enjoy a detour to Mt Stromlo Observatory (see Route Slip) which is open daily. The early hills are no problem, but don't be too surprised if the temperature is pushing up into the high 30s (Celsius). This will

ROUTE SLIP

Directions	R/S km	Ride for	Destination	Cum route km
END OF SECTION I			**TOTAL FOR ROUTE**	**103.1**
X-Murrumbidgee River	103.1		headwaters	103.1
L*-Blue Water Holes	98.1	5	camping area	98.1
L*-scenic lookout	94.3	3.8	view of Long Plain	94.3
end climbs	93.6	.7		93.6
Enter Kosciusko NP	71.1	22.5	Long Plain	71.1
begin climbs	65.3	5.8		65.3
L*-bush camping site	65.3		beside river	65.3
L	61.9	3.4		61.9
X-bridge (hill base)	61.8	.1	Goodradigbee R.	61.8
BR-Piccadilly Circus	51.1	10.7	top of hill	51.1
L*-Piccadilly Circus	50.7	0.4	Arboretum	50.7
dirt road begins	42.5	8.2		42.5
X-Condor Creek	39.2	3.3	begin climb	39.2
L*-Condor Camp	37.8	1.4	camping area	37.8
L	32.8	5		32.8
R-Brindabella Rd	25.7	7.1	Brindabella	25.7
L*-Cotter Dam	25.3	.4	camping area	25.3
R*-Casuarina Sands	24.1	1.2		24.1
R*-Mt Stromlo	16.5	7.6	observatory	16.5
L*-info map	16.4	0.1		16.4
BR-Cotter Rd	13.1	3.3		13.1
Join Cotter Road	10.6	2.5	Cotter Dam	10.6
R	9.3	1.3	Woden	9.3
BL	8.9	.4		8.9
R*-Western Creek	8.9			8.9
X-bridge	8	0.9		8
R*-National Museum	5.9	2.1		5.9
BR-over road bridge	2.8	3.1		2.8
BR-	2.5	.3	lake on left	2.5
BR-over hill	2	.5	beside lake	2
R-at T intersection	1.5	.5	see the lake	1.5
S-over bridge	1.3	.2		1.3
L-bike path	1.1	.2		1.1
L-Lakeside Hotel	1	.1		1
BR	0.5	.5		0.5
L-London Crt	0.4	.1		0.4
R	0.3	.1		0.3
Canberra-Billara St	0.0	.3	heading south	0.0
BEGIN SECTION I				

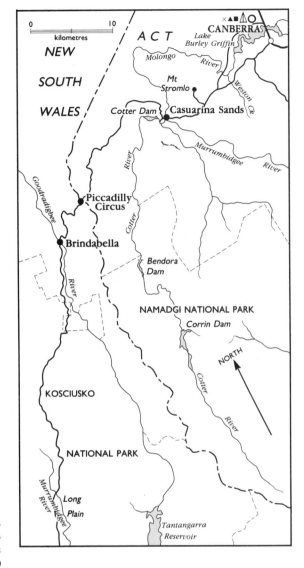

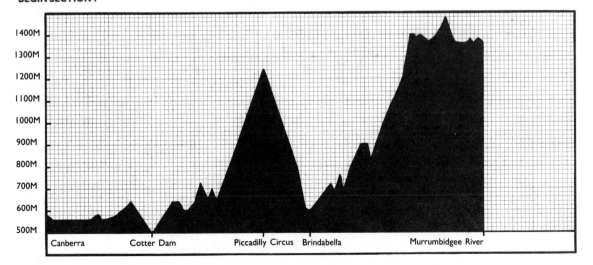

On ride line, each segment = 1 kilometre

make a swim in the Cotter River even more inviting. There's a riverside camping area and it would make an ideal stop for a relaxed first day's cycling.

Beyond Cotter, the climbing grade is steady but manageable and quickly gives you glimpses of little Cotter dam and Black Mountain tower (now in the far distance). Just before your big climb of the day, a road condition sign showing whether any areas are closed by snow, is an indication of just how cold this region becomes during winter. There are a couple of wasteful downhills before you cross the Condor River and start on *the* climb. Refill your water supply at Condor Camp, another possible early alternative stopping place. Unfortunately, it is impossible to guarantee the purity of many streams, so to avoid being laid low by a gastro attack, find some way to distinguish between the water you carry as drinking water and water to be boiled before drinking. At each night's campsite, boil up the next day's drinking water and let it cool overnight.

A short section of tar at the start of Piccadilly Circus hill is encouraging, but there are 600 m in 11 km to climb, so take it slowly. In the lowest gear at 6 kmph per hour height is gradually gained, though the dense foliage on both sides of the road dampens any appreciation of altitude. Just how steep the gulleys are is easily recognised as the land plummets downward beyond the outside edge of your panniers.

I'm not really sure whether the climbing grade increases towards the latter stages of the hill or whether it was just that I started to run out of energy. Either way, you'll cherish the few flatter diversions which appear as saviours just when it seems that the long, steep sections may never end. On these grinding ascents, try to keep away from the inside of tight corners as the road surface is extremely rough, making it very hard to keep traction. At the same time, be wary of oncoming traffic and impatient overtaking vehicles.

Piccadilly Circus Arboretum is a welcome sign as it signifies less than a kilometre to the top. Sadly, all the toil and struggle to bag this peak is cast away in one extravagant descent to Brindabella, though there is a leg-sapping little ascent on the way thrown in for good measure. Take care, the descent is a bone-jolting, knuckle-whitening spree akin to riding an untamed colt, particularly towards the latter half where some of the steeper hair-pin drops can cause terrifying brake fade. Just keep in mind that at the bottom you can take a restorative dip in the river's icy waters.

DAY 2: Brindabella to Murrumbidgee River

Distance ridden: 38.2 km;   Riding time: 4 hrs 18 mins;   Average speed: 8.8 kmph;   Maximum speed: 42 kmph;
Vertical metres climbed: 1140

Be sure your water bottles are full (four litres is the bare minimum), because without a shadow of doubt this is the hardest day's riding in the whole tour and on the severest part of the climb there is no water. Less than 40 km for a day's riding may seem a breeze, but 25 of those are steep climbing, gaining more than 1100 m, and all on rough dirt road!

Initially, you are riding up the Brindabella Valley where the morning light softens the ploughed fields. Each little rise brings a slightly different vista, backdropped by the mountain range you conquered yesterday. As the river is left behind, climbing becomes more intense — much more. The ascent is sustained and unrelenting and none but a calm, resolute attitude will have you over these mountains. For us, the day wasn't made any easier by initially disbelieving the height profile and fooling ourselves by wishfully thinking we had sped to a higher elevation than was true. This always leads to the soul-destroying belief that 'the top' will be 'just around the next bend'. A belief which, like as not, is dashed when the next bend reveals the track switch-backing up seemingly impossible grades to ride.

A friend of mine once described how someone on a bicycle tour became so tired and emotional that they dismounted, threw their bike into the middle of the road and burst into tears. After cresting my fifth false apex of the day, I knew that

ROUTE SLIP

Directions	R/S km	Ride for	Destination	Cum route km
END OF SECTION 2			**TOTAL FOR ROUTE**	**214.2**
Khancoban	111.1			214.2
L-Alpine Way	105.3	5.8	Khancoban	208.4
R*-Clover Flat	84.1	21.2	rest area	187.2
Toona Dam	77.1	7		180.2
L*-Oglivies Ck	70.7	6.4	rest area	173.8
L*-Bradley's Hut	62.3	8.4	rest area	165.4
Tumut Pond Reservoir	53.8	8.5	toilet/picnic area	156.9
L	46.3	7.5	Khancoban	149.4
R*-lookout Cabramurra	45.3	1		148.4
L*-shelter hut	45.3			148.4
L*-scenic lookout	40.5	4.8		143.6
begin dirt road	37.7	2.8	Kings Cross	140.8
Mt Selwyn	37.3	0.4	Skiing-day parking area	140.4
S-Mt Selwyn	34.9	2.4		138
BR*-Cabramurra	34.9			138
R*-3 Mile Dam	34.9		camping area	138
R*-Mining Museum	31	3.9	picnic area	134.1
R-Mt Selwyn	30.2	0.8	3 Mile Dam	133.3
L-Snowy Mtns Hwy	12.3	17.9		115.4
R*-Yarrangobilly	12.3		caves & hot springs	115.4
R*	9.1	3.2	to camping area	112.2
Murrumidgee River	0.0	9.1		103.1
BEGIN SECTION 2				

KEY

L = left   **R** = right   **S** = straight
BL = bear left   **BR** = bear right
X = cross   * = detour directions

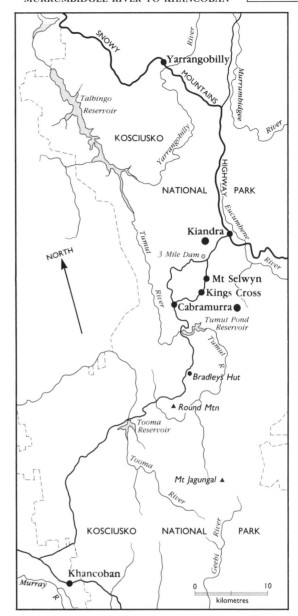

On ride line, each segment = 1 kilometre

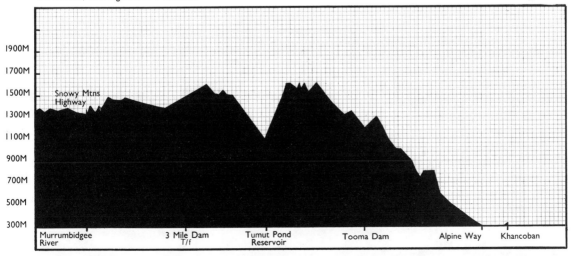

feeling intimately. Another chink in the armour of our minds was our lack of acceptance that the hydro-electric, high voltage power lines were irrefutable evidence of the road's destination, especially when the bloody things seemed to nudge the clouds.

To climb all day through tall trees, then come to an expanse of billiard table landscape called Long Plain (in Kosciusko National Park), is a strange, but wonderful experience. Even an enthusiastic headwind felt like nothing more than a slight hindrance. If you are set up for a few extra days camping then take the Blue Water Hole turn-off (see Route Slip) — it makes an excellent place for a rest day. We pushed on to the headwaters of the Murrumbidgee River and a little bush camp nestled into snowgums. Snowgums are sub-alpine eucalypts with strikingly beautiful bark. After

riding from 8.30 a.m. till 7 p.m., my down sleeping bag and self-inflating mattress felt like heaven on earth.

Kosciusko National Park

This national park (646 911 hectares) was created in 1967 through the concerted efforts of dedicated conservationists after cattle and sheep grazing had begun to cause considerable damage to the high country. It was originally a summer home to Aborigines who journeyed into the alpine area to gather bogong moths for celebratory feasts. The alpine area (above 1800 m) has about 200 plant species, many of which are unique to the Park. Best displays of wildflowers occur from late January to early February.

DAY 3: Murrumbidgee River to 3 Mile Dam (Half Day Rest)

Distance ridden: 34.8 km; **Riding time:** 2 hrs 14 mins; **Average speed:** 15.5 kmph; **Maximum speed:** 48 kmph; **Vertical metres climbed:** 360

Although this segment of the tour covers almost the same distance as the day before, it can be a half-rest day. Long Plain in the morning is a cool, gentle ride down a tree-fringed corridor flanked by grass plain. Meeting the smooth, tarred Snowy Mountains Highway will enliven both bike and rider. True, there are a few hills but they are a pleasant gradient and, once to the top of Bullock Hill, there is the scintillating experience of changing up onto the big chain wheel and cruising a 9 km descent to Kiandra.

Kiandra

Now a windswept, vacant landscape, back in the 1860s Kiandra was a raucous place. Gold had been discovered in 1859 and the fields were full of hopeful miners. Winter snows arrived and the miners on the diggings tackled this inclemency by introducing cross-country skiing to Australia and forming the world's second club. Today the National Parks and Wildlife Service has established an open air **museum** (see Route Slip) beside the Khancoban road, as well as the **Goldseeker's Track**. It starts on the left, just past the turn-off

to the Three Mile Dam campsite, and takes in 11 numbered sites including such things as sphagnum moss plants and an old stamper battery from the goldseeker days.

Three Mile Dam is a primitive campsite but a pretty one where your tent is ringed by snowgums. The dam was constructed in 1882 to supply sluicing water to the Kiandra goldfields, but today it's a home for trout. If you are planning to chase them, a fishing licence is required. Given a clear night, you should see the Southern Cross rising during the summer months.

Yarrangobilly Caves Side Tour

Turn right on joining the Snowy Mountains Highway, then left on the one-way Yarrangobilly Caves circuit road. The caves were discovered in the 1890s and **Castle Walking Track** was built of hand-hewn limestone in the early 1900s. There are also a **NPWS information centre** and **thermal pools** where the water is a constant 27°C.

DAY 4: Three Mile Dam to Khancoban

Distance ridden: 76.1 km; Riding time: 4 hrs 38 mins; Average speed: 16.3 kmph; Maximum speed: 70 kmph;
Vertical metres climbed: 1040

Three Mile Dam is just under 1600 m in altitude and early risers may see a summer mist slip from the surrounding land to float across the surface of the dammed waters. Valleys far below also generate mist which rises with the sun, turning the sky a soft grey. Around the camp, dawn also heralds a changeover of locals. Having dined elegantly all night, resident mosquitoes dozily drift away leaving your body free for the attentions of March flies. These biters love to hitch a ride and probe into some tender morsel of flesh when you are at your most vulnerable. Long slow hills are their preference. With your hands locked to the bike you are a submissive victim, so apply insect repellent, particularly around the ankles.

When you eventually break camp, be sure to check tyres for nicks, cuts or bulges, pannier frames for looseness and to adjust brakes. There are some awesome descents on this section since, although you will climb over 1000 m, you will rocket down 2180 m!

Ascending to Kings Cross on the only dirt road travelled for this day, there are blue-misted views across to Mt Jagungal (Mother of the Waters) in the far distance. By comparison, the other tree-cloaked mountains are mere dots in the foreground. There is a 30 km circuit walk to Mt Jagungal and back which begins at the junction of Tooma Road and Round Mountain fire trail.

Back on your bicycle, you pass by Cabramurra, Australia's highest town, before receiving the first big reward for hill climbing in the Kosciusko mountains. Tumut Ponds Reservoir is 400 m below and getting down to it is a spirit-soaring plunge — the road is smooth tar but watch out for loose gravel on some of the corners.

Alas, the only drawback with steep descents in the Snowy Mountains is that they are followed by ascents of equal sharpness. After a relaxing morning tea gazing at Tumut Pondage's deep blue water comes the climb of Round Mountain, 550 m in 5 km. The cooling breezes which swirled against your rapidly circling legs on the downhill run are replaced by shimmering heat. Beneath the bicycle tyres, black bitumen greedily soaks in the sun's rays then blasts it back on this slow ascent. Sweat runs down your face and drips onto your knees. You pump in the air and swallow a fly. It is summer in Australia, with a vengeance.

Little streams which gurgle and dance beside the road are an encouragement (soak a bandana and wear it wet), as are the airy views of Tumut Pondage below, then bigger mountains in the far distance. Altitude gains can produce extraordinary changes in temperature. Don't be too surprised if, when you lunch at Bradley's Hut, you are wearing a wind chill jacket to keep out the cold.

There are a few frustrating preamble hills after Bradley's before a cheery sign — 'Steep Descent' — signifies 38 km of downhill flying. If you are looking for a campsite, Ogilvies Creek (see Route Slip) is one of the prettiest alpine streams. Once out of Kosciusko and into cleared valley pastures before Khancoban, we found ourselves back in a breathless, hot summer's day. The pool at Khancoban Alpine Inn was never more appreciated.

DAY 5: Rest

Khancoban

This town (pop^n 600) was established when the Snowy Mountains Hydro Electric Scheme was being built. At one stage, over 7000 people were employed on the $820M project which collects waters from the Snowy and Eucumbene Rivers at high elevations, then turns them westward in tunnels cut through the Snowy Mountains to the Murray and Murrumbidgee Rivers. In the process, the waters fall more than 800 m and generate 3 740 000 kilowatts of electricity. You can use the same principle for chasing trout on board an inflatable raft down 15 km of the Swampy Plains River. There's an organised **fishing expedition** which includes a chicken and champagne lunch even if the fish aren't biting — details are available from the local tourist information centre in Khancoban.

DAY 6: Khancoban to Leather Barrel Creek

Distance ridden: 60.2 km;   Riding time: 6 hrs 33 mins;   Average speed: 8.4 kmph;   Maximum speed: 73 kmph; Vertical metres climbed: 1660

When you are facing a climb of Scammel Spur, your best asset is an early start and good spirits. Ascending Scammels is probably the most beautiful ascent of this tour. Initially, the clear cross light of early morning shows densely forested slopes in deep relief. You are pushing up through sharp-edged, red earth cuttings that can become unbearably hot later in the day. If there's no rush to your tour and the goal for the day is Geehi (a pleasant by-the-river campsite), then there's plenty of time to stop off at Murray One hydro power station for a guided tour.

Beyond Murray One, the warp of high voltage power lines is left behind and you are immersed in a strong aroma of eucalypts and surrounded by tall peppermint forests, their green and white bark wrapped around them and reminiscent of the spiralling pattern on barbers poles. These are superb trees, their crowns tower above you, while their bases are somewhere below in the hidden valley floor. The combination of elegant trees, rampant tree ferns and a continually changing chorus of bird calls, combine to make this a lovely valley, even if the last 10 km is an extreme incline.

Your attack of the very steep descent section may seem interrupted by the turn-off to Scammels Spur lookout. Don't ride past without seeing this, it is possibly the best lookout of the whole tour, commanding a view across to the western ramparts of Kosciusko's main range: two peaks of the Abbot Range, Mt Townsend (second highest mountain in Australia), Carruthers Peak, Sentinel and Mt Twynam. These are a wonderful collection of craggy-faced peaks, usually with some glistening white patches of snow stubbornly clinging to them.

At the time of writing, the tar surface continues to the Geehi river crossing where a new bridge is under construction (camping site to the right), but by the time you ride it the road may be tar all the way to Tom Groggin, beside the Murray River. Tom Groggin picnic/camping area is the place to look for the thickest concentrations of bush flies. Forget solar power, wind power and wave power, someone just needs to work on harnessing the power of the bush fly and Australia's needs will be provided.

From Tom Groggin the only way is up — up the hill known as Dead Horse Gap. One cyclist we met on the ride reckoned they should rename it Dead Cyclist Gap. Over the length of the hill, you ascend more than 1000 m in 18 km, a good climb at any time of day. Not making life for the cyclist any easier, it's a popular thoroughfare with a surface resembling a common Australian roofing material, corrugated iron. And it's loose and gravelly! Another handicap are the Tom Groggin flies which like to hitch a lift; looking at my partner's panniers, she must have been carrying at least 5 kg of the little blighters.

When we rode to Leather Barrel Creek camping area (half-way up to Dead Horse Gap) we were forced to walk sections due to steeply-banked corners of loose stones, errant vehicles and a gale-force headwind which threatened to literally push us over the edge of the road. At the end of such a day, a refreshing dip in icy Leather Barrel Creek was an ethereal experience.

TOUR 8: Amongst bushfire-killed trees on a great 400 m descent into Tumut Ponds Reservoir, New South Wales

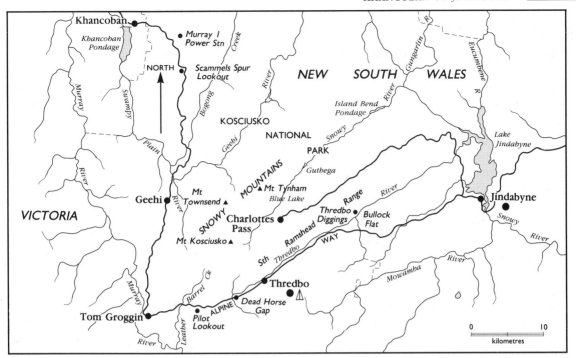

ROUTE SLIP

Directions	R/S km	Ride for	Destination	Cum route km
dirt road	53.1	7.1		267.3
R*-Tom Groggin	53.1		rest/camping area	267.3
R*-Geehi	31.8	21.3	rest/camping area	246
R*-scenic lookout	20.2	11.6		234.4
top Scammels Spur	17.6	2.6		231.8
L-Murray 1 Power Stn	9.6	8		223.8
L*-Murray 1 L/ot	8.5	1.1		222.7
L*-information sign	3.7	4.8		217.9
BL	2.3	1.4	Jindabyne	216.5
Khancoban	0.0	2.3		214.2
BEGIN SECTION 3				

Directions	R/S km	Ride for	Destination	Cum route km
END OF SECTION 3			**TOTAL FOR ROUTE**	**323.2**
Jindabyne	109			323.2
R	106.4	2.6	Jindabyne	320.6
L*-Bullock Flat	91	15.4	Ski Tube	305.2
L*-Thredbo Diggings	89.1	1.9	camping area	303.3
L*-Ngarigo	85.5	3.6	camping area	299.7
L*-Thredbo	76.1	9.4	Jindabyne	290.3
Dead Horse Gap	71	5.1		285.2
tar road	67.8	3.2		282
R*-Pilot lookout	66.2	1.6		280.4
L* Leather Barrel Ck	60.2	6	rest/camping area	274.4

On ride line, each segment = 1 kilometre

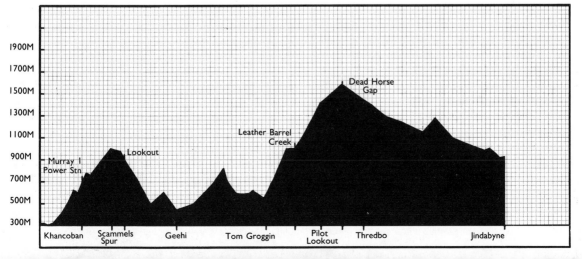

DAY 7: Leather Barrel Creek to Thredbo Youth Hostel (Half Rest Day)

Distance ridden: 15.9 km;   Riding time: 1 hr 42 mins;   Average speed: 9.3 kmph;   Maximum speed: 69 kmph;
Vertical metres climbed: 580

From Leather Barrel Creek there's little time to warm up stiff muscles. After 20 m of flat track you climb and in 10 minutes sweat is sure to be flowing freely. It may have been the benefit of a good night's sleep, but to me the second half of Dead Horse Gap, with its improved (although still dirt) road surface, was not as hard as the first. Passing traffic is lighter earlier in the day and there are a few drivers who, on seeing you, actually slow down to reduce the dust rather than speed up in an all out attempt to pass by.

The road is a series of switchbacks, right angles, steep pinches and tightly banked curves. At times, you feel as if suspended on a lofty, thin strip of gravel perched precariously before a precipice-like drop — there are plenty of trees to break the fall, however. Pilot Lookout is a tiny pull off but it gives you a glimpse of the Pilot (1831.5 m) and wild, blue-hazed landscapes to the south. The blue is sometimes spoiled by a less delightful brown smudge from bushfires which are prevalent at this time of year.

A magical transformation occurs beyond Pilot Lookout. Loose gravel becomes hot mix tar, a silky welcoming purr beneath your tyres. Dead Horse Gap itself is a little below the highest point of this climb, but to the right of the gap sign there are a few lovely old snow gums to rest a tired back against at morning tea. From this picturesque vantage point to Thredbo Village is a tuck-and-fly downhill.

Sitting on the balcony of the Thredbo Youth Hostel as night falls and looking across to ski-run covered hills, you may experience the sort of marvellous evening where, as the Japanese poet Oemaru wrote: 'Life flows away; people depart; only the moon remains.'

DAY 8: Rest

Vertical metres climbed (sitting): 560

W.R. Gainford managed the first bicycle ascent of Mt Kosciusko in 1898. Today you can take the Crackenback chairlift and walk the 6 km to Kosciusko or, at Bullock Flat (15.5 km down the valley from Thredbo), put your bike on the Skitube and ride to Kosciusko on the Summit track from Charlottes Pass (hire all-terrain bikes are available). Mt Kosciusko (2228 m) was named in 1840 by the Polish explorer Strzelecki because its round shape reminded him of the tomb of a patriot. If you have time and the energy, on your way back from 'Kossie' take a detour (turn right at the Kosciusko Lookout) through the wonderfully balanced tors of South Ramshead Range. These large scale balancing acts were created by *solifluction* — a process where the finer rock particles, wet from glacial meltwater, move gradually down a slope, leaving tors perched precariously in rock piles. If you are planning overnight treks, find a copy of *Snowy Mountain Walks* by Geehi Bushwalking Club, and *Beyond the Snowgums* by the National Parks and Wildlife Service (NPWS), and be sure to register your trekking intentions at the NPWS information centre.

DAY 9: Thredbo Youth Hostel to Buckenderra

Distance ridden: 91.4 km;   Riding time: 5 hrs 38 mins;   Average speed: 16.1 kmph;   Maximum speed: 75 kmph;
Vertical metres climbed: 880

After a heart-starter incline from Thredbo Village, the Alpine Way towards Jindabyne is a velvety smooth descent. High above you to the west are sure to be big drifts of snow, a reminder of last season's falls. There are a couple of nice campsites, Ngarigo and Thredbo Diggings (see Route Slip)

ROUTE SLIP

Directions	R/S km	Ride for	Destination	Cum route km
END OF SECTION 4			**TOTAL FOR ROUTE**	**431.5**
Namadgi NP	108.3			431.5
R	103.8	4.5	Canberra	427
BL	102.8	1	Canberra	426
Shannons Flat	102.8			426
BL	95.2	7.6	Canberra/Shannon Flt	418.4
BR	86.4	8.8		409.6
dirt road	85.8	0.6		409
X-Murrumbidgee R	85.8			409
R	83.6	2.2	Canberra	406.8
tar road	83.6			406.8
dirt road	76.4	7.2		399.6
R	73.6	2.8	Bolaro	396.8
L-Snowy Mtn Hwy	61.5	12.1	Tumut	384.7
Snowy/Murrumbidgee Divide	60.6	0.9		383.8
L*-Frying Pan Ck	59.8	0.8		383
L*-Buckendarra	50.6	9.2	camping area	373.8
S	36	14.6	Adaminaby	359.2
L-Adaminaby Rd	29.8	6.2	Eucumbene Dam	353
Berridale	29.4	0.4		352.6
BR	14	15.4	Berridale	337.2
Jindabyne	0.0	14.0		323.2
BEGIN SECTION 4				

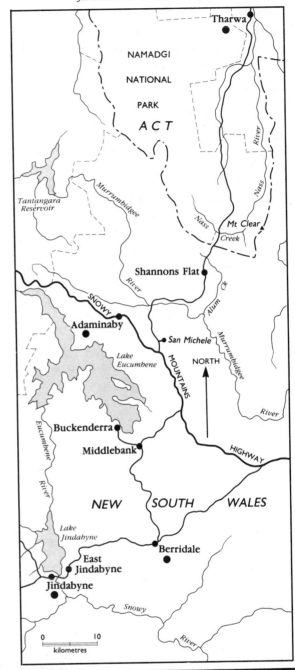

On ride line, each segment = 1 kilometre

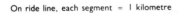

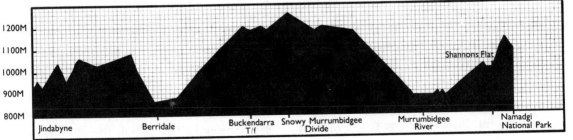

between Thredbo and Bullock Flat, where you can nestle beside the Thredbo River (be sure to boil this water before drinking), though they can be very popular during the summer school holidays.

Jindabyne

You don't need a sign to indicate the border crossing out of Kosciusko National Park. Parched yellow grasses, big-eyed panting cattle and dead and dying trees are all mute testament to that. There's a 140 m hill to tackle and a slight rise, before you slide down to the edge of Lake Eucumbene. The original Jindabyne lies at the bottom of the lake, but the new Jindabyne (pop[n] 1600) is on higher ground, overlooking this vast pond dotted with islands. The lake is a great place for **sailing, water skiing** and **trout fishing**, and there is a **cruise boat**, the *M.V.Kalinga*.

Though Jindabyne is at an altitude of 920 m, the road to Berridale can become excessively hot. Be sure you have enough water and stop for shade breaks — there's a nice spot at East Jindabyne. After the heated climbing to get out of Jindabyne, the last downhill into the little village of Berridale is welcome relief. Also welcome is turning off busy Alpine Way and on to Adaminaby Road, a meandering country lane. Unfortunately, this quiet road is basically a gentle to medium uphill for more than 20 km, but the landscape is one of open spaces, giant dark tors and big skies, so the kilometres roll past.

It was probably just me becoming tired and emotional, but scaling the last hill into Buckendarra is a monstrous exercise. With the hill won, Lake Eucumbene's cool blue expanse had an incomparably strong attraction to two hot, tired and dusty cycle tourers.

DAY 10: Buckendarra to Mt Clear Campsite

Distance ridden: 68.1 km;   Riding time: 4 hrs 58 mins;   Average speed: 13.6 kmph;   Maximum speed: 71 kmph; Vertical metres climbed: 540

There is no need to set an alarm at Buckendarra over the summer school holiday period. At the first change of night black to morning grey, a fleet of droning outboard motor-powered fishing craft will wake you. Drop back to sleep? Have no fear, the throaty roar of ski boats are sure to wake you again.

Once you rejoin Adaminaby Road, there's a consistent rise to the zenith where, for once, there is a sign. This is the Snowy–Murrumbidgee Divide, all water to the left drains to the Snowy River and all to the right drains to the Murrumbidgee River. Looking back just prior to the crest you can see the white-capped Snowy Mountains muted by far distant blues.

Snowy Mountains Highway has appreciably more, and faster moving, traffic but you are soon at the San Michelle turn off. (If supplies are low, take an all-tar detour to Adaminaby, home to the world's largest trout but a pretty village despite this landmark.) Regrettably the road quickly changes to bone-jarring gravel and takes you through dry, yellowed paddocks devoid of trees.

The only interesting rock formation has an unfriendly keep-out sign (there are many such signs on this section of the route). After the road takes a weird, sharp left turn and seemingly pointless backtrack, there is a tantalising little stretch of tar before it disappears upon meeting the Murrumbidgee River. Beside the road (on the prevailing wind's leeward side) is a pleasant picnic spot and the river beneath the bridge makes for an agreeable swimming hole.

Between the bridge and Mt Clear can be another very hot section of the tour, through some bone dry, hard country interspersed with stiff hills. Ensure your water containers are full before tackling it. Initially you follow the Murrumbidgee River and as each little rise is crested, the river's cool languid pools sparkle invitingly in the gulleys below. Unfortunately you part company with the river — it stays in New South Wales and you head for the Australian Capital Territory, via Shannons Flat. There are some tough climbs before a respite at Shannons Flat, but once you cross the Alum River (probably dry late in the summer), cycle

ROUTE SLIP

Directions	R/S km	Ride for	Destination	Cum route km
END OF TOUR			**TOTAL FOR ROUTE**	**517.3**
Canberra City	85.8			517.3
L-X bridge	84.4	1.4		515.9
R-at lake	81	3.4		512.5
R	79.4	1.6		510.9
L-overpass	79.3	0.1		510.8
S	77.9	1.4		509.4
L-city sign	77.4	0.5	X road	508.9
R-along footpath	77.1	0.3		508.6
S	77	0.1		508.5
R-city sign	75.1	1.9	keep canal on R	506.6
R-along footpath	74.6	0.5		506.1
L-over bridge	74	0.6		505.5
R-under road	72.7	1.3		504.2
X-traffic lights	72.4	0.3		503.9
X-traffic lights	71.5	0.9		503
L*-Canberra Nature Pk	70.6	0.9		502.1
Sign-Woden	69.6	1		501.1
BR	68.6	1		500.1
BL-underpass	68.6			500.1
follow white line centred bike path towards Canberra city				
R	68.2	0.4	Join bike path	499.7
R-Athllon Dr	67.6	0.6		499.1
S-traffic lights	64.2	3.4		495.7
L	62.3	1.9	Tuggeranong Town Cntr	493.8
L-double lane road	61.5	0.8		493
BR- X bridge	51.3	10.2	over Murrumbidgee R	482.8
Tharwa	51.1	0.2		482.6
R*-Cuppacumbalong	50.5	0.6		482
R*-Namadgi Visitors centre	48.5	2		480
Fitz's Hill	34.5	14		466
L*-Orroral	32.7	1.8	camping area	464.2
L*-scenic lookout	32.3	0.4		463.8
L*	28.1	4.2	toilets/water	459.6
tar road	20.6	7.5		452.1
X-Gudgenby R	20.6			452.1
L*-scenic lookout	16.3	4.3		447.8
R*-Shananans Mtn	8.1	8.2	walking track	439.6
X-Naas Ck	5.2	2.9		436.7
R*-Mt Clear	4.7	0.5	camping area	436.2
L*-Brayshaw's Hut	2.3	2.4	1903 bush hut	433.8
Namadgi NP	0.0	2.3		431.5

BEGIN SECTION 5

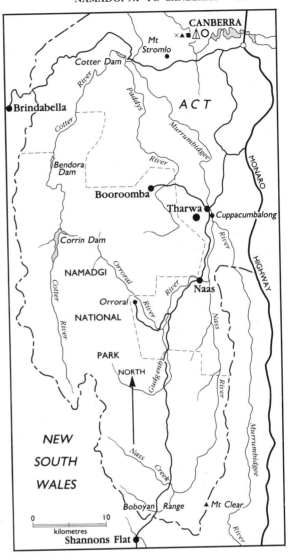

On ride line, each segment = 1 kilometre

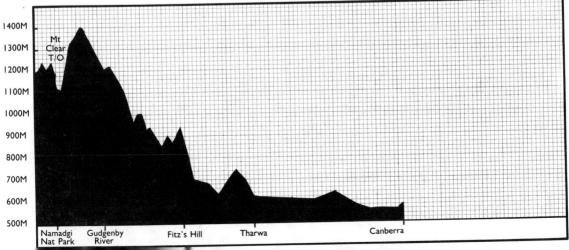

touring becomes climbing.

When we rode this section it was so hot that my fevered brain began to imagine the out-of-sync cicadas were lawn sprinklers. No such luck. Each time I stopped, the bush displayed what the Japanese poet, Basho, described in 'The stillness! Voices of cicadas pierce the very rocks'. Perhaps it was just an unusual afternoon. We had been awestruck by a midday display of thunder and lightning, then dumped on by a sunshower over lunch, but when it came time to attack the biggest climb of the day on Boboyan Road, not a cloud hindered the sun's burning rays. To sit quietly at Mt Clear's shaded campsite beside a demure stream (Naas Creek) and watch grey kangaroos at dusk is enchanting.

Namadgi National Park

This national park (94 000 hectares) was proclaimed in 1984 and covers 40% of the Australian Capital Territory. There are two low-key camping areas on the tour route, Mt Clear and Orroral, along with more than 140 km of walking trails and great rock-climbing at Booroomba Rocks. Highly recommended is the 1:100 000 Namadgi Map and Guide available in Canberra.

DAY 11: Mt Clear Campsite to Canberra

Distance ridden: 82.8 km;   Riding time: 5 hrs 36 mins;   Average speed: 14.6 kmph;   Maximum speed: 82 kmph; Vertical metres climbed: 680

Getting out of Mt Clear would rate as one of the steepest climbs on the tour, especially for the first two and a half of its 6 km. My clean, dry shirt had become a wet rag by the apex of the climb, but it is splendid to know that the most taxing effort is completed. However, there's little flat land up here. At times it seems like the ridge is barely wide enough to carry the road and is relying on densely-packed young snow gums to stop the whole lot sliding down the hill. Through pale thin trunks you can see a parallel mountain ridge fully cloaked in dense greens — beyond it, but unseen, is the Murrumbidgee River.

All-terrain bike riders will love the next 10 km. On a fully-laden touring bike however, coming down a surface of sliding shale is just a waste of 440 m of altitude. Crossing the Gudgenby River follows a brake-burning descent and it makes a perfect spot to calm frayed nerves, ease cramped hands and rinse off the morning's sweat and dust. Be careful where you tromp on sunlit rocks since harmless water skinks love to sunbake there.

Back on tar road, after a morning of climbing and clamped brake descents it's nice to know there are some fantastic freewheeling runs before Tharwa. On one particularly smooth steep hill (before the Orroral Creek Campsite turn-off), I clocked up my fastest run for all of the eight tours — 82 kmph! Be thankful that you are heading to Canberra, since in this direction Fitz's Hill is only an 80 m gain over 2 km. Cycling the other way, it is 240 m in 2 km!

Be sure to call in to the Namadgi Information Centre; their displays covering history and ecology are excellent. Cuppacumbalong (just before Tharwa) is also a treat, both as a perfect place for a celebratory lunch and to view superb examples of fine Australian crafts. At Tharwa you cross the Murrumbidgee for the last time before heading across open plains to Canberra. The city seems to come out to meet you — new houses, new roads are everywhere. This makes picking up the trunk route bicycle path tricky at times, but once on it you have a gentle, traffic-free conclusion to the tour.

APPENDIX A:
Recommended Reading

Touring

Bridge, R., *Bike Touring: The Sierra Club Guide to Outings on Wheels*, The Sierra Club, San Francisco, 1979

Winning, R., *Bicycling Across America*, Wilderness Press, Berkeley USA, 1988

Technical

Ballantine, R., *Richard's Bicycle Book*, Pan Books, London, 1984

Colligan, D. & Teresi, D., *The Cyclist's Manual*, Sterling Publishing Co., New York, 1981

Sloane, Eugene A., *Bicycle Maintenance Manual*, Simon & Schuster, New York, 1981

History

Birtles, F., *Battle Fronts of Outback*, Angus & Robertson, London

——, *The Lone Hand*, March 1910, March 1911, June 1912

Burston and Stokes, *Round About the World on Bicycles*,

Clune, F., *Last of the Australian Explorers*,

Fitzpatrick, Jim, *The Bicycle and the Bush*, Oxford University Press, Melbourne, 1980

Pearson, J., *Reminiscences Including Cycling Experiences*, Vale & Pearson, Sydney 1925

Smith, Patsy Adam, *The Shearers*, Nelson, Melbourne, 1982

This Australia, Vol 1, No. 2, 'Colonial Cycling', Vol 2, No. 1, 'War on Wheels'

Wells, H.G., *The Wheels of Chance*, London, 1898

General

Sloane, Eugene A., *The Complete Book of Bicycling*, Simon & Schuster, New York, 1980

Watson, R. & Gray, M., *The Penguin Book of the Bicycle*, Penguin Books, London 1984

Magazines

Australian Cyclist, Bicycle Federation of Australia, Inc.

Cycling World (Incorporating *Freewheeling*), Mason Stewart Publishing Pty Ltd

Background

Davidson, R., *Tracks*, Jonathan Cape Ltd, London, 1980

Illich, I., *Energy & Equity*, Marion Boyars, London, 1979

APPENDIX B: Touring Clubs and Bike Hire

Touring Clubs

Bicycle Institute of New South Wales, GPO Box 272, Sydney, New South Wales 2001

Bicycle Institute of Queensland, PO Box 753, West End, Queensland 4101

Bicycle Victoria, PO Box 1961R, Melbourne, Victoria 3001

Cycle Touring Association of Western Australia, PO Box 174, Wembley, Western Australia 6014

South Australian Touring Cyclists' Association, PO Box 304, Norwood, South Australia 5067

Fair Go for Cyclists Tasmania, Environment Centre, 102 Bathurst St, Hobart, Tasmania 7000

Organised Large Group Bicycle Tours

New South Wales:	Sydney Spring Cycle — October
	Sydney to the Gong ride — November
Victoria:	Great Victorian Bike Ride — December
South Australia:	Hawker to Adelaide — September/October
Tasmania:	Great Tasmanian Bike Ride — February
Western Australia:	South-West Tour — November
Northern Territory:	Kakadu Safari — June

Commercial Bicycle Tour Operators

Bike Moves, PO Box 642, Unley, South Australia 5061

Bogong Jack Adventures, PO Box 221, Oxley, Victoria 3678

Tailwinds Bicycle Touring, 15 Sargood St, O'Connor, Australian Capital Territory 2600

Tropical Cycling, PO Box 5155, Cairns, Queensland 4870

Out & About Bush Experiences, 49 Jersey Ave, Leura, New South Wales 2780

Touring Bike Hire

Bicycle Hire Sydney, 31 Glebe Pt Rd, Glebe, New South Wales 2037

Rent-A-Cycle Tasmania, 36 Thistle St, Launceston, Tasmania 7250

Hillman Cycles, 44–46 Grantham St, West Brunswick, Victoria 3056

APPENDIX C: Bike Shops Australia-wide

(List courtesy of the Retail Cycle Traders Australia Inc, as of 1 March 1991)

AUSTRALIAN CAPITAL TERRITORY

Houdine Camping Sport & Leisure, Cnr Nettleford & Cohen Sts	Belconnen Town Centre 2617
Canberra Bicycle Centre, 11 Woolley Street	Dickson 2602
Canberra Cycles P/L, 70 Newcastle Street	Fyshwick 2609

NEW SOUTH WALES

Taylor Cycles, 344 Brunker Road	Adamstown 2289
Hadley Cycles P/L, 617 Glebe Road	Adamstown 2289
Maurice Mathé Cycles, 5 Park Avenue	Adamstown 2289
Alstonville Cycles & Mowers, 63 Main Street	Alstonville 2477
The Armidale Bicycle Centre, 248 Beardy Street	Armidale 2350
Ashfield Cycles, 353 Liverpool Road	Ashfield 2131
Alvis Cycle Co, 68–70 Auburn Road	Auburn 2144
Avalon Bicycle Centre, Shop 2/23 Old Barrenjoey Rd	Avalon 2107
Redback Cycles P/L, 404 Darling Street	Balmain 2041
Star Sports P/L, 32 Arthur Street	Baulkham Hills 2153
Stead Cycles & Sporting, 29 Landor Street	Beresfield 2322
Blacktown Cycle Centre, 5 Alpha Street	Blacktown 2148
Fit & Free Cycles P/L, 617 Princes Highway	Blakehurst 2221
Bomaderry Cycles, 61A Meroo Street	Bomaderry 2541
Daisy's Cycles, 65 Gypsum Street	Broken Hill 2880
Ye Olde Bicycle Shoppe, 9 Church Street	Bundanoon 2578
Lets Go Bikes, PO Box 531	Byron Bay 2481
Camden Discount Cycles, 184 Argyle Street	Camden 2570
Fishers Ghost Bicycles, 164 Waminda Avenue	Campbelltown 2560
Cardiff Cycle Centre, 34 Veronica Street	Cardiff 2285
Norscott Cycles, 82 Barker Street	Casino 2470
Bob Wallis Cycles, Cnr Collingwood & Orlando Sts	Coffs Harbour Jetty 2450
Concord Sports Store, 46 Crane Street	Concord 2137
Cooma Sports & Cycles, 130 Sharp Street	Cooma 2630
Dee Why Beach Cycle Stop, 15 The Strand	Dee Why 2099
Huddle Sport & Leisure, 293 Cressy Street	Deniliquin 2710
Rockets Toy & Sports World, 31–33 Napier Street	Deniliquin 2710
Try-Cycle-Way, 144 Victoria Road	Drummoyne 2047
Kenny's Mowers, PO Box 95	Drummoyne 2047
Wheeler Cycles, 193 Brisbane Street	Dubbo 2830
ABC Dural Cycles Sports & Toys, Shop 17 Dural Mall, Kenthurst Rd	Dural 2158
Eastwood Cycle Works, 265 Rowe Street	Eastwood 2122
Engadine Cycles, 26 Station Street	Engadine 2233
Calypso Cycles, C/- PO Box 167	Enmore 2042

Ettalong Bike Shop, 203 Memorial Avenue	Ettalong 2257
Cycology, 242 Victoria Road	Gladesville 2111
Inner City Cycles P/L, 31 Glebe Point Road	Glebe 2037
Valley Sports 'N' Toys, 36 Church Street	Gloucester 2422
Eclipse Cycles & Fitness, 378 Auburn Street	Goulburn 2580
Schaffer's Cycle Works, 145 Prince Street	Grafton 2460
Hornsby Cycle & Sports Store, 169 Pacific Highway	Hornsby 2077
Jack Griffin Cycles, 186 Byron Street	Inverell 2360
Central Coast Cycles P/L, 118 Wyong Road	Killarney Vale 2261
Kingscliff Cycle Centre, 3/110 Marine Parade	Kingscliff 2487
Kirrawee Cycles, 146 Oak Road	Kirrawee 2232
Kurri Tackle & Cycles, 123 Lang Street	Kurri Kurri 2327
Lane Cove Cycles, 3/98 Longueville Road	Lane Cove 2066
Lavington Cycles, PO Box 572	Lavington 2641
Harris Cycle Co, 85 Keen Street	Lismore 2480
Jetty Cycle Works, 306A The Entrance Road	Long Jetty 2261
Maitland Cycle Centre, 339 High Street	Maitland 2320
Wheeler Cycles, 87 Pittwater Street	Manly 2095
Maroubra Cycles, 787 Anzac Parade	Maroubra Junction 2035
Just Cycles, 115A Maitland Road	Mayfield 2304
Westlakes Cyclery, Shop 13, 99 Dora Street	Morisset 2264
K & M Ward Cycles, Unit 14 Ford Street	Moruya 2537
King Cycle Works, 32 Market Street	Muswellbrook 2333
George's Cycle & Sport, 223 Concord Road	North Strathfield 2137
Nowra Cycle Centre, 11 Haigh Street	Nowra 2541
Kervel Cycles, 86 Central Avenue	Oak Flats 2529
Boulton Cycles & Marine, 116 Summer Street	Orange 2800
Woolys Wheels P/L, 82 Oxford Street	Paddington 2021
Beacon Cycles, 67 Howard Street	Padstow 2211
Bike Barn & Triathlon Ware, 7 Victoria Road	Parramatta 2150
Port Push Bikes, 5/155 Horton Street	Port Macquarie 2444
Graham Seers Cyclery, Shop 1 Port Marina, Park Street	Port Macquarie 2444
Quakers Hill Cycle Centre, Shop 2, Cnr Douglas & Railway Sts	Quakers Hill 2763
Centennial Park Cycles, 50 Clovelly Road	Randwick 2031
Cranks Bike Shop, 92 Pacific Highway	Roseville 2069
Sakeys Cycle Centre, Shop 7, Campbells Corner	Scone 2337
SouthSide Cycle Centre, 49–51 Skinner Street	South Grafton 2461
South Tweed Bicycle Centre, 13 Blundell Bvde	South Tweed Heads 2486
Champion Cycles, West Lane	St Marys 2760
Blackman Bicycles, 59 Queen Street	St Marys 2760
Stanmore Cycles, 208 Parramatta Road	Stanmore 2048
The Edge Cycle Centre, 789 King Georges Road	Sth Hurstville 2221
Durban Cycles, Shops 3 & 4, Durban Road	Sutherland 2232
Clarence Street Cyclery, 104 Clarence Street	Sydney 2000
Tamworth Bicycle Co., 280 Peel Street	Tamworth 2340
Bourke's Bicycle Centre P/L, 35 Pulteney Street	Taree 2430
Cyclesport International, 276 Pennant Hills Road	Thornleigh 2120
Toukley Bicycle Shop, Shop 1, 10 Hargraves Street	Toukley 2263
Twin City Cycles, 121 Wharf Street	Tweed Heads 2485
Ulladulla Cycles, Shop 22 The Plaza, 107 Princes St	Ulladulla 2539

Wagga Motor Cycle Centre P/L, 119 Fitzmaurice Street	Wagga Wagga 2650
Kidsons P/L, 107 Fitzmaurice Street	Wagga Wagga 2650
Ryans Cycle City, 68 Nelson Street	Wallsend 2287
Bikecology, Unit 6, 401 Manns Road	West Gosford 2250
Westleigh Cycles, Shop 15, Eucalyptus Drive	Westleigh 2120
The Bicycle Shop, 195 High Street	Willoughby 2068
Windsor Cycles, 293 George Street	Windsor 2756
Woodsy's Wheels, 3/58 River Street	Woolloolga 2456
Yagoona Cycles, 454A Hume Highway	Yagoona 2199

NORTHERN TERRITORY

The Penny Farthing Bike Shop, 26 Elder St	Alice Springs 0871
Centre Cycles, Shop 3, 9 Lindsay Ave	Alice Springs 0871
Wheelman Cycles Stores P/L, PO Box 1365	Darwin 0801
Rosettos Sports Centre P/L, (1) Smith Shopping Mall	
(2) Casuarina Shopping Centre	Darwin 0801

QUEENSLAND

Cycle Brothers, Shop 18, Discount Shopping Ctr	Alexandra Hills 4161
Ashmore Cycle Centre, Shop 51, Ashmore Shopping Ctr	Ashmore 4214
Aspley Cycles, 8/611 Robinson Road	Aspley 4034
Beenleigh Cycles, 5/102 York Street	Beenleigh 4207
Life Cycle, 276 Petrie Terrace, Normanby	Brisbane 4000
Edward Street Bicycle Centre, 160 Edward Street	Brisbane 4000
Bicycles Pacific Fair, Pacific Fair Shopping Centre	Broadbeach 4218
Trinity Cycles Works, 146 Grafton Street	Cairns 4870
Berretto Bicycles, 724 Gympie Road	Chermside 4032
Cooktown Bicycle Sales & Repairs, Charlotte Street	Cooktown 4871
Caves of Coorparoo, 185 Cavendish Road	Coorparoo 4151
Sam's Cycles, 142 Auckland Street	Gladstone 4680
Balmoral Bike Shop, 121 Riding Road	Hawthorne 4171
Southport Bicycle World, 4 James Cook Esplanade	Hollywell 4216
Bike Trekkers Aust, 153 Eagle Street	Longreach 4730
Kessels Road Cycles P/L, 3/579 Kessels Road	MacGregor 4109
Hodgkinson's Bicycle People, 164 Victoria Street	Mackay 4740
Eddleston Motors & Cycles, 39 Constance Street	Mareeba 4880
Cycle World, 161 Bazaar Street	Maryborough 4650
Wilcox Bike Shop, 326 Kent Street	Maryborough 4650
Curly Dann Sports Store P/L, PO Box 184	Mount Isa 4825
Nambour Funtastic Centre, 47 Howard Street	Nambour 4560
Skate Cycle & Leisure, Shop 28, Nerang Fair	Nerang 4211
Thommo's Bike Shop, 118 Elphinstone Street	North Rockhampton 4701
Nundah Cycle Centre, 25 Station Street	Nundah 4012
Oxley Cycle Centre, Oxley Plaza, Cook Street	Oxley 4075
Palm Beach Cycles, 4/15 Palm Beach Avenue	Palm Beach 4221
Cooper's Cycles, PO Box 82	Palm Beach 4223
Murray Cycle Works, 82 William Street	Rockhampton 4700
Tucker's Cycle Inn, Cnr Richardson Rd & Alexandra St	Rockhampton 4701
B.B.C. Cycles, 4 Scarborough Street	Southport 4215
Cycle & Surf Inn, 3 Stevens Street	Southport 4215

Allans Cycles Pinelands, Pinelands Plaza Cnr — Sunnybank Hills 4109
Leader Cycles, Shop 12, Taigum Shopping Town — Taigum 4034
Kev Olsen's Cycles, 6 Robertson Street — Toowoomba 4350
Toowoomba Bicycle Centre, 3 Thackeray Street — Toowoomba 4350
The Big Bike Shop, 2938 Pacific Highway — Underwood 4119
Allan's Cycles, 1921 Logan Road — Upper Mt Gravatt 4122
Xpress Mowers & Cycles, 98 Grafton Street — Warwick 4370

SOUTH AUSTRALIA

Blackwood Bicycle Centre, Shop 3, 276 Shepherd's Hill Rd — Eden Hills 5050
Rob Hahn Bicycle Shop, 63 Murray Street — Gawler 5118
Holdfast Cycles, 768 Anzac Highway — Glenelg 5045
Trak Cycles, 170 Montague Road — Ingle Farm 5091
Kingston Sports Store, 23 Charles Street — Kingston 5275
Exeter Cycles, 270 Fletcher Road — Largs North 5016
Morvale Cycles, 212 Main South Road — Morphett Vale 5162
S-J Cycles, 5 Mitchell Street — Mt Gambier 5290
Jim Lynch Cycles & Sports Shop, 123 Commercial Street — Mt Gambier 5290
Bruce Dowdell's Cycles, 46 Gray Street — Mt Gambier 5290
Brooks Cycle Depot, 63 Bridge Street — Murray Bridge 5253
Challinger's Bikes & Bicycles, 65 Mortlock Terrace — Port Lincoln 5606
Lincoln Cycles, PO Box 1077 — Port Lincoln 5606
Riverland Sports P/L, 145 Murray Avenue — Renmark 5341

TASMANIA

Noel von Bibra Cycles, Shop 3, 142 William Street — Devonport 7310
Ken Self Cycles, 124 Elizabeth Street — Hobart 7000
G A Fletcher Cycles, 9 Wilmot Road — Huonville 7109
Treadlies, Shop 27, Channel Court Shopping Centre — Kingston 7050
McBains Cycles P/L, 10–14 Paterson Street — Launceston 7250
Sandy Bay Cycles, 13 Gregory Street — Sandy Bay 7005
Wicks Auto Parts & Cycles, PO Box 241 — Smithton 7330

VICTORIA

Abbotsford Cycles, 299 Johnston Street — Abbotsford 3067
Ken Kim's Sports Store, 92 Pier Street — Altona 3018
De Rose's Altona Sports & Cycles, 82 Pier Street — Altona 3018
Lardner Bros, 198 Barkly Street — Ararat 3377
Ashburton Cycles & Sports, 277 High Street — Ashburton 3147
Avoca Cycles, 123 High Street — Avoca 3467
Bacchus Marsh Toy & Cycle Centre, Shops 2 & 3, The Complex — Bacchus Marsh 3340
Warren Meade Cycles, 75 Main Street — Bairnsdale 3875
Bairnsdale Bicycle Centre, 209 Main Street — Bairnsdale 3875
B D Action Sports, 191B Main Street — Bairnsdale 3875
Shaw's Cycling Centre P/L, 614a Skipton Street — Ballarat 3350
Gove Cycles, 524 Doveton Street North — Ballarat 3350
Cycle City, 35 Armstrong Street North — Ballarat 3350
Navajo Everything Bicycles, 408 Sturt Street — Ballarat 3350
Bayswater Sportscene P/L, 687 Mountain Highway — Bayswater 3153
Squires Sports Store, 45 Nunn Street — Benalla 3672

Ross Hardings Bicycle Centre, 66 Queen Street	Bendigo 3550
Darryl Gilmore Cycles, 344A Hargreaves Street	Bendigo 3550
In Gear Bike Shop, 275 Burwood Highway	Bennettswood 3125
Mac Cycles, 210 Dorset Road	Boronia 3155
Exercycle P/L, 980 Whitehorse Road	Box Hill 3128
Gray's Cycles, 1029 Whitehorse Road	Box Hill 3128
Bayside Cycles, 395 Bay Street	Brighton 3186
Brooklyn Cycles, 557B Geelong Road	Brooklyn 3025
Campberwell Cycles, 732 Burke Road	Camberwell 3124
Borsari Sport Centre, 193 Lygon Street	Carlton 3053
Simon King Cycles, 503 Station Street	Carrum 3197
Superior Cycles & Sports, 89 Mostyn Street	Castlemaine 3450
Mainline Cycles P/L, 494 Nepean Highway	Chelsea 3196
Chelsea Sports Store, 333 Station Street	Chelsea 3196
Corsair Cycles, 265 Charman Road	Cheltenham 3192
Cheltenham Cycle Centre, 290 Charman Road	Cheltenham 3192
Clayton Cycles & Repairs, 303 Clayton Road	Clayton 3168
Melbourne Bicycle Centre, 37 Queens Parade	Clifton Hill 3068
Spurway Cycles, 42 Sydney Road	Coburg 3058
Coburg Cycles, 245 Sydney Road	Coburg 3058
The Bike Shop, 53 Corangamite Street	Colac 3250
Cowes Bike Hire & Repair Centre, 43–47 Thompson Avenue	Cowes 3922
Bicycle Barnes, 182 Mt Dandenong Road	Croydon 3136
Bicycle Super Store, 240–248 Princes Highway	Dandenong 3175
Kingsbury's Cycles, 101–103 Foster Street	Dandenong 3175
Dandenong Cycle Centre, 175 Lonsdales Street	Dandenong 3175
Dingley Bicycle Centre, 2 Pethybridge Close	Dingley 3172
Top Gear Cycles, 4 Mitchell Street	Doncaster East 3109
Drouin Cycles, 82 Princes' Way	Drouin 3818
Centurion Bicycle Centre, 169–171 Boundary Road	East Bentleigh 3165
Olsen Cycles, 215A McKillop Street	East Geelong 3219
Centreway Cycles & Sports, 30 Centreway	East Keilor 3033
East Kew Cycles, 1361 Burke Road	East Kew 3102
Action Cycles, 157 Waverley Road	East Malvern 3145
Lawton Cycles, 228 Pakenham Street	Echuca 3564
On Your Bike, Shop 3, 212 Darling Street	Echuca 3564
Pauls Sports Store, Shop 17, Eltham Mall	Eltham 3095
Warren's Sport & Recreation, 387 Main Road	Emerald 3782
Bicycle Depot, 545 High Street	Epping 3076
Essendon Cycles, 54 Rose Street	Essendon 3040
Ferntree Gully Cycles, Shop 1/48–52 Forest Road	Ferntree Gully 3156
Shorters Bikes & Sports Store, 56 Mountain Gate Shopping	Ferntree Gully 3156
Giramondo Cycles & Knitwear P/L, 700 Nicholson Street	Fitzroy North 3068
Beasley Cycles, 127 Buckley Street	Footscray 3012
Ted The Toyman, 265 Barkly Street	Footscray 3012
Glenns Sports & Gifts, 41 Main Street	Foster 3960
Peninsula Star Cycles, 48 Payne Street	Frankston 3199
Pedal Power Bike Shop, 4 Young Street	Frankston 3199
Frankston Bicycle Centre, 16 Beach Street	Frankston 3199
De Grandi Cycles & Sport P/L, 68–72 Mercer Street	Geelong 3220

Glen Waverley Cycles, 106 Kingsway	Glen Waverley 3150
Glenroy Cycles, 78 Wheatsheaf Road	Glenroy 3046
Diamond Valley Bicycle Centre, 129 Main Street	Greensborough 3088
B. & C. Cycles & Mowers, 87 Vines Road	Hamlyn Heights 3215
Hampton Bicycles, Shop 22, 449 Hampton Street	Hampton 3188
Lawrencia Cycles, 756–758 Glenferrie Road	Hawthorn 3122
Christie Cycles, 80 Burwood Road	Hawthorn 3122
Junction Cycles, 205 Camberwell Road	Hawthorn East 3123
Healesville Toyworld & Sports, 203 Maroondah Highway	Healesville 3777
Heywood Sports Store, 29 Edgar Street	Heywood 3304
G & D Cycles, 4 Sharp Street	Hoppers Crossing 3029
Wimmera Wheels P/L, 31 Urquhart Street	Horsham 3400
Ivanhoe Cycle Works, 1079 Heidelberg Road	Ivanhoe 3079
Kurzke Cycles, 139 High Street	Kangaroo Flat Bendigo 3555
Accent Cycles, 315 High Street	Kew 3101
Buckys Trading Post, 530 Mt Dandenong Road	Kilsyth 3137
Stan Apostola's Sports, Shop 4, Lalor Plaza, Darebin Dr	Lalor 3075
West Gate Sports, 159 Railway Avenue	Laverton 3028
Manning Sports & Cycles, 108 Main Street	Lilydale 3140
Alexander's Cycles & Sports, 74 Johnson Street	Maffra 3860
Malvern Mowers & Cycles, 37 Station Street	Malvern 3144
Maryborough Cycles, 86 Nolan Street	Maryborough 3465
City Cycles, 269 Lonsdale Street	Melbourne 3002
Melton Cycles, 45 Bakery Square	Melton 3337
Col Jones Cycles, 114 Balcombe Road	Mentone 3194
Brighton Cycles, 132 Church Street	Middle Brighton 3186
The Penny Farthing Cycle Shop, 100 Canterbury Road	Middle Park 3206
Hodgson Cycles, 106 Pine Avenue	Mildura 3500
Maxfield's Sports & Records Centre, 5 Moore Street	Moe 3825
South Road Cycles, 487 South Road	Moorabbin 3189
Spokes Bicycles, 22 Brice Avenue	Mooroolbark 3138
Wedgwood Sports & Cycles, 148 Main Street	Mornington 3931
Mornington Cycles, 160B Main Street	Mornington 3931
Howie's Bicycles P/L, Shop 3, Station Street	Mt Evelyn 3796
Reynolds Lightweight Cycle, 1 Dunoon Court	Mulgrave 3170
Sam's Sporting Centre, 67A Clyde Street	Myrtleford 3737
Narre Cycles, 1 Webb Street	Narre Warren 3805
McQuade's Newport Sports Store, 320 Melbourne Road	Newport 3015
Campione Cycles, 356 Pakington Street	Newtown 3220
The Bicycle Factory, 380 Latrobe Terrace	Newtown, Geelong 3220
Smith's Sports & Cycles, 81 Nelson Street	Nhill 3418
Noble Park Cycles, 41 Buckley Street	Noble Park 3174
Marshall's Cycles, 57 Alkira Avenue	Norlane 3214
Complete Cycles, 417–419 Maroondah Highway	North Croydon 3136
Niddrie Cycles & Toys P/L, Shop 1, 318 Keilor Road	North Essendon 3041
Numurkah Sports Store, 36 Melville Street	Numurkah 3636
Ian Hendry Cycles, 10 Park Lane	Ocean Grove 3226
Pakenham Sports & Cycles, 10 Station Street	Pakenham 3810
Cycles Woodrup, 25A Bank Street	Port Fairy 3284
Logan's Cycles, 38 Barkly Street	Portland 3305

Resa Accessories, 76 Edwardes Street	Reservoir 3463
Mascot Cycles, 308 Bridge Road	Richmond 3121
Gordon Hill Cycles, 86 Maroondah Highway	Ringwood 3134
Eastwood Cycles, 114 Railway Avenue	Ringwood East 3135
Shoes 'N' Sports, 47 Perrin Street	Robinvale 3549
Jemmima's, 57 Main Street	Rutherglen 3685
Boyd's Service Station, 163 Main Street	Rutherglen 3685
Barlee's Cycle Centre, 384 Raymond Street	Sale 3850
Mallard Cycles P/L, 89 Macarthur Street	Sale 3850
Sandringham Cycles, 20 Station Street	Sandringham 3191
Seaford Cycles & Sports Store, 113B Nepean Highway	Seaford 3198
Don Ash Cycles & Sports Store, 134 High Street	Shepparton 3630
Mikeron Sports Store, 61 Fryers Street	Shepparton 3630
Goldcross Cycles, 124 Bayswater Road	South Croydon 3136
Morton Cycles, 282 Park Street	South Melbourne 3205
PRM BMX Equipment, 1144 North Road	South Oakleigh 3167
The Freedom Machine, 401 Chapel Street	South Yarra 3141
Springvale Bike Shop, 261 Springvale Road	Springvale 3171
St Kilda Cycles, 11 Carlisle Street	St Kilda 3183
Boag's Cycles & Sports, 124 Gold Reef Mill	Stawell 3380
Mr Les T. O'Halloran, 14 McCrae Street	Swan Hill 3585
Gibson's Cycles & Sports Store, 261 Campbell Street	Swan Hill 3585
Tatura Sports Store, 141 Hogan Street	Tatura 3616
Freewheeling Cycles, 1889–1893 Nepean Highway	Tootgarook 3941
Sports Plus P/L, Shop 1, Palm Court, Bell Street	Torquay 3228
Woods Cycle Centre, 45 Vincent Street	Wangaratta 3677
Active Outdoors Sport, 38 Palmerston Street	Warragul 3820
Jones Cycles, 2B Goldfields Shopping Plaza	Warrandyte 3113
De Grandi Sportscene, 180 Timor Street	Warrnambool 3280
Watsonia Cycles, 365 Greensborough Road	Watsonia 3087
Keith Park, 47 Anderson Street	Werribee 3030
Hillman Cycles P/L, 46 Grantham Street	West Brunswick 3055
Ford Cycle Works, 96 Bell Street	West Heidelberg 3081
Whittlesea Cycles & Sports, 47 Church Street	Whittlesea 3757
Lardner's Newsagency, Main Street	Willaura 3291
The Circle Cycle Centre, 241 Kororoit Creek Road	Williamstown 3016
Progress Bicycle Co., 82 Chapel Street	Windsor 3181
Matthews & Co P/L, Jack Hore Place	Wodonga 3690
Quick Wheel Cycles, PO Box 453	Wodonga 3690
Wodonga Bicycle Repair, 30 High Street	Wodonga 3690
The Hub Cycle Centre, 12 McBride Avenue	Wonthaggi 3995
Holman Cycles, 186 Commercial Road	Yarram 3971
Yarrawonga Sports Store P/L, 94 Belmore Street	Yarrawonga 3730

WESTERN AUSTRALIA

Albany Bike Sales, 2 Albany Highway	Albany 6330
Canning Bridge Cycles, 886 Canning Highway	Applecross 6153
Australind Village Discounts, Shop 14, Australind Village	Australind 6230
Plaza Bikes, 75 Spencer St	Bunbury 6230
City Cycles, 15a Princep Street	Bunbury 6230

175

Avocet Cycles, 27 St Quentin Street	Claremont 6010
Bill's Bikes, Rear 39 Forrest Street	Collie 6225
Ambassador Cycles, Unit 2, 460 Canning Highway	Como 6152
Oliver Cycleland, 166 Canning Highway	East Fremantle 6158
Bassendean & Guildford Cycles, 149 James Street	Guildford 6055
Hannan Street Cycles, 266 Hannan Street	Kalgoorlie 6430
Johnston Cycles, 78 Boulder Road	Kalgoorlie 6430
Bill Gordin's All Bikes N' Gear, Shop 2, Village Kingsley Drive	Kingsley 6026
Everything Bicycles, Unit 4 Olga Plaza	Maddington 6109
Cycles Mandurah, 152 Mandurah Terrace	Mandurah 6210
Push 'N Pedal Cycles, 139 Pinjarra Road	Mandurah 6210
Skyway Bicycle Co, 167 Great Eastern Highway	Midland 6056
Garry Suckling Everything Bicycles, Unit 3, 150 Russell Street	Morley 6062
Fleet Cycles, 66B Adelaide Street	Morley 6062
Ward Cycles, 2 Wellington Road	Morley 6062
Padbury Bike Shop, 15 Noranda Avenue	Morley 6062
Mosman Cycles, 543 St Leonards Mall, Stirling	Mosman Park 6011
Mount Cycles, 379 Oxford Street	Mt Hawthorn 6016
Prestige Cycles, 126 Angove Street	North Perth 6006
Gordonson Cycles P/L, 374 Murray Street	Perth 6000
Runner's World, 5 Fitzgerald Street	Perth 6000
Bill Gordin's All Bikes 'N Gear, 77 Wanneroo Road	Stuart Hill 6060
Hi-Way Cycles, 170 Albany Highway	Victoria Park 6100
Cambridge Cycles, 334 Cambridge Street	Wembley 6014
Burrendah Cycles, Shop 22, Southlands Centre	Willeton 6155

ACKNOWLEDGEMENTS

After many years of riding and touring I began work on this book at the invitation of Kirsty Melville from Simon & Schuster Australia. Little did I realise how much time was involved in designing, researching, riding, photographing and writing a book on bicycle touring.

Creating the height profiles required countless hours in the Mitchell Library, Sydney, poring over 1:100 000 topographical maps. I would like to thank Con and the staff of the Mitchell for their help and patience.

Travelling to the start and from the end of most tours I was fortunate to be able to fly with East West Airlines — The Leisure Airline. Each time my bike arrived undamaged and at the right destination.

Thanks to the South Pacific Hotel Corporation, I was occasionally able to forgo my tent, enjoying stays at the Capital Parkroyal in Canberra, the Gold Coast International and Coral Coast Resort at Cairns. Thanks also to the Australian Youth Hostels Association — their hostels are a boon to cycle tourers of any age.

I also appreciate greatly the assistance of the Tourist Commissions of Tasmania, Western Australia, Victoria, South Australia, New South Wales and the Australian Capital Territory.

Thanks to Steve and Colin of Cranks bike shop and to my equipment suppliers, Karrimor, J & H and Trangia.

Though I rode two of the tours solo, for the remainder I was blessed with good companions. My thanks to Rhonda and Mick Barrett, and Karen Mead (Tour 2), Chris Hood (Tour 3), Mick Vickers and Liz Hopper (Tour 4), Sonja and Geof Thompson (Tour 5), Debbie Buck and John Kirkpatrick (Tour 7), and Shelley Cartledge (Tour 8).

My special gratitude to Shelley for the thankless task of helping with the preliminary editing of the manuscript.